# The Best of Gowanus

*New Writing from Africa, Asia and the Caribbean*

*Edited by:*

**Thomas J. Hubschman**

**Gowanus Books**
**http://www.gowanusbooks.com**

The Best of Gowanus
New Writing from Africa, Asia and the Caribbean

© 2001 by Thomas J. Hubschman

Cover art by Eric and Isaac Black

Published by:

Gowanus Books
473 17th St. #6
Brooklyn, NY 11215-6226


ISBN 0-9669877-2-1
LCCN:2001116427

Printed in the United States of America

http://www.gowanusbooks.com
info@gowanusbooks.com

# Contents

# Introduction

*By* Thomas J. Hubschman

Since I myself don't like being told in an introduction to a book like this the plots, strengths and weaknesses of the writing contained therein whose quality I am quite able to judge for myself, I won't burden the reader with anything similar here. But as the publisher you must permit me some enthusiasms.

*Gowanus* was not a project I was obliged to undertake because there was not enough good writing on the Net. Even before the first issue came out in June, 1997—a century ago in Internet years—there were plenty of quality publications: *Blue Moon Review* (*Blue Penny Quarterly*, in its former incarnation), *Morpo Review, Kudzu, In Vivo* (no longer publishing) and many others. The world didn't need yet another ezine devoted to the work of talented First World writers. What *was* lacking was a venue for their brethren living in parts of the world where the Internet was not yet so strongly entrenched but where the human imagination most assuredly was, perhaps even more so, and seemingly against all odds. Knowing those writers were out there, and that no one—at least, no one I knew of at the time—was looking to provide them with a forum of their own, ignited the spark that became *Gowanus*.

Even my best hopes were exceeded by the submissions I began to receive almost immediately. Norma Kitson, the late South African author and political activist who spent her final years in Zimbabwe, contributed "Parking Ticket" and also put me in contact with Fanuel Jongwe, a talented young Harare author. A seasoned journalist at Trinidad Express newspapers by the name of Anthony Milne appeared out of the ether and has contributed to every issue. Another veteran journalist, this time from Pakistan, Abbas Zaidi, claiming never to have written any fiction (a protest I still find hard to believe) began to produce one remarkable short story after another, as well as articles and essays that stand out not just as examples of fine writing but speak eloquently for the "ethnically cleansed" and culturally repressed in parts of the world not given much attention in the US. We in the West forget that life goes on elsewhere pretty much as it does in our own part of the globe, and matters just as much to those who live it. The strong oppress the weak, religious and tribal arrogance wages holy war on tolerance as it did in Bosnia and Rwanda and still does in the Middle East and even in the United States of America. Such wrongs are endured and even transmuted into something noble through wit, imagination and a passion for truth which those of us who live in relative ease and peace can only admire.

But *Gowanus* is not a political publication. It has no axe to grind. The only criterion for getting into its electronic pages is a quality of writing that delights and challenges its editor and readers. Fiction is, in any case, the best advocate for any cause, as is the well-wrought personal essay. Human imagination is still the greatest force on the face of the earth.

The stream of excellent talent continued. Anjana Basu, a writer of immense talent, contributed excerpts of two novels either one of which is worthy of a major literary prize. She also contributes wry, powerful snapshots of Indian life and mores, as well as book reviews that are more worth reading (IMHO, as we say on the Net) than are most of the volumes she reviews.

Other writers from the Indian subcontinent abound. Is there any modern civilization—other than the Irish—who have such a genius for story-telling?

Ly Lan, an established Vietnamese author, contributes brilliant fiction of her own as well as sensitive translations of other Vietnamese authors.

You will also find in these pages an essay on Kosovo by a Croatian refugee that gives a better sense for what has happened to that blighted part of the world better than any ten TV documentaries; a story of flight and porpoises; a critique of South Africa's Truth and Reconciliation Commission's failures in the case of two prominent actors in the apartheid struggle, one white and one black; a first-hand account of the appalling conditions under which the Dalit, the so-called Untouchables, still live.

But if I go on I will only end up recapitulating the table of contents. The short stories and essays in this anthology, gleaned from the pixels of its Internet progenitor, represent some of the best contemporary writing to be found anywhere. A big claim, and certainly not an unprejudiced one. But if you don't agree, the publisher (myself) will gladly refund the purchase price. Try getting that kind of warranty from Borders or Barnes & Noble for the latest postmodern phenom!

What is contained in this volume is called the "best" of *Gowanus*, but there is hardly anything that saw publication on the *Gowanus* website during the last four years that doesn't deserve inclusion. Only economic and publishing practicalities have reduced the girth of this book to what you hold in your hands.

If there happens to be anything amiss herein, I take responsibility. But for the existence of *Gowanus* itself and now for the print anthology you must thank my wife Luella who supported this venture wholeheartedly from the outset and without whom there would have been no *Gowanus*; Ellen Larson who provided the critical impetus and professional expertise to see this book into print; Isaac Black who insisted that this child be conceived and then contributed out of his own pocket to ensure its success, along with the beautiful cover design and artwork; and, not lastly, Richard Cumyn whose friendship has kept me afloat when I was ready to sink into discouragement and without whose editorial help this book would be poorer.

But mostly, we all—publisher and readers alike—owe thanks to the wonderful authors all around the world who continue to burn with the passion that is the parent of all good art and who generously share that passion and their talents with the rest of us in these pages.

Brooklyn, New York
January, 2001
tom@gowanusbooks.com

# The Crowded Business of Beauty

*By* Anjana Basu

The beauty business has finally hit Calcutta. Perhaps it was always there, but it went unnoticed: everyone was busy being conservative and pretending that studies were the "in" thing—two pigtails and a shoulder bag, walking demurely to school. But then Suzy Sen hit the Miss Universe headlines and demureness was out—even though she was Delhi, she had the Bengali surname and relatives in Southend Park. And what Sushmita Sen failed to accomplish, Bipasha Basu did full force with her Ford Supermodel title in Mumbai. Suddenly beauty contests stopped being anti-cultural. Which brings us to the Miss India prelims—Calcutta's main taste of Mumbai glamour.

The first thing to do, of course, is get hold of a ticket. The word is out that the invitations have been sent and now you have to find out who you know who can organize you one. After all those parties around Christmas and New Year, this promises to be one of those things you shouldn't miss—at least, not if you want to be mistaken for "somebody."

It's such a small thing to make a fuss about, a blue card with a graphic of a white face and sweep of black hair, but it gets you into the third lap of the Miss India finals, and that's the closest you're going to get to Miss India unless you happen to have contacts in Mumbai. Miss Beautiful Smile, Miss Personality and Miss Talent is what it says on the back, with cocktails starting at six p.m. Well, that's a terribly early cocktail hour, though it is theoretically after sundown, so you start scrabbling through your cupboards for a set of glad rags that aren't too well worn. The males have this notion that dress is formal, which means doing the jacket and tie thing all over again, but everyone's willing to suffer a little for an evening of starlight and twenty-two-year-old beauties. Especially the ones who went through Miss Beautiful Eyes at the Taj Bengal two years ago.

This time the venue is at a well-known country club instead of a five-star hotel. Chinese lanterns festoon the entrance, which is tucked discreetly down the drive so that curious passersby are not hanging outside the gates. I spent some time waiting for my companions near the club's Golf Shop, so I was able to take in a few unusual sights. Like a huge tourist bus which swept in and disgorged brown sweaters, children and shawl-wrapped wives. I kept peering into the bus, thinking that surely a few would-be Miss Indias were tucked in the depths and that the whole thing was some kind of elaborate camouflage. But, no. Instead, more brown pullovers congregated at the entrance, until you began to wonder whether a monkey cap would soon appear and the whole proceedings be transformed into a Food Fair or some other kind of melee. "Very middle class," muttered a few people near me who were quite ostentatiously sporting their blazers and designer wear.

Anyway, we all trooped down the designated gate, wondering whether the description "glitterati" had been changed for the evening because the crowds there were so unglittery, judging by the monkey-capped crowds. The cocktails were a fight all around the seating area, with hostesses frantically diving to look for liquor glasses hidden under their noses. "No, Madam, no glasses in the seating area, please," I was told. Others who held their glasses lower were more successful, or perhaps they were just ignored. There were snacks with the cocktails, but each bearer was promptly surrounded by fifty pairs of hungry hands, so it was best, taking into account the warning announcements that told you to sit down before the lights were switched off, to just do so and concentrate on the feast of beauty that lay ahead. The food smells tormented you, but there were Céline Dion and Barbara Streisand soothing you on the muzak.

Twelve judges were announced by a Los Angeles Miss India who glimmered dimly on a distant horizon decorated with more Chinese lanterns. Shilpa Shetty had the men murmuring and thinking that their evening was made—never mind if they didn't get to see the Miss Indias. There was also, in view of the fact that the contest was sponsored by Colgate, a dentist on the panel. Then the pictures of the girls bounced on and off the screens—twenty-five of them merging into three—Swarnima, Pranamika, two Shwetas, poor things, one with a "v" and one with a "w," what were they going to do if one of them won? —all aged between eighteen and twenty-two. "You mean to tell me she's eighteen?" muttered the twenty-six-year-old at my side. "She doesn't look eighteen from any angle." I told her it was the make-up.

The unstated theme of the evening was, "Making the Calcuttans feel Important." Reshma murmured, *"Kaemon accheyn babumoshai?"* ("How are you, gentlemen?") and went on to hint at Tagore's contribution to the Bengali psyche. There was talk of all the important sons of Bengal: Tagore, Satyajit Ray, Leander Paes and Saurav Ganguly. Remo Fernandes, with his Microwave Pappadum band, announced that he had rarely met more sensitive audiences than the Bengalis and so what if Calcutta didn't have the glitz and the granite, she had soul. Raageshwari, of MTV fame, coming on later with Duniya and parroted the Bengali phrases she knew while her father stole all the pullovered hearts with three bars of *rabindrasangeet*.

In the middle of this was the bouquet of beauties in purple gowns flashing leg up to the thigh. "Why on earth are they wriggling so much?" demanded the twenty-six-year-old, watching a tightly swathed purple derriere advance and retreat. The twenty-six-year-old was, of course, a *she*. The men were gaping, in between passing rude remarks. I remembered Miss Beautiful Eyes in Arabian veils two contests ago. She lounged on silken cushions in a desert tent while the judges gazed soulfully into her deep lustrous eyes—all fifteen pairs of them. What did they do to Miss Beautiful Smile? Did the dentist pull out his instruments and tap thirty-two ivories? However, that was another country.

Miss Talented was, as usual, a strain on the judgement. They danced, they sang, they emoted. Some of them choreographed their own dances and performed in red and silver outfits. "Shilpa Shetty should be pleased," someone muttered. In the meantime delicate drizzle descended on the lawns of the Tollgunge Club and before I could ask, "Is this dew?" a female voice said, "My god, she danced and it started raining. What'll happen when the next one starts singing?"

The rain started a steady trickle of people for the exit—there was only one exit. Anticipating a stampede, I joined the departure. Cell phones rang as we jostled. "Yes, yes, answer that phone," said one of the pullovers. The organizers were undecided as to whether to offer people the blue slips again so that they could get back in if they wanted to, though by the time I reached the exit I was lucky enough to be given one. But it was getting late, too late to have had no dinner, and the car and driver were waiting streaked white with crow droppings in the parking space under the trees.

# Ethnic Cleansing of the Kafirs in Pakistan

*By* Abbas Zaidi

In all the languages spoken in Pakistan, *kafir* means "infidel" and Kafiristan means "Land of the Infidels." (Kafir also means "infidel" in Arabic.) Yet, ironically, Kafiristan in Pakistan is believed to be a paradise. Located in the northwest part of the country, its lakes, waterfalls and green forests teem with wildlife, snow and mellow sun.

But it is not just the place itself that fascinates. The beauty of the women there, part-fairy and part-human, as the story goes, can make a man lose his religion. "When a Kafir woman drinks water you can see it streaming down her throat. One can count the veins on her body," is the standard text regarding the Kafir woman's delicateness.

Who are these Kafirs?

The advent of the Kafirs in the northwest of Pakistan—what is known now as the Kalash Valley, consisting of the Birir, Bumboret and Rumbor sub-valleys—and southern Afghanistan, predates the birth of Islam by several centuries. Today, the Kalash Valley is a part of Chitral, a large administrative region in northwestern Pakistan. The Kafirs are believed to be descendants of the warriors who arrived with Alexander the Great and decided to stay on. Historically, the Kafirs have remained an isolated ethnic group who were left undisturbed by both the Muslim rulers of India and by the British Raj. Many Western historians during the Raj were surprised to find the Kafirs' physical resemblance so similar to their own that they proudly declared that they and the Kafirs were of the same stock. As such, the Kafirs were allowed to freely practice their ancient customs, including ritual alcohol consumption, promiscuous dancing and ritual sex.

The tragic watershed in Kafiri history came towards the end of the nineteenth century when in southern Afghanistan their population was decimated in the name of Islam. The Afghan ruler at that time declared that the Kafirs either would be converted to Islam or wiped off the face of the earth. The Afghan campaign was a total success, and the dawn of the twentieth century did not see a single Kafir living in Afghanistan as a Kafir. Even the names of their villages were Islamised.

The Kafirs on the Pakistani side of the border were spared genocide thanks, one might suppose, to the Raj. In 1947 the Raj ended and Pakistan came into being, but the Kafirs continued to lead their lives as they had lived them for centuries. The legends about the beauty of the Kafir women and the landscape continued in a quasi-orientalist mode. Every so often one heard about someone marrying a Kafir woman and bringing her home, though no one ever actually saw one. (In legends and tales about Kafiristan the Kafir men are significant by their absence.)

It was only in the early 1970s that the people of Pakistan began to hear about the Kafirs in the national media, when Kafiristan was facing famine. Thanks to then Prime Minister Zulfiqar Ali Bhutto, a tragedy was averted and he became the Kafirs' hero.

But then came the CIA-sponsored *jihad* in Afghanistan and, in 1979, Iran's Islamic Revolution. Ayatollah Khomeini challenged, among other things, the US, the Arab monarchies and Pakistan's military dictatorship. Pakistan's progressive religious groups also became inspired by the Iranian Revolution and started planning for a revolution in Pakistan. A curious mix of Islam and Marxism, some were extremely anti-American and anti-Soviet; some preferred the atheistic Soviet Union to the anti-Islamic United States and had made socialist friends in Afghanistan; some were pro-Khomeini because Khomeini had challenged the US as no one had ever done before. Hence, the Iranian Revolution unified them into an anti-American front. They called the Afghan refugees of those days "the absconders" and the *jihad*-wagers "the CIA agents."

General Zia ul Haq, Pakistan's longest-reigning dictator to date, was the *enfant gâté* of the Saudi Royal Family, with a proven track record of loyalty to his masters in Jordan as well. The US needed a strongman in Islamabad to offset pro-Iranian, anti-American sentiments and to oppose the Soviets on its behalf. Hence it became vital to divide Pakistan along sectarian lines. Only the Deobandi-Wahabi (see end note 2) version of Islam could produce the desired results. So, in order to out-Khomeini Khomeini, the General introduced his own brand of Islamisation. That same year Zulfiqar Ali Bhutto was hanged with the full blessing of the US government. 1979, that *annus mirabilis*, marked the beginning of the end for the Kafirs.

14

In 1981 Ronald Reagan provided a multi-billion-dollar "aid" package to help Pakistan intensify the Afghanistan *jihad*. General Zia called upon the nation to go one step further than the government in bringing Islam to every village and hamlet of Pakistan. As a result, countless Tablighi (proselytizing) parties confronted every Muslim and non-Muslim Pakistani preaching the Deobandi-Wahabi version of Islam. Coincidentally, that year saw klashnikovs and heroin begin to penetrate every nook and cranny of Pakistan. The Kafirs got the first taste of things to come when some Tablighi zealots illegally occupied a large cultivated piece of their land in Bumboret and built a mosque.

What happened after that is not hard to imagine. The Afghan refugees and the Pathan Tablighi parties (now known as the Taliban) seized nearly seventy percent of Kafir land during the period 1981 to 1995. They built mosques and seminaries where, in addition to learning the Koran by rote only, students learn the arts of war, techniques that are used against India in Kashmir and against Muslim and non-Muslim religious minorities within Pakistan as well as against "infidels" elsewhere. The first fruit of the Afghanistan *jihad* for the Kafirs was the decimation of the Kalash forests and wildlife by the Afghan refugees. As the vegetation grew sparse, the Kafirs' cattle met the same fate as their forests, and the traditional Kafir means of livelihood was irreparably destroyed.

Once the Afghan refugees and the Tablighis became entrenched in Chitral, forced conversion of the Kafirs began. Gun-toting Tablighis made it clear that in order to go on living in Pakistan (Pakistan means "Land of the Pure") the Kafirs must convert to Islam. For the Kafirs any place beyond the Kalash Valley is as alien as Mars. Kidnapping and forced marriage—and hence forced conversion—of the Kafir women to the Muslims, mostly Tablighi Pathans, continues to this day. These women are not allowed to see their relatives unless the relatives also convert. It is no secret that many of them are sold at auction. Men are circumcised against their will. The Tablighis carry klashnikovs as a matter of routine and have killed many Kafirs who resisted conversion to Tablighi Islam. By contrast, no Kafir is allowed to carry a gun.

The poverty of the Kafirs has also been a major factor in their conversion to Tablighi Islam. Within the Chitral society they are completely ostracized for being "Kafirs," a term that illiterate people (and illiteracy in Chitral is the norm) understand to mean "infidels." The government does not give loans to Kafirs; the police and the judiciary have never taken any action against the appropriation of Kafiri land by

Tablighis. The only source of income for the Kafirs are the Tablighis, who lend them money at high interest. Since the Kafirs cannot pay off these loans, the only course left for them is either to convert or surrender their properties to the Tablighis.

While electricity, available through gasoline generators, and tap water are accessible to every Muslim in the Kalash Valley, and loudspeakers relay *azzan* and Koranic recitations throughout the day, there is not a single Kafir house that has electricity or a water tap. Their living conditions are indescribable. The Chitral winter is Siberian. The mosques and seminaries have heaters and warm water. The Kafirs' houses remain dark all winter, and they have to melt snow for drinking water. They cut wood to make fire. Their houses are actually large single rooms that remain shut for the six months of winter. Humans and animals live in them together. There are no toilets. One can only imagine the stink and the lack of sanitation. In summer, people use the open fields to relieve themselves; in winter they relieve themselves inside their houses, the same as their animals. One finds human and animal waste everywhere.

There is not a single hospital or even a minor dispensary in the whole of Kafiristan. The Tablighis have 4 x 4 jeeps, but few Kafirs have any kind of vehicle. Many Kafirs have died, when basic emergency aid could have saved them, such as during childbirth. The Kafiri diet is basic and monotonous, and one rarely sees either a male or female Kafir who looks physically strong. The women's veins show plainly because of their malnourished state. Their characteristic long necks are dirty, and you only have to come close to one to know that they seldom get to take a bath.

Needless to say, Kafir culture is now nonexistent, thanks to the Tablighis. In the 1980s it was thought that the Kafirs as a distinct cultural group would become extinct by the end of the century. But they still linger on, though their number now is no more than two thousand. The government of Pakistan takes great pride in having established the Kalash Foundation "to preserve and propagate Kafir culture." But the facts speak otherwise. It is true that the Kalash Foundation has somewhat slowed the steamroller of Tablighi Islam. But it has not done anything positive for the Kafirs. No effort has been made to give their language written documentation, and there does not exist even a single standard text devoted to Kafiri culture.

Visitors to the Kalash Valley have to pay a toll to enter. The toll ticket given to the visitor is jokingly called "the zoo ticket." The Kafirs and what is left of their culture have been preserved merely to cater to the exotic tastes of generals, bureaucrats, politicians and foreign dignitaries. Thanks to the Kalash Foundation, the Kafirs have become little more than anthropological artifacts. The World Wildlife Federation has been crying blue murder over the fact that only five thousand tigers remain in their natural habitat. Who cares that only two thousand Kafirs remain, despite a captivity-*cum*-protection program supposedly accorded them by the Pakistani government?

Meanwhile, the Tablighi are pushing to convert the few remaining pagans, and it is unlikely the Kafirs will last very long into the twenty-first century. Kafir culture will end up—like so many indigenous cultures elsewhere—in the "cultural centers" of the big cities under the oversight of the Ministry of Cultural Affairs. One may surmise that in future the converted Kafirs and their progeny will be engaged in fighting Indians, the religious minorities of Pakistan and "infidels" elsewhere. Meanwhile, in order to edify and entertain their audiences, Muslims employed by the Ministry of Cultural Affairs will stage exhibitions of Kafiri culture, dressing up and posing as the Kafirs whom the government and the Tablighis have systematically eliminated.

**Notes:**

1. I felt compelled to write this article after reading the chapter "The Islamization of the Kalash Kafirs" in Akbar S. Ahmed's *Pakistan Society* (Oxford University Press, Karachi, 1986). I was appalled to read that the author, "the Margaret Mead of Islam," did not once touch upon the destruction of the Kafirs. He does mention the "formidable social, and psychological pressures resulting from [the Kafirs] being viewed as "dirty" non-believers by aggressive and powerful neighbors," but ends his chapter on a high note of optimism that everything for the Kafirs will be all right in the course of time. Maybe he could not appreciate the true nature of the situation because at the time of his writing he was an important member of General Zia's bureaucracy.

2. A word about the Tablighis and their version of Islam. Within the Sunni sect in Pakistan and India there are two major sub-sects: the Brelvis and the Deobandis. The Deobandis are very close to the Wahabis of Saudi Arabia in their literalist interpretation of Islam. That is why the Deobandis and the Wahabis work side by side, from politics to

*jihad*. The ubiquitous proselytizing groups in Pakistan and elsewhere are overwhelmingly Deobandi. The Deobandis believe that except for themselves and the Wahabis all other sects of Islam are heretical and must be exterminated. In the 1970s it was chiefly the Wahabis and the Deobandis who succeeded in having the Ahmedis declared non-Muslims in Pakistan, a declaration later constitutionalised by General Zia, himself a Deobandi. The Sipa-e-Sihaba of Pakistan and the Taliban of Afghanistan are Deobandi financially supported by the Saudi Royal Family. It's interesting to note that within Sunni Islam the Deobandis and the Brelvis are not found anywhere outside India and Pakistan. The creation of these two sects was one of the masterstrokes of the Raj in its divide-and-rule policy.

3. The Kafirs have become the victim of Tablighis Islam. Islam, however, is a religion whose God—Allah—by His own claim is, *inter alia*, the Beneficent, the Benevolent and the Merciful. Allah strictly forbids Muslims to carry out forced conversion.

# Uncles and Crooks

*By* Abbas Zaidi

"Uncle Mian is coming next week," Niki said. "He comes home every year, richer than ever. He must be the richest man in Manchester. I heard this time he is coming with his English wife and will build a mosque here."

"Go ask your mother to make me tea," Uncle Khizar shouted back in his usual way. Niki stole a look at me and smiled in the usual way and I gave her the usual, stealthy smile back. Uncle Khizar had been a hot-tempered man ever since he returned from England fifteen years ago, but his recent kidney problems and confinement to a wheelchair had made him even more irritable. Diabetes, his latest ailment, had affected his eyesight as well.

No one resented his outbursts.

"The last time someone wanted to build a mosque, you told the head of the rival group that it would create sectarian tension, and the plan was abandoned. But this time you don't seem bothered," I said to him.

"Ah, but this time my great friend Mian is providing the moolah."

"But, Uncle, if you are against something, you don't let it happen," I persisted.

"What is in the news today?" he replied, ignoring my objection.

I started my daily ritual of reading from the *Lahore Times*.

"'General Zia says democracy is a sham; Pakistan's salvation lies in Islam alone. He also said that the reason he hanged former Prime Minister Bhutto was because Bhutto headed a corrupt, unIslamic government....'"

"Next story," Uncle commanded.

"'The Lahore High Court has ordered the release of Haji Usman who chopped off his sister's and her lover's heads when he found them in a compromising situation. The learned judge said that Usman did the right thing because no honorable brother could tolerate...'"

"Next!"

"'A man cheated his widowed mother-in-law out of all her wealth and then kicked her out of her own house. She is begging on the streets now. She has requested that the authorities...'"

"Next!"

"'An old woman claims her brother got her house transferred to his name through fraud....'"

"Why do you read me such stories every day? You have no shame. I will tell my sister that her son reads me offensive news only to spite me."

"But, Uncle, I don't make the news."

"Stop barking and start reading the international news."

I never complained about Uncle Khizar's outbursts. Apart from being an invalid, he had been like a father to me. He brought me up when my real father passed away, kept me and my mother in his house, took charge of the vast properties my father owned and engaged me to his only child, Niki.

I read him the international news, ignoring any item about Britain. He hated news about Britain.

"'Nigerian Crooks Having Field Day in Southeast Asia,'" I read from the headline of a news feature, then went on to another. Uncle Khizar cut me short, "Go back to the other one."

"'Rich Southeast Asians have become the target of Nigerian crooks. These crooks write them letters on behalf of "officials in very high government positions," offering commissions as high as "a few million US dollars" if the latter allow them to transfer huge amounts of money to the Nigerians' accounts....'"

"That's enough for now," Uncle interrupted. "What animals human beings are! Well, nothing new about that."

He lit a cigarette, took a few pulls, exhaled and began staring into space. I stood up to leave, but he stopped me.

"Listen up," he said and resumed his seemingly trance-like state. After a while he said, "You know who is the perfect nemesis of a greedy man, even if he is an evil genius?" Without waiting for my answer, he said, "It's a crook. A crook promises everything, even the moon, to the greedy man. You can go now."

I left, assuming I would not see him again until the next morning.

But that evening my mother said, "Go downstairs. Your Uncle wants you."

When I entered the living room I saw Uncle sitting on the sofa with a newspaper in his hand.

"Read the rest of the news about the Southeast Asian gulls," he said, handing me the same newspaper I had been reading to him that morning.

"'The impression left—and left deliberately—by the Nigerian crook is that the money he has in his possession has been illegally obtained from the Nigerian exchequer. The greedy gull goes along with the scheme. Within a few days he receives an envelope from the crook that contains some documents, "originals" and photocopies. He is then asked to deposit a substantial amount of his own money into a given account number which will "cover the initial transfer/taxation fee." Which he does happily and hopefully....'"

"We will read the rest later," Uncle said. "I have to go for dialysis."

Next morning Uncle Khizar was in a rage and did not want to see me. He was sitting by himself out on the lawn.

"What is the matter?" I asked Niki. This was one of the few opportunities Niki and I had, as a betrothed couple, to sit alone together and chat. Auntie did not mind such meetings, but Uncle would never have allowed them.

"Mother just told him Mian is arriving next week. You know, Mian has married and is bringing his wife along. Since she is coming to Pakistan for the first time, Mother thought we should invite them for dinner. But Uncle became furious."

"But Auntie has never shown any liking for Uncle Mian before. He comes home to Pakistan every year, but she has never invited him to the house."

"Yes, but she says this time he is coming to build a mosque in the village. She still thinks he is a rotten egg, but for once he is going to do a good deed. We don't have a mosque in our village."

In the afternoon my mother sent me down to see Uncle Khizar.

"Read the rest of the story about the Asian gulls."

I began: "'The money transfer is followed by a correspondence between the victim and the crook. In every letter, the victim is asked to put still more money into the designated account. Sometimes he is asked to visit Nigeria for "final discussions." He is provided with a complete itinerary for his visit, which includes meetings with "important Nigerian officials" and "prospects of future cooperation." Upon reaching Nigeria the victim is received by uniformed "government security persons" at the airport and taken to a high-class hotel for negotiations with "interested parties." The result: the victim loses whatever money he has left, and even his passport. All the "officials" disappear after the victim is penniless.

"'One victim reported that he sold everything in his house in order to receive huge commissions from a Nigerian crook; another borrowed a fortune from a bank. The governments of Singapore, Malaysia and Indonesia have used mass media to inform their people about the Nigerian crooks. Yet people continue to do business with these unsavory characters.'"

When I had finished Uncle said, "You remember I was telling you about a crook's promising the moon to a greedy man?"

"I remember."

"You know what happens next to the greedy man? I will tell you: A disaster happens."

I decided to broach the topic that had created such a fuss that morning. "Your friend Uncle Mian is coming as usual. But this time I think it is different. You know about the mosque...."

Uncle Khizar glanced toward me, then quickly looked away. His eyes were moist with feeling. He said, "You know my friend Mian is doing well in Manchester. He started as an assistant manager of a nightclub. Now he has his establishment."

It was not the first time Uncle Khizar had become reverential at the mention of Uncle Mian.

I said, "But I've heard he could not pass even his "O" levels and his English is terrible. I can't understand how he was even allowed to enter Britain. He had no future, even in Pakistan. How come he did so well in Manchester?"

It was the first time I ever took the liberty to speak my mind about this subject to Uncle Khizar.

He gave me the look of a full-grown adult who is talking to a toddler. "Why don't you ask the Asian gulls?"

I did not understand, but I continued, "You did a BBA in Manchester. It should have been you who stayed, not Uncle Mian. Mother tells me you wanted to return to Manchester, do an MBA and get a good job. I'm sure you could have succeeded. At that time Britain was a good place for us—still well before Thatcher's time."

"Yes, I wanted to," he almost whispered.

"What happened?"

"I wanted to leap ten years ahead of myself. I wanted a job I could only have gotten after ten years' hard work," he said with a sad smile.

"But why?" I persisted.

Suddenly he sat up straight and snapped, "Why don't you ask the Nigerian crooks?!"

Uncle Mian arrived. The news spread immediately, and the villagers came out to see the "Mem Sahib" who had married a Pakistani. Ours was a village of no more than six hundred people. All of them were proud that a white woman had married one of us. Except for Uncle Khizar and myself, no one in the entire village could speak English, but they wanted to tell the Mem Sahib how happy and honored they were to have her visit their "old and small" village so unworthy of her presence. I went as well to pay a visit to Uncle Mian and his wife, but they were too tired by then to receive anyone. But before I could leave, the prayer leader of the neighboring village appeared; his son would be heading up Uncle Mian's new mosque.

"Allah be praised," the prayer leader said. "Last night I saw Prophet Muhammad in a dream. He said that Mian's wife had converted to Islam and both of them would go to paradise after their death."

"Allah be praised! Mian be blessed!" some villagers shouted. Before letting us go, the prayer leader made everyone offer a special thanksgiving.

Next morning I found that Uncle Khizar had left the house early to preside over a village gathering at which a compromise candidate was to be chosen for the city council election.

In the afternoon our house-cleaner arrived in a clearly agitated state. She asked Auntie, "Are there any blacks in England?"

"No. At least, I have not seen any in my husband's photos from Manchester," Auntie said.

"But Mian's wife is black! And we thought she would be a fairy-tale white woman like the ones on the TV."

"Then, she is not from England. Mian is a liar."

"The milkman says she will become white because she has converted to Islam," the housekeeper added wistfully.

23

A week passed, but Uncle Mian had still not come to visit us. Neither had Uncle Khizar been to Uncle Mian's house. It was Mian who would have to pay *him* a visit. But Mian was apparently busy with plans for the new mosque. Uncle Khizar did not even mention him, though he did have a private conversation with the would-be prayer leader of the mosque.

One morning when I was reading him the *Lahore Times*, Uncle Khizar said, "Find me more news about the Asian gulls."

There was a small item about a Singaporean who had committed suicide after losing all his money to Nigerian crooks.

"A brave man," Uncle said. "He has rid himself of shame, embarrassment and worry."

"But it is wrong to kill oneself. Anybody can be duped. Why don't the Asians get together and work out a strategy to beat the crooks at their own game?"

"You," Uncle replied, "believe in nothing-succeeds-like-success. But I believe in nothing-fails-like-failure. If you fail, even though you are a genius and your failure is just pure coincidence, you are finished and everything you have achieved through your hard work is over with."

Next day Uncle asked, "Is there any more news about the Asian gulls?"

"There is no news today. But why is it you never ask about the crooks? You seem interested only in the gulls. If your greedy-man-and-crook theory were spread throughout Southeast Asia, many poor souls could be saved and you would be canonized," I said only half-seriously.

Uncle Khizar gave a hearty laugh, the first I could ever remember seeing from him. "Don't you know God's mill grinds slow, but sure?"

Next morning mother told me Uncle Khizar had gone out early to attend a meeting about which he had not said anything to anyone in the house. I rushed down to have tea with my fiancée. Afterward Niki went to have a look at the bed of roses she had planted in our garden, and I went to visit Auntie, who was busy in the kitchen. I started talking about Uncle Khizar's friendship with Uncle Mian. She said, "I have never told you this, because I did not want to hurt your uncle or Niki. But if he had listened to me he would be a successful man today."

"What mistake did he make?"

"After passing BBA from Manchester, your uncle wanted a job that was possible only if he had also done MBA. He decided to return to Pakistan because his childhood friend, this cunning Mian, had written to him that he would find him a high position in Pakistan's Ministry of Finance, through his own uncle who was a very highly placed officer there. Obviously no such uncle existed. Mian took your uncle's passport, which still had a valid visa in it, replaced it with his own photo and went to Manchester. The result is before you," she said.

In the evening Uncle Mian dropped by to invite us to participate in the foundation-stone ceremony for the new mosque. I was not home at the time.

Next day I pushed Uncle Khizar's wheelchair to the ceremony. Uncle Mian looked very solemn and saw to it that Uncle Khizar sat beside him during the proceedings. After a recitation from the Koran, Uncle Mian made a long speech about his struggle in a faraway land where Islam faced a number of threats. Then he praised General Zia and his Islamization policy. Looking at Uncle Khizar, he concluded, "I am building this mosque from money I have saved after working day and night for the sake of this village. Allah is kind to me, and I am a lucky man. Throw me into a river and I will come out with a fish in my hand and a pearl in my mouth."

After the ceremony Uncle Mian invited his childhood friend to visit his house and meet his wife. He embraced me affectionately and offered to help me find a job in Manchester when I had finished my degree. Then he added, "Even if you don't finish your degree I can still get you into England. There are many Pakistani girls there who need a suitable match like you."

I thanked him and glanced toward Uncle Khizar, whose expression betrayed nothing.

There were seven or eight other guests sitting in Uncle Mian's living room, including Mian's wife Julie, who seemed a very lively and sociable woman. We all sat and talked for a while. Then Julie and Uncle Khizar got together and conversed in low voices. Uncle Mian was sitting at a distance from them, but was constantly looking their way. Both she and Uncle Khizar seemed very pleased with themselves, especially Uncle. Soon the other guests left and the two uncles went to one end of the room to talk by themselves.

"Uncle has done a very noble deed," I said to Mian's wife, without believing a word of it.

"Yes," she said, "but, you know, the credit really goes to me. His nightclub has been doing great business, and he wanted to do something for his village that could win him respect. At first we calculated that the mosque would cost Khizar more money than he was willing to spend. But then I told him what to do and the result is before you."

"What was it you told him to do?"

"That," she laughed, "is a trade secret."


On the way home I told Uncle how Julie had referred to her husband as "Khizar" instead of "Mian."

He chuckled. "Mian has left Manchester for good. You know why?"

"Why?"

"He has been evading paying his taxes for quite some time. Unlike in Pakistan, tax evasion is a big crime in Britain and one is punished severely. So he has said goodbye to Britain. He wanted to set up a business in this country, but since the Pakistani government has started deducting Islamic *zakaat* he has put his money into his wife's account in her home country. She is going there tomorrow, and Mian is expected to follow her some time next month. You know, she is an income tax lawyer. He is extremely nervous about all this, but he has been assured that his money, when pooled with some other peoples', will benefit him to the extent that he will be a very, very rich man."

"Where is her home country?" I inquired.

Uncle turned toward me, trying to hide his glee behind a look of circumspection. "Didn't you know? Julie is a Nigerian."

"You mean, she..."

"Why was the cunning fox killed?"

Before I could reply, he supplied the answer: "Because he bought a ticket to Nigeria!"

He looked up from his wheelchair, chuckled, winked, then gave a roaring laugh, his shining eyes full of triumph.

# Bridges and Trees

*By* Ellen Larson

"No Nile, no Egypt...." So sang the fishermen as they rowed up the misty river, setting their nets in the gray hour before dawn, wrapped to the eyes in threadbare robes against the cold. "...No Egypt, no Nile."

Abdul Rahman Mohammed, sitting at the edge of the water behind the policemen's barracks in a cramped Cairo suburb, saw them every morning as he washed. He was a long way from Aswan in Upper Egypt where his mother, wife, son and infant daughter lived in a mud-brick house, but the fishermen and the river were the same. He cupped his hand, dipped it into the water and thought, 'Far away to the south, Nouzha is reaching into the water, washing herself just as I am. Maybe that little ripple was caused by the movement of her hands.' An ibis floated out of the sky, contracted its graceful wings and settled onto a half-submerged and rusted wheel rim a little way from shore.

Later, neatly dressed in his black winter uniform with matching beret, gaiters and boots, he joined his comrades: slim young men sporting narrow mustaches; naive young men straight off the farm; undistinguished young men fulfilling their military obligation at the lowest level of service. Together they clambered into the back of an open truck (the "cattle truck," they called it as a joke) and bounced along the roads to the spacious Cairo suburb of Maadi.

As it neared the first post, the truck slowed. Mahmoud Abdul Moneim and Mohammed Ali Mohammed hopped off, while Ahmed Ali Ibrahim and Ahmed Saied, whom they were relieving, scrambled up. The young men laughed and hooted as Ahmed Saied's rifle strap snagged on the sagging tailgate and he was forced to jump off again. The driver, Ahmed Behnassoui, grinned at them in the rearview mirror and revved the engine. Struggling to unhitch himself, Ahmed Saied had to run hard to keep up.

As they picked up speed, Abdul Rahman reached out and hauled Ahmed Saied into the truck, making sure the young man didn't stab himself with his bayonet. Abdul Rahman was older than the others—he had chosen the security of a second tour, small though the pay was, rather than the uncertainty of looking for work as a laborer in Cairo or the assured poverty of returning to his village—and thus had the responsibility for providing moral guidance. His name, one of the hundred names of Allah, meant "servant of the merciful," and he never forgot his duty to live up to it.

When the truck reached his post, Abdul Rahman hopped down nimbly, holding his rifle high on his back. He gave a gallant wave to Ahmed Behnassoui as the truck jounced over the bridge and rumbled away. Samir, his new partner, yawned and wandered a few paces up the road. The young man placed his rifle butt on the ground, folded his arms on top of the barrel and closed his eyes. He would not wake up until something worth watching occurred at one of the grand villas across the road. Abdul Rahman stretched his limbs, walked over to the bridge, placed a hand on its stone parapet and inspected its foundation. His post was an old friend and he liked to spend a few minutes each morning remaking its acquaintance, although he didn't expect to learn anything new.

There were policemen at all the major intersections in Maadi as well as at other important locations—railroad crossings, mosques, schools and, of course, bridges. Abdul Rahman's bridge carried Mostafa Kamil Road, the main market route, across the canal and into the Maadi *souk*. Abdul Rahman was proud to have a post of such importance, and prouder still because of the unusual beauty of the place.

The canal had run parallel to the Nile, two kilometers inland, since the beginning of memory, carrying irrigation water to the narrow strip of farmland on the east bank of the River. It was eight meters wide, two meters deep, straight as an arrow and had steep banks. Like most canals in Egypt, the water was motionless, unless a breeze rippled its surface, and reddish-brown. Also like most canals in Egypt, it was dotted with floating islands of water hyacinth, much to the annoyance of the bargemen who had to pole through it, and the farmers whose irrigation ditches it clogged. But what made this particular stretch of canal special were its eucalyptus trees. Their smooth trunks stood like pillars on either bank, sturdy branches holding up a leafy canopy that shaded the waterway—a silver-green colonnade running through modern residential Maadi as the mighty boulevards of stone had once run through the temples of the pharaohs. Although there were many trees and gardens in Maadi—foreigners and rich people who lived there could afford the luxury—none was as beautiful as Abdul Rahman's eucalyptus. They had been set in the ground as saplings some six or ten years previously. Abdul Rahman had it on good authority that the great Gamal Abdul Nasser himself had ordered their planting.

After admiring the trees in the morning light and checking for traffic on the canal, Abdul Rahman turned his attention to the little area at the east end of the bridge he considered his territory. Who knew what mayhem the policemen on the night shift had created in his absence? He liked to keep the ground swept clean, but others didn't care where they threw their bits of paper, cigarette butts and rubbish. He liked to keep the tin drinking-cup in a recess of the parapet, but he often found it down by the canal on a jutting rock or even lying on its side on the muddy bank. Abdul Rahman always shook his head at this; this new batch of policemen seemed more careless than the last.

A horse clip-clopped over the bridge, its harness bells jingling, pulling a flatbed wagon piled high with sweet potatoes. Fruit and vegetables—tomato, okra, mango and cucumber—from the outlying farms were brought to the *souk* every morning along this route. Abdul Rahman greeted the driver cheerfully and folded his arms across his breast to watch the rig go by. The dark red horse stepped eagerly, looking very flashy in his green and red harness. The low sides of the wagon were painted green and red and yellow. The colors reminded Abdul Rahman of his childhood home far to the south: green for the lush fields of sugar cane and *berseem* clover, red for the dark Nile mud and yellow for the sun and the sand.

After picking up the stray bits of trash, Abdul Rahman rearranged the loose stones and pieces of broken masonry to suit his fancy. The previous night had been cold, and the policemen on duty had lit a fire for warmth, moving some of the larger rocks to make a little hearth. Abdul Rahman, however, liked to keep the largest stone, which was shaped like a boat, at the foot of his favorite eucalyptus tree where it made a comfortable seat. So, as on most winter mornings, he had a little struggle shifting it back into place.

Not that he spent much time seated. For most of each day he remained on his feet, as ramrod straight as the trees, standing close beside the bridge, greeting passersby, sometimes walking a few paces down the road to stretch his legs. But for a little while each day, usually after midday prayers, Abdul Rahman liked to take his ease, and at such times he liked to sit and feel the bark of the eucalyptus against his back. At such times he watched the reflection of the trees in the canal, and studied the goings-on of the insects clinging to the long grasses bobbing by the water's edge. He only moved enough to wave a slow hand at the passing canal boats, content to watch the pilots wave back with equal tranquillity. It was at such times that he knew he would be signing up for a third tour.

At midday, year in and year out, rattletrap donkey carts trundled by, operated by pairs or trios of rag-tag children. At each villa along the road, one or two of the children would leap off the cart and disappear into yard or entranceway, returning with bags or cartons full of garbage, which they piled onto the high-sided carts. Abdul Rahman did not greet these children cheerfully. He sniffed to show his disdain, and shouted at them in a loud voice if they came too near when he didn't want them—and in a louder voice when he did. In the latter instance, they approached warily, took with feigned terror what bits of refuse he gave them, and scampered away. Then Abdul Rahman sniffed again. They were the *zebeleen*, the garbage people, socially inferior. They lived in the City of Garbage by the Hills of Mokkattem and had no education, no religion and no law. But they did a good job collecting the garbage, year in and year out.

In late spring, when the days grew hot and then sweltering, the policemen put on their white summer uniforms with matching white berets. Born and bred in the furnace of Upper Egypt, they did not mind the heat. Only when the holy month of Ramadan—during which they took neither food nor water from dawn to dusk—occurred in summer did some of them suffer. Then they sat swooning, their heads fallen forward on their knees, sweat beading on their sallow faces. But while others sagged, Abdul Rahman stood at his post as usual, alert and cheerful, greeting the gardeners and tradesman as they passed by on their bicycles or with their pushcarts. He kept in the shade of the eucalyptus trees, but it was his pride to remain upright and smiling when his younger comrades were limp and fainting in the scorching heat.

It was also his delight during Ramadan to say a prayer and take the first sip of water after the cannon was fired at sunset. The food he carried with him for *iftar*, the breakfast, was no different than what he ate during the rest of the year—bread and white cheese, with perhaps a pickle or two—but it always tasted better during Ramadan. And there was a generous lady who lived in the flat-topped villa across the way who never failed to send out a plate of delicacies for him: tangy apricots, spicy rice cooked with raisins and sweetmeats, *molukhaya* and *omali*, which slipped down the throat so easily at the end of a meal. Those were happy times which matured into happy memories to savor in the after months.

As the memories collected over the years, Abdul Rahman began to notice that some things were changing, and not all for the better. When he first came to Maadi children celebrated the holy month by dancing along the roads in groups after *iftar*, swinging their Ramadan lanterns and singing. But as time passed, the streets became empty in the evenings, and the children preferred to stay indoors and watch quiz shows on television while their parents continued the feast till dawn and then slept the day away to shorten the fast.

Abdul Rahman frowned on all such shirking of duty. He tried to make the long trip to Upper Egypt to see his family at least once a year, to bring them the little money he had saved and to help with the harvest. During these visits he fathered two more daughters, and his wife Nouzha began to keep chickens. But the cost of the train ticket went steadily upward, and one year he did not go at all, entrusting the money to a friend who was himself making the trip south. After his little son died, he went home even less often.

At the end of Abdul Rahman's fifth tour the captain called him into his office and told him it was time to depart the police force and return to his family. But Abdul Rahman knew the money he was able to send his family as a policeman was the most he could ever hope to make, given his lack of skills and the fierce competition for even the most menial jobs. And though he did not say so, he dreaded the prospect of leaving his beloved Mostafa Kamil Bridge. So he further delayed the already endless process of completing his paperwork, and merely shrugged when his sergeant stared hard at him and said he had heard he was leaving. Abdul Rahman clung to his routine, determined to wait the situation out. After a few months the sergeant ceased his comments and once again took Abdul Rahman's presence for granted. After a year had passed, the captain stopped asking him if he had gotten his discharge papers stamped yet.

Time drifted by—a day, a month, a year—much like the last. But one memorable day in late summer, word filtered down that the government was going to fill in the canal. The fields on the east bank of the Nile grew nothing now but tall apartment buildings, and the people in them had no use for brackish irrigation water. Pipes, filtration units and sewer systems were what they wanted. Modern technology was turning the desert, even far from Cairo, into farmland. Maintaining the canal—the yearly dredging and the upkeep of the secondary ditches—was too expensive for the sake of so few farms. Abdul Rahman was heartsick at the prospect of the coming destruction and thought, This would not have happened in Gamal Abdul Nasser's day.

For many weeks, he stood at his post and watched the noisy, ugly trucks bring in sand from the desert while teams of barefoot, gray-garbed workers, laborers he might have joined had he not become a policeman, shoveling the sand into the empty canal. In his waking dreams he pictured the eucalyptus trees lying stricken on the ground, their broken branches scattered on the road, and felt tears streaming hot down his narrow face. His youthful partner told him he cared for the trees more than he did for the ladies, and then laughed when Abdul Rahman could not explain why he felt as he did.

But after the canal was filled in and the work crews had left, the double row of eucalyptus trees still stood. The grass grew quickly in the shallow depression that had been the canal, and bushes were planted that would bear tiny red and yellow flowers in spring. The following year, and every year thereafter, children came to play on this new shady lawn. Families picnicked there on Sham El Nassim, the spring holiday named in honor of Smelling the Breezes. After months of dust and noise, Abdul Rahman's life returned to normal. But there were two differences. First, to get a drink of water he had to walk down a side road to the public water urn (a red-clay vessel shaped like a headless, narrow-waisted woman, with a flat rock on top to keep the animals out). Second, Abdul Rahman kept his post by the bridge alone.

The filling in of the canal had been swift and painful. Other changes occurred so gradually that he didn't notice them until they were complete, at which time he could only shrug in resignation. One day he realized it had been a long time since he had been able to make the trip to Aswan, and although relatives continued to bring him news of his family, his wife and children seemed very far away, and he did not think of them so much anymore. His mother had died, and their little farm had been rented out. Eventually, Abdul Rahman took a second wife, a young woman crippled from polio who was the sister of

Ahmed Behnassoui, the driver. For two years they lived in a room hard by the policemen's barracks, from which he still caught the cattle truck each morning. But then the young woman died, and he moved back to the barracks, and did not look for another wife.

When he was young Abdul Rahman had giggled and whistled along with the others when a girl of questionable virtue walked by, although even then he had felt guilty about doing so. *"Taali, zibadi!"* the bolder ones called if a girl's skirt showed a bit of plump white calf—"Come here, white yogurt!"—or worse. Then they whistled and hooted as she hastened away. But eventually Abdul Rahman conquered the demon within him and stopped joining in such games. One day he spoke harshly to a young policeman he caught behaving in such a fashion, shaming him into silence. In his heart, he did not like to see a girl immodestly dressed or walking alone down the road, but he knew it was none of a policeman's business.

He had to remind himself of this fact more often than usual the autumn the Generous Lady's granddaughter came to visit. She was very modern, and it was hard for Abdul Rahman to keep the disapproval from his face when he saw her going out with boys from college or sitting wearing shorts on the chaise lounge in the yard. She was disgracing her grandmother, he thought. He said nothing, but spent much time shaking his head, his usually cheerful expression fixed in a censorious scowl.

That year during Ramadan the granddaughter sometimes brought Abdul Rahman his *iftar* plate. Each time he thanked her humbly, but she was very ungracious, as if the task she was forced to perform were beneath her. He was surprised, therefore, when one evening she chose to speak to him.

"I've always wondered something," she said, eyeing him with condescension. "What exactly do you do here?"

"I guard the bridge," said Abdul Rahman politely.

The girl regarded him with large, intelligent eyes. Then she glanced toward the greensward between the trees and at the road that crossed it. "What bridge?"

Abdul Rahman shrugged, but then placed his hand on the stone parapet that still bordered the road for eight meters. The girl looked at the parapet, unimpressed, and went back to the villa.

As each autumn turned to winter he wondered if the weather was not getting colder with each passing year. As he grew older, he found it harder to keep warm in the cold months, although he wore all the clothes he owned under his black wool uniform. The other policemen made fun of him, calling him "clothes store," but what could he do? Most other things were growing harder each year as well. Everything, in fact, except the fasting during the holy month of Ramadan. That grew easier.

The open cattle trucks were replaced by large blue vehicles with blue canvas tops, but the tradition of saving the brakes for emergencies still held, and Abdul Rahman's hop off the tailgate was not as spry as it had once been. There was a new driver who had little sympathy for him and sometimes played games with him, much to the delight of his comrades who thought it was a good joke that such an old man kept amongst their ranks. Their laughter was not pleasant, but Abdul Rahman endured it with good humor. One day he tripped in a pothole while scrambling after the truck and fell hard, breaking his arm. That was a difficult winter, for the arm was slow to heal and never worked quite right again. The captain spoke harshly to the driver and to the men who had been on the truck, and after that Abdul Rahman had no further trouble with them. But this too saddened him, for he knew he and his colleagues were separated by a barrier he could no longer cross.

But the basket man, his red and green woven wares piled impossibly high on his head, still liked to stop and pass the time of day. He never failed to assure Abdul Rahman that his bridge was a fine location for peddling—such a nice shady intersection. Likewise, the knife-sharpener who trundled by on Tuesday afternoons pushing his heavy handcart always stopped to speak with him—although he only talked about the growing stiffness of his legs and what medicines he was taking to bring about the return of his youthful vigor. One day Abdul Rahman mentioned that the doctor had said there was something wrong with his kidneys, but the knife-sharpener seemed quite wounded at this presumption on Abdul Rahman's part, so he did not bring it up again.

Besides the peddlers, Abdul Rahman still enjoyed exchanging greetings with the street sweepers, women of his own age dressed in black who appreciated his trees and his politeness. And the latest generation of *zebeleen* children still appeared daily, shouting at each other as they scampered from villa to villa. They tore past Abdul Rahman in their efforts to keep up with the lopsided donkey cart while the lucky driver laughed and beat his little gray donkeys, their noses to the ground as they strained under their load.

The Generous Lady across the way did not leave her villa any more. She suffered from a mysterious complaint that involved daily shots from a visiting pharmacist, limited movement before noon and a preference for hushed whispers. But she did not forget Abdul Rahman. At least once a week, even when it was not Ramadan, she sent her servant, Nabila, to him laden with a sampler of tasty foods as well as advice on how to avoid a cold that winter or how he should stay in the shade next summer. When the government put the new sidewalks in, they broke the water urn on the nearby side road and did not replace it, but from then on Nabila brought Abdul Rahman water in a plastic bottle every day, and he felt himself very well off indeed.

In the evenings, Abdul Rahman liked to hobble down to the River behind the police barracks, where he would sit on a rock and enjoy the close of the day.

"No Nile, no Egypt...." So sang the feluccamen, sitting curled at the bases of their tall masts as they carried the tourists up and down the river at sunset. Their white sails swept graceful arcs across the deep blue sky, reminding him of the wings of the ibis he had seen in his youth. "...No Egypt, no Nile." On a clear night he could see the pyramids of Giza behind the tall palm trees across the river: unconquerable monuments to the past.

One morning in mid-winter, Abdul Rahman was slower than usual getting up. He was tired because he had been too cold to sleep, and he could not pass water. He struggled to pull his boots on and get to the truck before it left. "Don't go," said a colleague, concern evident in his eyes. Helping hands lifted him onto the truck, and when he arrived at his post the driver came to a complete stop and waited until Abdul Rahman was safely on the ground.

He did not have the strength to stand on his own, but it was without regret that he lowered himself onto his favorite rock and leaned his back against the gnarled eucalyptus. Mercifully, the air was still and he was not uncomfortable. He closed his eyes. When he opened them it was midday and warm. He closed his eyes again and enjoyed the heat of the sun on his face. He opened his eyes and watched a pack of schoolboys hurry by, carrying books and satchels. It was mid-afternoon. Time seemed to be passing rapidly. He closed his eyes again.

At the end of the day the setting sun shot red and yellow rays through the treetops and touched his face. He opened his eyes and looked around. The rich light enflamed the poinsettias that grew head-high along the stone parapet, and they glowed as if from an inner source, throbbing red and gold. He slid sideways off the rock and slumped onto the ground, face downward. He thought he had come to his final resting place, until strong hands pulled at his shoulders till he was half sitting, supported by the rock and the tree roots.

"What's wrong, *ya Hajj*?" came an anxious voice. He smiled at the words; he had always been a little sad that he had never been on the Hajj, and the use of the honorific—although still premature—pleased him. He opened his eyes to see the Generous Lady's granddaughter—now a married woman and a mother herself, he had heard—kneeling beside him.

"Nothing is wrong, lady," he said.

Her eyes were as intelligent as ever, and he saw she understood what he meant. "Can I get you anything, *ya Hajj*?" she asked.

His mouth was dry. "A glass of water," he said.

"Nabila!" The granddaughter's voice was sharp with urgency.

He closed his eyes again, and opened them when he felt the granddaughter's hand behind his head and the glass at his lips.

The water tasted very sweet. He licked his lips, refreshed. He looked up into the granddaughter's face, and smiled.

"Don't cry, lady. I am not worth your tears."

The granddaughter shook her head. "You are our life's blood."

He heard no more.

The Generous Lady turned over in her bed when her granddaughter told her what had happened, and as Nabila rushed off to prepare herb tea, tears gathered on her puffy pink and white face and wet her pillow. The basket man when he heard the news said, "By the grace of Allah the beneficent and the merciful," and out of respect sat for a while on the boat-shaped rock, until a passerby woke him from his reverie demanding to buy a basket. The *zebeleen* children stopped and stared in awkward silence but, remembering the consequences that awaited them if they lingered too long, raced away after the donkey cart. Abdul Rahman's captain shook his head and signed an order dated six years previously directing him to remove the non-existent Mostafa Kamil Bridge from the list of police posts.

The eucalyptus trees stand there still.

# Confessions of a
# Left-handed Trinidadian Cook

*By* Anthony Milne

One evening in a Port of Spain bar an extraordinary young woman looked my way and said: Do you cook? I immediately began a lecture on the joys of creole cooking and my theory that the male Trinidadian creole (I actually meant French-creole, local white, in the broadest sense) is often a fine cook. I cited the culinary talents of my grandfather, uncles and male cousins and said that I too had inherited the gift.

I had missed the point, of course, and the opportunity. I lack the killer instinct. I am too theoretical and impractical, too caught up in my own cloudy, imaginative world, too absent-minded. A lazy, left-handed procrastinator, my short-term memory is appalling. Many years too late I see she was asking: Will you cook for me?

And I would have, of course.

But I really do have some hereditary culinary talent, enhanced by experimental inclinations which spring naturally from that cloudy imagination of mine. I needn't go into detail about the special dexterity required of left-handed cooks, since every single kitchen utensil is designed for those who work from the other side.

My father claims to have taught my mother to cook, though I have never seen him create anything more original than a fine pair of toasts. Somebody else, I understand, taught her how to drive. In the end she chose the cook over the driver. She doesn't regret it. My father's father, when he took a break from prosecuting people for tax evasion, made excellent black-beef stews, with plenty of burnt brown sugar. He was still cooking well into his eighties. His buljol and souse were unparalleled.

My uncle Terence, when he is not drawing deeds or preparing briefs, is an absolute master in the kitchen, especially with morocoy, quenk or lappe. I once got into trouble with the environmentalist lobby by quoting his recipe for stewed morocoy. Four or five of my male cousins are excellent cooks. One of them has helped manage a restaurant; another is a chef in one of London's best hotels.

Another uncle, a hunter as well as a cook, built his own large, two-burner, stainless-steel device to cook big soups and wild meat. He kept it in the garage and worked there while he imbibed and played Wagner records at a volume way above the legal limit.

My aunts, of course, are all superb creole cooks. What I would have done without my aunts I will never know. Theirs has been an undying, always forgiving, welcoming, belly-filling love.

I myself am nowhere near as talented as my uncles and cousins. But black-beef stew I too do well, sometimes with dumplings, sometimes with many other things. I can roast a fowl, seasoned uniquely, though I am really a flesh person, not a bone person. In this way I am unlike most members of my family. When they are through with a chicken leg there is nothing left. No trace of bones, feathers, nothing. I can make a reasonable pilau, though the rice may sometimes turn out too soft or too grainy. It's a matter of timing. The best cooking is done slowly. As the French say: *Avec de la patience on arrive tout.*

Often I am too hasty. The blood rushes to my head. It has got me into trouble in other ways. Ask the Four Roads, Diego Martin, police. My fried bakes are something to behold, and often to taste. I make a good cup of coffee, and I don't mean instant, which I never use. Otherwise I survive on oats, unboiled, with raisins, sugar and milk. I doubt anyone in Trinidad has consumed as much raw oats as I have. It is one of the few foods I eat that is really good for me. I detest all greens and most fruits, especially when ripe.

In my early youth, I am now ashamed to say, I slaughtered an immense number of birds, lizards, crabs and other creatures with a Diana .22 air rifle. Some of these creatures I plucked, cleaned, fried carefully and devoured. I can tell you there is very little flesh on a ground dove or bluebird. But, being close to the bone, it is sweet. Keskidees I never tried. I will one day soon if they persist with the racket they make outside my bedroom window at five in the morning.

Once or twice I have taken the life of a ramier or manicou with a shotgun. I kept a small snake once and used to strike down mabouyas with a broom to feed it. I wouldn't do this again. The truth is that I now find it almost impossible to kill. I make an exception for mosquitoes, big cockroaches that fly into my bedroom at night, and fat rats. When I have had enough of them I carry out a pogrom.

My pacifism has reached the stage that I won't even go fishing. This is only partly out of principle. Mostly it is a matter of emotion. I am terrified at the thought of suffering and the finality of death. My own and others. This includes plants. I have seriously thought of starting a Society for the Prevention of Cruelty to Plants. No one thinks they have feelings. I don't know why.

This does not mean I am a vegetarian. I tried it once, but the withdrawal symptoms, the need for cooked flesh, were too great, like my desire for a daily dose of rice. Let someone else do the killing and dressing, I'll do the cooking. I became a vegetarian partly out of necessity when I was a student. The philosophical impetus came from a reading of the Mahatama's autobiography. But he was celibate and ended up eating only fruit and nuts. That was going too far.

As a homebody I have an interest even greater than cooking: plants. Especially wild, exotic plants found in the forest. Everyone laughs when I tell them about my potted timarie. They stop laughing when I tell them that people in Holland pay quite a lot for what they call the "sensitive plant."

The word timarie is French-Trinidadian patois: *Ti-Marie*, from the French *Petite Marie*, "Little Mary" Some distant relative of mine must have thought its tiny leaves, closing when touched, looked like praying hands. If I had any entrepreneurial spirit I would start a timarie farm and export the best of them to Amsterdam. But without any business sense, I follow the timarie's example and merely pray to win the lotto.

My timarie is just one of a number of selected plants I keep. Though I don't sweep or cook as often as I should, I think I've inherited my maternal grandmother's green thumb. She must have got it from the long line of St Kitts planters she was descended from. A couple hundred years ago, one of them, a Miss Burt (their family name) married a friend of the great Dr Johnson.

Her husband, a physician, spent most of his spare time writing a five-volume poem on sugar cane. When I told a colleague I liked going into the bush to find wild plants, he said I was one in a million. That may be true, but not in this instance. There can't be only half of another person like me in the Republic.

Avid orchid collectors often risk thorny undergrowth, mapepires and tarantulas in search of specimens. All plants come originally from the bush. They were all wild till somebody tamed them. Then botanists produced hybrid versions. The undiscerning eye looks at the forest floor and sees only tangled weeds. Look more carefully, distinguish them individually, and you find the most beautiful things.

I have a shrub with pale green leaves that turn silver in the sunlight. I don't mean the familiar little shining bush, though I have one of those too. A man in Tamana, describing the mysteries of the hill, told me there were trees with silver leaves. I knew right away what he meant. I like ferns too. Many kinds are found all over Trinidad, especially at high elevations such as along the road to Maracas. If you go high enough, up to El Tucuche, say, above 2,000 feet the air and vegetation change abruptly. I got a miniature balisier there which thrived well in the garden but hardly ever flowered.

At the Aripo savannah there are curious specimens, like the tiny insect-eating sundew and a rare little ground orchid with yellow flowers. I broke all the rules and took home one of these orchids. It did well till its pot fell over one day. At Fig Walk, deep in the Matura Forest there is a tree like a banana you probably won't see anywhere else. A friend and I once walked so far into this forest we had to overnight. Luckily, there was a clear stream nearby full of fat crayfish, and nothing crawled over us while we lay in the bush, trying to sleep.

The next day an old hunter said he often slept in the forest, curled up between the big roots of a mora. My friend walked out of the forest the next day carrying a young fig tree. I took it to a botanist as an excuse to see and talk to her, and we fell in love. But I was never sure whether she preferred the fig tree or me.

People in Trinidad judge plants, trees especially, for their usefulness and tradition. When you build a house you must have an orange, a mango, and a zaboca. These are all fine trees, but if I ever have a house I will plant a flamboyant first.

I like growing trees in pots. I can't claim to know much about bonsais, though I have a book about them. I have a banana tree in a big pot in the verandah and a magnificent flamboyant in a much smaller pot. Also a small palm, and a frangipani I've thought of planting out at the family plot in Lapeyrouse. (For some reason there are frangipanis in cemeteries all through the West Indies.) Have you ever been into a field of flowering coffee trees? The air is filled with the sweetest scent. I kept a coffee tree once. It lived for years but didn't get taller than three feet and never flowered.

One of my favourites is the bois canon, with a long, slender white trunk and leaves that look like crumpled hands when they fall to the ground and turn brown. (A man from Guyana told me it is called conga pump there. In Jamaica it is called the trumpet tree and makes a weeping sound before a hurricane hits). I planted one recently in the deep window box in the verandah. It is still small and the landlord doesn't know, so don't tell him. Someone warned me it was bad luck to plant a bois canon, but I decided to chance it.

My tulsi bush, which Hindus consider sacred and plant beneath jundi poles, should keep evil forces at bay. It is also meant to keep away mosquitoes, though I can't testify to this.

Also in my window box are two vines, a creeping plant with white-veined green leaves, and a pau pau tree about six foot tall. I don't think it will get any bigger. A concerned aunt advised against leaving it there. She said pau pau trees use up a lot of oxygen. I told her I don't need much. The pau pau tree has flowered, but there is no sign of fruit. It may be a male. The usual advice in cases like this is to cut off the top and place an upside-down container on it to stop water running down into the trunk. This will change its sex. But that is the last thing I would want to do, so we are both likely to remain childless bachelors.

Also on the verandah is an old bougainvillaea with white and purple flowers. It was there when I moved in. It grows on the burglar-proofing, with a little training, and is forming an arch over the gate.

Looking after these plants, watering them, pruning them and watching them grow, means I have little time for other household chores. But I don't think you can die of dust, and a bowl of uncooked oats, raisins and sugar is wonderfully nutritious.

# Letter from Halifax

*By* Richard Cumyn

*Halifax, November 12, 1998*

I remember hearing, long before I had visited Nova Scotia—fabled province of schooners and pirates, smuggled rum and buried treasure—that Peggy's Cove, a half-hour's drive south of Halifax, had been chosen the most picturesque place in Canada. More breath-taking geography can be found elsewhere in this country, in the high Arctic, the Rocky Mountains, Cape Breton, the Gaspé Peninsula, or Newfoundland. To try to describe it—a few brightly painted houses, some fishing boats beside a seaweed-covered dock, a tall white lighthouse anchored to a mooring of granite jutting into the entrance to St. Margaret's Bay—beggars the beauty of the place. Nor do colour photographs do it justice, although a plethora of these bucolic stills, with their Crayola reds and blues and salt-bleached whites, adorn calendars and coffee table books *a mare usque ad mare*. No, you have to walk up the hill into the village, past the carved granite memorial to those lost at sea, and then down beyond the lighthouse and onto the smooth rock—not too close, for every year someone is swept into the icy swell by a rogue wave—to be fully romanced by Peggy's Cove.

The sign says that only sixty people live in the village now. Not many earn their livelihood fishing anymore. The restaurant, which boasts the best clam chowder in the region, serves a steady influx of tour bus travellers year round and, along with a craft shop or two, is the main employer. The residents grumble quietly about shutterbugs tramping through their flower beds in search of the ideal camera angle, but they don't complain about the intrusion as much as they used to, back when the spot first became a destination. The place has become somewhat of an artificial construct in the last twenty years, not quite a theme park, but not quite a real fishing village either. Without paying visitors it would surely cease to be populated.

Over the years many people have made unintended landfall there, to be ministered to by doctors, priests or undertakers as the case demanded. The waters in the area are notoriously dangerous to ships, and there are wrecks spanning centuries strewn across the floor of the continental shelf. The sea in its bounty and its rage has left its indelible mark, on the rock and on the faces of those whose people are buried in the thin soil. These are no strangers to calamity. A stretch of good weather, like a run of good luck, is usually tempered by the remark, "Ah, yes, but we'll pay for it soon enough." They know well the late-night vigil for a missing boat or a ship in distress.

For all this, their knowledge of pain, their long history of loss, nothing could have prepared the residents of St. Margaret's Bay for what happened in the late hours of September 2, 1998, when Swiss Air flight 111, en route from New York to Geneva, went down in waters 10 kilometers off the Cove, and all 229 passengers and crew perished. And nothing suited Peggy's Cove less than did its transformation into an impromptu command center for the armies converging there: police, armed forces personnel from Canada and the United States, journalists, politicians, doctors, forensic pathologists.

In the first hours after the crash—so loud it shook houses and woke residents up and down the coastline—local news coverage used the term "rescue effort." But as the light came up the next day, giving the motley fleet of small vessels a clear look at the debris field, and as the magnitude of the crash became clear, they stopped talking about finding anyone alive. The plane hit so hard that only the landing gear remained recognizable. The RCMP kept anyone not involved in the search away from the coastline as the gruesome task of retrieving evidence and determining the cause of the crash continued. Peacekeepers returned from Bosnia, seasoned police veterans of highway accidents, and doctors whose job it is to reassemble mangled bodies were shocked speechless by what came ashore bit by bit.

Much of the plane has not yet been retrieved even as I write. The heartrending task of identifying body parts, mainly through DNA matching, continues. Both of the so-called black boxes, the flight data and voice recorders, may have stopped working before the plane's crew knew anything was wrong with the electrical system, before the cockpit filled with smoke and caught on fire. The theory that faulty wiring insulation caused a complete electrical failure has yet to be proven conclusively. An eyewitness said he saw the plane's cockpit on fire as it passed overhead. Retrieved pieces of melted metal from the cockpit suggest that intense heat and smoke concentrated there were such that the flight team could not have been sitting at the controls for the last few minutes of the flight, that they either succumbed at their places or fled aft. After jettisoning fuel before turning towards Halifax International Airport to attempt an emergency landing, the plane suddenly dropped, hitting the water nose-first and disintegrating on impact.

Swiss Air flew the victims' relatives to Halifax so they could see the place where the airplane went down. They were put up at hotels in the city and driven out to Peggy's Cove. All along the route were make-shift signs expressing condolence. One was a simple Swiss cross, white on red, and the number 111 written below it. Even as the salvage operation continued, news coverage showed small groups of people, dressed in dark suits, standing, holding onto each other for assurance and stability on the bare outcrop, and gazing far out over the waters.

We knew them the instant we saw them coming out of the Lord Nelson Hotel not far from where we live. Such a loss marks a person, sets her apart in a protective bubble of grief and detachment. They had a gravity, an air of nobility about them. One of the mourners said on television that she was happy—happy!—that the last thing her father saw before he died was this magnificent meeting place of land and sea. The water was surprisingly blue and calm that day, the sky clear. To look out as they did that day, shading their eyes from the warm sun, upon a gravesite so glittering and smooth and unmarked by what it contained, must have been a baffling experience. How could so placid a scene have been the location of such horror?

The families attended church services in Peggy's Cove and Halifax. The names of all 229 were read aloud. Some family members rose to speak about those who were now so suddenly and inexplicably absent from their lives. As one woman waited at the front of a church for her turn to speak, she tried to hold back her tears, and searched in her purse for a handkerchief. Those who had congregated, as much to address their own grief as to show support for the grieving, waited, held their collective breath, watched her dissolve by increments in front of them, and were impotent in their silent concern, until a little girl came forward with a tissue, handed it to the woman, and then all walls came down.

In 1912, many of the unclaimed bodies from the Titanic were brought to Halifax for burial. In 1917, when a ship loaded with munitions collided with another in the harbor, Halifax was devastated by the largest man-made explosion ever experienced, one that would not be surpassed in magnitude until the atomic bomb exploded over Hiroshima in 1945. One of those giving a eulogy to the Swiss Air dead reminded his listeners of this point to say that Nova Scotians can offer, if not the comfort of a miracle, then at least empathy. They know about loss and will never be hardened or insensitive to grief. Pilgrimages to this watery grave will be quiet, anguished, and intensely private. Who would willingly profit from such sadness as this?

# A Betting Man

By Vallath Nandakumar

Mohan felt the coolness on his damp body as he walked through the dark passageway from the bathroom into his bedroom. Selecting a clean white loincloth, and a shirt with buttons down the front that he could easily remove in the temple, he finished dressing.

His mother was in the gods' room doing her daily 9 a.m. ritual of offering bananas and parched rice in silver dishes to the gods. "Did you dry your hair properly, Mohan?" she called out mechanically.

"Yes," Mohan answered with a trace of impatience, although water was dripping in tickling streams down his neck.

"Well, take an umbrella. The sun is too hot. And remember, if you go to the temple, to break a coconut for Ganapathi."

Umbrella! Mohan disdained to reply to his mother, and with a jaunty upward flick of his ankle, he folded his *mundu* up like a kilt, put on his sandals, and walked out into the hot April sunshine.

His grandmother and her brother were sitting on the porch. Mohan paused to let his eyes adjust to the brightness outside.

"Where are you going in this heat, Mohan? Don't you have exams to study for?" his grandmother Kalyani Amma demanded. She was a dignified old woman, past eighty, but her eyesight and hearing were still sharp. And her tongue, thought Mohan. That was the sharpest. She was the matriarch and the ruler of the Konnath family, even though her brother Krishnan Nair was the titular head, the *karanavar*.

"I have to do things," Mohan muttered evasively, and hurried down the porch steps to the little shelter over the gate to their yard.

His great-uncle Krishnan Nair said nothing. An old man with a long white beard, he never took any interest in family matters, being concerned solely with his poetry. "Visual poetry," the critics called it,

46

and it seemed to just play on the peculiarities of the Malayalam language and the stringing together of syllables. But he was famous. Mohan sometimes reflected that he seemed to not live in this world. Although the Konnath family wealth had dwindled in the last few generations, there was still enough left to support the family, the income being eked out with the help of people like Mohan's father. Most of the paddy fields and fruit orchards were managed by Mohan's uncles and other granduncles, since Krishnan Nair did nothing as worldly as estate management. The world must have poets too, he would counter lamely in the rare moments when he chose to respond to his sister's criticism of his lack of interest in family affairs.

Mohan decided to take the long way to the temple, avoiding the potholed and dusty main road with its open lorries and horse-drawn carriages. His friends were loafing about outside their "club," a tiny room which they had rented out from the shop owner Pillai in front. Pillai sold bananas, cigarettes and fresh limejuice, and bantered with the boys when he was between customers.

The clubroom was sparsely furnished, with a rough table with a surface covered with carved initials and doodles, a couple of benches and a chair or two. The club's recreational equipment consisted of a couple of worn packs of cards, a cricket set, and a soccer ball. The main entertainment value of the club lay in its members, however, who could always be assured of finding a friend to chat with if they managed to escape there from under the watchful eyes of their parents. In addition, the room was tucked away from prying eyes, and was thus the ideal getting-away place for teenage boys trying to assert their independence. Mohan looked around quickly to make sure that none of his relatives were on the street, and asked the shopkeeper for a cigarette.

"And a piece of peanut candy." The peanut candy was essential to remove the cigarette's smell before he reached home.

"Four annas," the shopkeeper said. "When are your exams?"

"In four weeks," said Mohan, putting his cigarette into his pocket. "Plenty of time to study," he added defensively, even though studying was the last thing that would have occurred to the shopkeeper, who had not even studied up to his 10th standard.

Mohan peered into the dim interior of the clubroom. His friends stopped their heated card game. "Come on over and join us for a while. We have some details to discuss about tomorrow's match. You are playing, aren't you?"

"Yes, of course," said Mohan, walking over. "I hear Velan's hand has healed, and he will be their goalie."

"I know," said one of the boys. "And we have to have a seven-a-side game. Many of the other fellows are studying for their high-school exams."

"Mug-pots," he said scathingly. "Can't rely on them."

"Going to the temple?" another boy asked with a sly smile. "Are you going to see your goddess?"

Mohan started, and the others roared with laughter. He hadn't known that they guessed his secret passion for Parvathi, and that he went to the temple every Friday morning to catch a glimpse of her. Friday was the day unmarried girls went to the temple of Siva and Parvathi, the gods who blessed marital bliss, and his beloved-from-afar dutifully went to pray to her namesake goddess for a good husband.

"She won't even turn around to look at him," the boy with the sly smile teased.

"Poor Mohan."

"Oho?" Mohan replied, stung. "What do you know," he added, smiling mysteriously and squaring his shoulders.

"Well, if you two are such a hot item, prove it," his taunter challenged. "Bring back some jasmine flowers from her. After all, jasmine is the flower of love." He imitated a coy girl as he said "love," and all of them laughed again. Like jackasses, Mohan thought disgustedly.

"Bet!" he said aloud. "If I bring it back, you must pay for my cigarettes and peanut candy for a month. Otherwise I will pay."

"Agreed," nodded the other, grinning, and they shook hands, while another boy "cut" their hands apart with his own to seal the wager.

I am a total fool, he thought moodily to himself. She will kill me if I ask her for jasmine flowers, and I will look like an idiot in front of my friends. Or worse, she will act surprised and tell me that she had always thought of me as a "good friend" or a "brother," and embarrass me. She might never speak to me afterwards. These thoughts occupied him until he reached the temple.

On arriving, Mohan took his sandals off, let down his folded loincloth and entered, just remembering to take his shirt off. He did not want to get caught by the temple manager for entering with a shirt. Men had to approach the god without vanity, with breast bared. Too bad women don't have to remove their blouses, he laughed inwardly.

He did however get a chance to satisfy his curiosity in the mornings, when he went to the bigger Vishnu temple early every day, before sunrise. The red light of dawn would just be breaking, and he would walk to the nearby river, and swim in the men's *kadavu* by the red laterite stone steps. The water would be cool and quiet, and when he looked towards the women's side, he could often see them washing their clothes and bathing with their breasts bared. Of course, he was just curious, he would tell himself, suppressing a pang of guilt, as he dried off and put on clean clothes for the temple. It is because our society is so orthodox and sick that people gossiped even when I talked to a girl, he would think vehemently. This in the land of the Kama Sutra, the great treatise on sex and love! Look at the West, where boys and girls freely interact! He felt sure that the boys in the West did not constantly think of girls' bare bodies. Of course, he wouldn't want everyone to look at Parvathi's hidden charms.

The brief swim in the river always left him refreshed for the whole morning. His grandmother told him she was impressed by his dawn temple visits, even though she was an old woman and knew the ways of the world, and had guessed that piety was only one of the reasons he was so regular. Although she dominated him mercilessly, Mohan could in fact deal with his grandmother better than with the rest of his largely female family.

The temple smelled of burning oil and camphor, and he heard the buzzing beat of the *edakka* drum showing that the main morning ritual had started. Mohan stepped over the high granite step into the inner courtyard and stood aside with folded hands, waiting for the door to the inner shrine to open. The temple was crowded, and he felt hot. In between muttering prayers, he let his eyes wander while he searched for "her" in the crowd. Suddenly the door opened and displayed the statues of the god Shiva and the goddess Parvathi, decorated with flowers and illuminated with oil-lamps. A little boy rang the big bell furiously, just as he, Mohan, had as a little boy whenever he had managed to secure that privilege. The priest circled the image with a small plate with burning camphor, and passed the plate to the worshippers so that they might touch the flame to their eyes and pray. May our egos be burnt up like the camphor, leaving nothing behind but the brightness of true knowledge. Mohan closed his eyes and prayed to the gods for success in exams, and then for strength, wisdom, and knowledge. He murmured the Sanskrit prayer asking their blessings as parents of the universe, as inseparable from each other as word and meaning.

Suddenly he felt a hand on his shoulder. "What, Mohan? How are matters with you? We haven't seen you at our place for many days!" He looked around to see Parvathi's aunt, a kindly old woman who frequently came by to his place to gossip with his own grandmother and mother. Parvathi looked on and smiled agreement with her aunt.

"Uh, yes," he stammered, and looked at Parvathi. She was looking divine, he thought, in her cream muslin with the green border, and he continued to stare at her figure.

"Well?" the aunt asked again. "When are you coming?"

"I will come by this morning," he said, his chest constricting at the thought of the bet he had made. "Will you be home?"

"Where else can we be? Be sure to come. Leela has made some new sweets, and you must taste them. Take some *prasadam*," she added, referring to the sandal paste from the priest, and drew a mark on his forehead. She and Parvathi left to finish their worship. Parvathi paused to glance back at him, and their eyes met for a moment before she turned away.

Mohan's gaze followed her until she disappeared round the corner. He was about to leave too, when he remembered the coconut for the elephant-headed Lord Ganapathi, the remover of obstacles. He walked to the offerings counter, and asked for a coconut.

"One rupee," the dour man at the counter told him, and handed over the coconut. He had a thread crossing his chest, signifying that he was of a high caste.

Mohan took the coconut and went to the shrine of Ganapathi, where he paused a moment. He meant to pray for success in his exams, but another silent prayer came unbidden to his mind as he dashed the coconut against the granite stone. It broke into many pieces, which a little boy standing by picked up and took to one of the temple buildings. He himself picked up a couple of pieces, for his mother would be sure to ask him for a piece of the god's coconut.

On the way out, he saw the gray temple elephant swaying to and fro, and when he approached, the elephant held out its trunk to him. Mohan placed one of the pieces at the end of the trunk, which quickly disappeared into its cavernous mouth. The elephant blinked and held out its trunk again, but Mohan shook his head and walked out, putting on his shirt and sandals.

He walked to his father's house, his mind still on his last prayer. His father lived very near the temple, and visited his mother in the evenings after dinner, spending the night at her house. Mohan himself belonged to his mother's family, and his uncles were his father figures, to train him and discipline him and guide him in the ways of men. Mohan was, however, very close to his own father, and went there almost every day.

His father was on the porch reading the paper, and put it down when Mohan came. Mohan fell into a reclining canvas chair, and his father called out to his sister to bring some water. Mohan greeted his aunt and gulped down the warm ginger water, and proceeded to tell his father all about his trouble with his class notes and the difficulty of getting books from the library at exam time.

"I may be able to send for books from Madras, if you give me a list of what you need," his father said. "And if you get good marks in your high-school exam, you know that I want you to go to Madras and study for your degree."

"Oh, no, Father, it is too much trouble to get books from Madras," Mohan protested. "And I don't know whether I want to go all the way there to study. I don't know anybody there, and Madras is even hotter than here."

"Nonsense. You must get your degree in a good university. You are a good student, if somewhat easily distracted, and you must make the most of your life when you are young. Have you been practicing yoga like I asked you to improve your concentration?"

Mohan did not like the idea of leaving his soccer friends, and especially Parvathi, he told himself. Who knows what would happen if he left? She might marry someone else, and even though she was only fifteen now, he would be away for three years, and she was sure to get a hundred marriage proposals by then. And he felt happy where he was: his parents were nearby, he had his friends for company, and he led a carefree life, punctuated only occasionally by the intrusion of any conflicts or responsibilities.

Neither did he want to broaden his mind. After all, everything there was to learn by traveling could be learned in his own town. He supposed that he took after his great-uncle Krishnan Nair in that respect. But there was a sense of inevitability at the whole thing. His life was beginning to move with a momentum that he could not stop or even direct.

He left his father's house and made his way to Parvathi's, stopping on the way to buy some flowers. He decided that he was going to give her some flowers, even if he couldn't get her to give him any. She was in the garden when he reached there. Barefoot and reaching high, she was pruning twigs from a hibiscus bush, while her blouse stretched over her figure. The sunlight falling on her bare midriff highlighted the fine downy hair on her skin and blurred its outline. Mohan stared as long as he was able, and then called, "Parvathi!"

"Mohan!" she exclaimed. "So you finally made it here. You haven't forgotten me after all!"

Mohan flushed in confusion, and felt sweat breaking out on his palms and under his arms. He tightened his grip on the flowers in his hand. Parvathi laughed, and Mohan flushed again.

"You know my father wants me to go to Madras to study at the University," he said. "I don't want to go for three years."

"Of course you should go. You will do very well," she said encouragingly. "And won't you be back for vacations?"

"I suppose so. But..." he stammered. "What will you do in that time?" The pressure of his yearnings propelled the question from him. It floated in the air between them like a piece of thistledown, and Mohan willed his mind to blow on it and urge it towards her.

"I will wait for you," she said suddenly. Her tone held a faint surprise, as if he should have known that already.

Mohan's bewilderment at this set his mind spinning. What does she mean, he wondered? She was even a minute ago laughing at him. For a moment he wondered whether she was teasing him. But he shook off his racing thoughts and, seizing the moment, walked up to her.

"You must wait," he said mustering up all his confidence.

With that, the knot in his stomach unraveled itself and his anxious sweat dried up. All the fears and doubts that he had been living with disappeared like a pinch of dust would in a puff of her breath. It was suddenly as if he had known her to be his for years, or maybe through many past lives.

"Give me the flowers from your hair as a symbol of your commitment. I will give you these." He handed over the yellow marigold flowers he had just bought, still damp in their banana leaf wrapping. They were slightly crushed and their scent was strong, and he wasn't sure whether they were the type girls wore in their hair, but he didn't care about all that any more.

Without a word, Parvathi removed the flowers from her hair and held them out to Mohan. She seemed to hold her face out to him along with the flowers, and suddenly Mohan felt a madness come over him. He gripped Parvathi by her shoulders, and planted a kiss clumsily on her nose and lips. It was his first kiss. Then, snatching the jasmine flowers from her, he turned around and walked away without waiting to see her expression.

Outside he pulled out a single flower and stuck it behind his ear, tossing the rest away. He only needed one.

His friends saw his jaunty walk when he passed them, although they did not notice his flower.

"So, did you get the flowers? I don't see any," his betting friend called out.

"No, I didn't get anything," Mohan said. "Cigarettes and candy on me for the next month." He then lit his own cigarette openly, and with Paradise in his stride, sauntered home.

# Memory's Nest

*By* Paul Toth

Exhausted from the four hundred miles of driving that day, Charley sat on the couch, a small one with just enough room for a big man like himself. The shades were drawn, but there were no neighbors to see him, only a town twenty miles away that as yet had no idea his house had suddenly been repossessed by Julia's widower. To them it remained unoccupied just as it had in all the years since her father died. They thought about the house only occasionally, perhaps when driving by on their way to the Interstate when they might say, "I wonder if she's ever coming home?" until the last few months, when they said, "Looks like she's never coming home now...thank God."

It was then that he saw what he called Julia's ghost, which was actually just the darkness at the edges of his vision. He preferred thinking this way. In order to feel differently about something, he simply called it by a different name. So "ghost" was preferable to his actual memory of Julia. The ghost, unlike his wife, was quite friendly, happy that he felt better now, encouraging him to relax and enjoy his remaining years. In fact, earlier that day the ghost had actually thanked him for the time he had spent with it-her. "I regret my black moods," the ghost said, "which you endured and eased for me." She, Julia herself, would never have said such a thing in real life. Nor would she have **ever placed fresh ice cubes in his drink or returned some portion of the bed covers** (which she routinely gathered about her head, trying to forget he existed).

"Yes, well," he said to himself. He located the barely used briefcase he had purchased so many years ago, took it around the back of the house, found a large rock and began hammering the leather. He continued doing so for fifteen minutes. By then it could be called a battered old briefcase. "You are my companion of many years," he lied to it, "and you have stayed with me since my first days in practice. You've faithfully carried my prescription pads and my coffee-stained notes and about 1,203,002 pencils, and for that I thank you by never, never parting with you, no matter how soiled your appearance, despite your holes and creases and the embarrassment you have often caused me in the presence of others."

He went inside to the bathroom. There was no electricity, so he had to lean close to the mirror to see his reflection. He studied his hair, pulling it back against the top of his head, stroking his newly regrown beard. He saw that his glasses were much too straight. He removed them, bent the frame a little to the right, then pushed the nose rests apart so that when he put the glasses back on they slid down his nose. His old face emerged. He remembered who he had been before he met Julia: Dr. Galuszka.

"I'm afraid," he said, looking at his reflection but pretending to be talking to a patient, "this is not the news we had hoped for." He shook his head, pretending to hold an X-ray toward the outside light. "It could be worse, however," he added. "We have to learn to balance things, to see them in perspective. We can't think only of the good or only the bad."

He returned to the living room, picked up the phone and ordered the electricity, gas and telephone services restored. Then he collected his briefcase and set out for town.

It was a pleasant enough drive, but as Charley approached town he noticed nothing remained of the memories he had of it. Perhaps it was because of the way the color had all drained out of the photos in the old scrapbook, but the town seemed brighter, with chain stores and restaurants having replaced the small-town businesses his wife so hated. "That ridiculous place?" she would say whenever he mentioned taking a trip back to visit her father. "You have to be retarded to live there. If my father wants to see me, he can take a plane and visit me here. It won't kill him."

The town actually reminded him of certain parts of Los Angeles, as though two square blocks had been cut out of that sunny city and dropped into the middle of Virginia. It disconcerted him to see the exact same chain restaurants and drugstores in such a pastoral setting. He had, after all, decided to return here because it was almost as far as one could get from Los Angeles (the reverse motive for his wife's moving them to LA).

"This is a gigantic city, Los Angeles," Julia used to tell him. "We have the money, we have the ability to travel anywhere we want and eat anything we want, and yet you stay in your same little corner, the same little box, as though you're on twenty-four-hour guard duty." "You've got your friends," he'd tell her, knowing she preferred to socialize without him.

"It's true, I do have friends. And why? I'm a gregarious woman. I can't live like a redneck's wife, going to your patients' funeral receptions, sitting at card tables in some church cafeteria, picking over fried chicken. It's makes me sick just thinking about it."

"That's just how you see it."

"How I see it? Charley, do you know what a doctor is? A glorified janitor. I won't live with a janitor. A doctor is worse than a janitor, which is worse than the freeloader you are now."

"Maybe I'm just not the man you want. Why don't you accept that and let me go back to being a doctor?"

"First of all, that's ridiculous. How are you going to start practicing thirty years later? How will you treat your patients, with castor oil? Why can't you enjoy what I've made of you rather than always thinking you have to achieve something?"

"The terrible things I used to say," the ghost butted in. "I realize now how I must have hurt you. And what incredible patience you had not to strangle me."

"That's all right," Charley said. "No need to apologize. If you knew what I was thinking whenever I held a fork or passed a knife…."

"Bullshit," Julia said.

He scanned the strip malls for a familiar local hangout, but even the bars seemed to have been imported from other places. There was not a single place called Ray's or Lucky's where he might sit down, ease his way into a conversation and say, "You may remember my name: Dr. Charles Galuszka. I'm back in practice, so if you ever need a checkup…." But he also knew that even if such a place existed, such a conversation would never happen. He never started conversations with strangers and, because he radiated discomfort, only rarely and by necessity did strangers begin conversations with him. He kept on driving.

"Well, Dr. Galuszka," he imagined (then forgot he was imagining) a stranger beside him saying. "You don't remember me, but I remember you. I had an appointment with you a long time ago, but then you and your wife moved away. How long did you practice, three months? You must have really fallen for her. Me? I never moved. I never traveled. What's the point? Things trail after you, residue and scrapbooks, dust mites. My name's Harold Wicker. I'm a plumber, retired. With a profession like that, I never had a chance. Don't call me Harold. Call me Harry, Charley. Unless you prefer Charles. I bet she called you Charles.

"Yes, I knew Julia. It's easy to get to know everybody here. I knew all about you too, and you were only here three months. You've come back into that cave you call your self to see what's left. Strip-mined, plumbed of natural resources. You should see my house: Home of the Strip-mined, nothing but ghosts. I hear a thousand voices, all the time, every single minute. There's ghosts in my mind too. I've got comedians, kings, pickpockets, any kind of bastard you can think of. I can't get any sleep.

"Did she ever talk about me, compare me to you? I bet that pissed you off, didn't it? Happened to me too. Never a good comparison. I bet her first boyfriend, some little shit three feet tall, I bet he had it up to here with her talking about fairy-tale princes. Any goddamned thing she can think of to cut your nuts off, she'd do it. 'A plumber!' she used to say to me. 'A toilet cleaner!' 'That's right,' I'd say, 'a necessary and important profession,' and she'd shake like she was having an earthquake. But with all her promises, I started thinking about it. Why not? My dad worked hard enough for ten men. That left nine more after me who wouldn't have to work. I tried living with her for a summer, the one before you first came to town. I lived like a king. She had it worked out we'd move together—New York City. All I had to do was not eat dinner with the goddamned salad fork. But then, every time I ate anything that summer, staring across the table at her with that salad fork in my hand...you know. Her spidery nature couldn't help but emerge."

Charley watched the rows and rows of corn stream past, splitting the moonlight and, remembering, said, "The day before we left, a plague of caterpillars covered the house."

"That happened every year," Julia said. "It had nothing to do with you."

"Well, now I'm lost," Charley said, and though the moon was swelled full with light he did not know how to navigate by the night sky. "I'll be goddamned if I know which way to go." An untrained captain, piloting a ship lost in a sea of corn, he said, "So then, tell me what to do. I'm listening."

"If I were you I'd drink myself to death," Julia said.

"Fall in love, and forget about me—her—us," the ghost said.

"No, no, no," the plumber said. "I'll tell you what I'd do. Actually, I'll tell you what I've done. I mean what I did all those years ago, between when I told her to get lost and when she made you get lost. I retired from that part of life is what I did. I told myself, Harry, Harold, Wicker, that part of life is gone for you now. Most people need something to recover from—a hangover, sickness, anything—before they get to dusk, to music. But I tell you, say goodnight to that spidery bitch. Tell him, ghost. You're just playing with time, thinking about her the way you do. Playing tricks with your mind."

"Yes," the ghost said.

Harry said: "Would you like us all to come together now, your little Greek chorus? Even Julia, for we need her wasp-filled throat to sing this tune."

"We all agree on this?" Charley asked.

Julia sighed. "Harry's right this time: I have to sing with these fuckers if that's what you want."

They sang a terrible-sounding song, arrhythmic, full of grunts and moans. It was a song that would give anyone a headache. Charley's head did indeed begin to ache, fiercer and fiercer until he could hardly see. Then the car shot into a cornfield, straight across the rows. Ears of corn splayed off the windshield into the blackness. The tires caught mud ruts, choked, spun, slamming over row after row. Then the car seemed to find its way onto a road—certainly he himself had nothing to do with its sudden achievement.

"Here I am," he said, realizing he was in control again and, even more surprisingly, alone and not hearing voices. He saw his symptoms clearly now. They made sense like a once impossibly complicated math problem made clear. "There's nothing wrong with you at all," he said. "All of these things have just been in your head, and if you scratch your ass you'll see it turns red as any ass should when scratched." Talking to ghosts, having conversations with a wife's ex-lovers, hearing Julia's recriminations at this late date, all of these were as strange to contemplate as pining for a childhood security blanket or a set of bicycle training wheels.

That night he put his ghosts all away in the attic where no one but spiders would visit them again and he dreamed of new strangers who had never heard his name or the name of anyone he knew. And, despite feeling quite odd and not a little frightened, he was glad at the mystery he found outside himself. He was glad at the stretch of time he found there too, which passed so naturally that eventually it just disappeared like the faded yellow lines in a parking lot.

# The Lady and the Tiger

*By* David Herman

Both were accused kidnappers and murderers. Each unleashed a reign of terror during which men and women were tortured and killed for incurring their personal displeasure. She was the Mother of the Nation; he the Priest from Hell. Winnie Madikizela-Mandela and Gideon Johannes Nieuwoudt. The Lady and the Tiger.

Their characters are so disparate, it takes a great leap of imagination to discern the similarities, but the very distance between them created an irresistible magnetic charge pulling their fates together. And yet only a few brief years ago they were diametrically opposed representatives of two sides in a battle that was patently void of any gray area. He stood for the oppression of the country's majority by whatever means necessary; she waved the banner of human dignity.

It was a battle I witnessed from the safety of exile in London. My contribution to the struggle lay in not buying South African wine. In the mid-1960s I had fled South Africa, a teenager, terrified of what I might face as a white soldier in the apartheid Republic's army. When I returned in 1999, I was keen to see how the new South Africa was dealing with its past on the eve of its second free elections. I found the invaders being thrashed in the only battle that mattered: the cricket match against the West Indies.

On a late afternoon in Soweto, 1999, Nelson Mandela and Thabo Mbeki kicked off the election campaign in the dusty soccer stadium. Mbeki, Mandela's handpicked successor, was not a rousing speaker and was delighted when his speech was interrupted by a tumultuous ovation. It took a moment till he realised the crowd's applause was not for him but for a lone figure strolling slowly across the pitch. Winnie had arrived, stylish charismatic ex-member of the royal family, fashionably forty-five minutes late. The throng *toyi-toyied* in delight. With much grinding of teeth, Mbeki acknowledged the interloper. "Viva the president of the African National Congress Women's League!" "Viva!" roared the crowd. In the first game of the season against the new establishment, it was 1-0 Winnie.

At about the same time, ex-Special Branch Colonel Gideon Nieuwoudt, loner, inarticulate ex-member of a fraternity of cruel and robotic cops, was having less success with his PR campaign. Nieuwoudt had visited Zwide, Port Elizabeth, the home of slain anti-apartheid activist Siphiwe Mtimkulu. He went to request a reconciliation with Mtimkulu's family. The ceremony was brief. Mtimkulu's son smashed a flower vase over Nieuwoudt's head. Mrs Mtimkulu smuggled Nieuwoudt out of the back door, avoiding the angry mob that had gathered in front of the house.

Lost in the melee of ongoing life were the amnesty decisions of the Truth and Reconciliation Commission. When the hearings ended, a report was delivered to Mandela amidst a furore of debate. The amnesty decisions began to trickle in, and it didn't look good for some of the players. But round the *braai*, or barbecue, where South Africans hold their clan meetings, the talk was of cricket. If it's politics you're interested in, it's still about cricket.

"It's a disgrace," said a black newspaper editor between bites on his *wors*.

"The selectors have chosen only one black for the team, and he's the reserve. My eight-year-old son, a cricket fanatic, is proud to be South African and proud to be black, but he's supporting the West Indies."

The reserve is called the "twelfth man" in cricket. The twelfth man can field in place of an injured player. The twelfth man can run for an injured batsman but cannot bat. And here's the rub. In the arcane game that is cricket, the twelfth man has another duty: he serves the team drinks during the tea break. Not exactly a revolutionary position for a black man in the new South Africa.

The Truth and Reconciliation Commission was set up in South Africa in order to lay old ghosts to rest. Nobel Peace Prize winner Archbishop Desmond Tutu, a man of infinite patience, compassion and good humour, was installed as chairman. The commission's brief was awesome, but the path to amnesty simple and straightforward. Perpetrators of crimes, some of them guilty of gross assaults on human rights, had to step forward, give an open and honest accounting of their crimes and provide a political motivation. The Commission would provide them with full amnesty in return.

Simple, it would seem, till one ran into the likes of Nieuwoudt. He had the answers to a lot of questions, but he wasn't much good at telling the truth. They tried to stimulate his memory with a few pointed questions. How did you torture Mukuseli Jack? Where did you bury Siphiwe Mtimkulu? When did you shoot the PEBCO 3? Why did you let Steve Biko die?

Nieuwoudt denied none of these crimes associated with his name, but stubbornly refused to tell the truth. He stuck to the cover-up stories concocted with his colleagues in the Special Branch. He resisted breaking ranks, notwithstanding the risk that he would be denied amnesty.

Trivial, you might think, unless you were the wife or the son or the mother of one of his victims. They had to put aside their desire for retribution, had to be prepared to watch the men who tortured and killed their loved ones walk free in return for acknowledging what happened.

Nieuwoudt had five separate hearings in front of the Truth and Reconciliation Commission during which he brushed aside troublesome questions with blunt disdain. Nieuwoudt was a ruthless interrogator and, by his standards, these enquiries were a cakewalk.

No one was putting a wet canvas bag over his head and holding it fast till he choked and begged to breathe. None of his inquisitors was beating him with a steel pipe and, Nieuwoudt certainly knew, he was not going to end up naked in the back of a pick-up truck with severe brain lesions, slowly dying, like Steve Biko.

Not wanting to see the killers walk free, Biko's family opposed the amnesty process. They took their appeal all the way up to South Africa's Constitutional Court. In some of the most gently understanding language one is ever likely to hear in a judicial process, the appeal was turned down.

The judges accepted the validity of the applicant's concern. "The results may well often be imperfect and the pursuit of the act might inherently support the message of Kant that 'out of the crooked timber of humanity no straight thing was ever made.'"

But in conclusion the judges restated the reasoning behind the amnesty process. They explained that there appeared to be no other mechanism to force perpetrators to reveal their crimes. Families of the victims would now have the truth they so desperately desired. Truth that would empower them while "the country begins the long and necessary process of healing the wounds of the past, transforming anger and grief into a mature understanding."

The judges reckoned without Gideon Nieuwoudt. They also underestimated the power and resolve of Winnie Madikizela-Mandela.

1977 was a crucial year. Winnie Mandela was the visible spirit of the ANC in South Africa. Nelson Mandela had spent more than a decade on Robben Island, serving a life sentence. After years of being harassed, tortured and held in solitary confinement, Winnie was banished from her home in Soweto and dumped in Brandport, a sandy desolate village in the middle of nowhere. She wrote a friend, "The solitude is deadly. Social life is the nightly raids and funerals! Yet there's something so purifying about exile, each minute is a reminder that blackness alone is a commitment in our sick society."

Nieuwoudt's star, by contrast, was on the ascent. 1977 found him in Pretoria in the old synagogue that had been converted into a court for Nelson Mandela's treason trial in the early 1960s. Nieuwoudt was one of the Special Branch Policemen who stood accused of the murder of Steve Biko. Biko it seems, was killed not because he was regarded as such a prominent enemy—in fact the policemen involved knew little to nothing of the black consciousness movement—but because he refused to stand during his interrogation. He insisted he should sit. Nieuwoudt was outraged by the arrogance of this black man who needed to be taught a lesson. As it turned out, a deadly lesson.

It took Magistrate Marthinus Prins less than three minutes to deliver his verdict: No one to blame. Biko had been eliminated, his death declared an accident. The police had lied, the district surgeons had lied and the magistrate's priority was not truth but support of the apartheid regime. Nieuwoudt was on a fast track to promotion.

By the mid-1980s, South Africa was in turmoil. The ANC's tactic was to fight the regime by making the Black Townships ungovernable. There were riots and killings. Winnie Mandela was back in Soweto and had become a formidable figure. In the Eastern Cape, Gideon Nieuwoudt was amongst the small band charged with restoring order. The government had been embarrassed by the publicity the Biko hearing received in the foreign press. Henceforth, victims of the Special

Branch would either disappear or have their deaths laid at the doorstep of rival black factions.

Witness the case of the Motherwell bombing. Four black Special Branch colleagues of Nieuwoudt were blown to bits in their car in the little town of Motherwell. A police investigation concluded the bombing was the work of the ANC.

By 1997, the Special Branch had more than its fair share of image problems. No longer protected by the apartheid courts, and now being offered the carrot of amnesty in return for full confessions, cops were coming forward and admitting to torturing and killing opponents of the old regime. But they were hedging their bets, admitting only to the more obvious crimes and hiding behind the old saw, "We were only following orders."

Then a cop broke ranks and revealed Nieuwoudt was behind the Motherwell bombing. Nieuwoudt applied for amnesty to the Truth Commission. He did it, he said, because he discovered the four Special Branch officers had secretly joined the ANC. Wasn't he afraid the police bomb expert would identify the explosive not as Russian but as South African police issue? Not really: Nieuwoudt was the investigating bomb expert.

It turned out that the reason for the killing was other than he claimed. The four black officers had been caught ripping off secret funds and threatened to expose the Security Branch of having killed a group of activists if they were charged. Nieuwoudt, known to his colleagues as Mr Fixit, soon sorted it out.

Amnesty could be granted to people already convicted of crimes if they met the commission's requirements of full disclosure and political intent. A perpetrator of a crime denied amnesty was left open to prosecution for their acts. Their testimony before the Amnesty Commission was not admissible in a criminal court.

Nieuwoudt was denied amnesty for the bombing. He faced twenty years in jail if convicted in a criminal court.

Nieuwoudt had been feared throughout the Eastern Cape Townships. It was rumoured he masqueraded as a priest on his nighttime visits to activists' homes, hence the moniker, the Priest from Hell. Siphiwe Mtimkulu disappeared one night. He'd had a history of meetings with Nieuwoudt.

Mtimkulu's mother sat at the TRC hearings clutching a plastic bag with the only remnant she had of her son, a small piece of his scalp with some hair attached. Siphiwe Mtimkulu had been poisoned in prison, causing his hair to fall out. The poison left him confined to a wheel-chair. His mother described what her son told after he was released from his first session at the Nieuwoudt clinic.

Siphiwe said he had been brutally tortured. He told his mother he had been starved for days and then chained naked to a rock at the sea-side while Nieuwoudt and a colleague barbecued spare-ribs. They threw the stripped bones in the sand at his feet.

Nieuwoudt admitted to the TRC that he later murdered Mtimkulu, but he denied torturing the crippled student leader. He claimed that he drugged him and then shot him in the back of the head while he slept. Then, he said, he burned the body and scattered the ashes in a river. Mrs Mtimkulu did not believe him. Nieuwoudt claimed he eliminated Mtimkulu because Mtimkulu was a danger to public order. Mrs Mtimkulu believed her son was killed because he had the temerity to sue the police for poisoning him.

Nieuwoudt was the product of a strict Dutch Reform Church up-bringing. His lawyer to the Truth Commission gently suggested to him:

"The church of which you were a member also decided at synod level, that the policy of separate development as it was termed by the Government of the day could be justified in terms of the Bible."

"That is correct," Nieuwoudt said, and continued, "The way I understood it is the following, that all measures should be used to pro-tect the government of the Republic of South Africa and to keep them in power, and whatever methods would be used, would be justifiable."

While Nieuwoudt was going about his dirty business in the East-ern Cape, Winnie Mandela had become, to all intents and purposes, a warlord in Soweto. She must have felt untouchable and, to a degree, she was. Protected by the Mandela name, she trod roughshod over the black leadership. Furthermore, the authorities felt that Winnie was, in effect, an unwitting ally. Her reign of terror and the mayhem it was creating, not only in Soweto, but also amongst the ANC leadership, were more effective than anything the Security Branch could devise. Winnie was out of control. With her husband in jail, she seemed to believe that she was the rightful leader of the resistance movement within South Africa and that anyone who challenged her was an enemy of the cause.

She inhabited an unsavoury world peopled by charlatans, petty thieves and informers, a world whose epicentre was the backyard of her home in Soweto, the headquarters of Mandela United Football Club. The team members were Winnie's foot soldiers, in a league of their own. They tortured and killed with impunity. There are theories, and then there are theories, regarding Winnie's transformation. It was said that she took to drink and drugs during the lonely years of isolation. It was said that the police broke her during one especially nasty and long period of solitary confinement.

In the rooms and outhouses of the Mandela compound, people were also tortured and killed. Their crimes? They had thwarted Winnie or one of her henchmen. The justification? If they upset Winnie they must be government informers. Two youths had revolutionary graffiti carved into their limbs and torsos and the wounds rubbed with battery acid. A pregnant woman was assaulted by Winnie and later assaulted again by a group of the "footballers." She had had the temerity to fall in love with one of Winnie's part-time chauffeurs who also happened to be one of Winnie's part-time lovers.

On television, I had watched Nelson Mandela and Winnie walk hand in hand out of prison when he was freed after twenty-seven years in jail. My heart soared as they raised their clenched fists. I had agonised during Winnie's trial and was pleased that she escaped, knowing little about the world behind those dark curtains in Townships like Soweto. Then, slowly, the universe of Winnie Mandela began to reveal itself to the public eye.

Bombshell after bombshell exploded. Winnie was subpoenaed to appear before the Truth and Reconciliation Commission. She admitted nothing and was not asking for amnesty. This was during a special hearing into the activities of the Mandela United Football Club. Eighteen accounts of murder, kidnapping and torture were laid before the Commission. In a full week of hearings, the world heard the stories of men and women who had suffered the same kind of fate at the hands of Winnie and her followers that activists had endured at the hands of Gideon Nieuwoudt and his colleagues in the Special Branch.

During six days of hearings, witness after witness told harrowing stories condemning Winnie. A father wept when he told how he had never forgiven himself for not rescuing his son when Winnie drove him by his house, badly beaten, before he was murdered. Archbishop

Tutu had to deliver a solemn warning to the audience after one of the victims' mothers was threatened by Winnie's entourage in the washroom during a break in the proceedings. Winnie sat in the hall with her bodyguards providing her cool drinks and presenting her with flowers.

The last day of the hearing was Winnie's turn. It was her chance to soar above the squalid days of inhumanity and reclaim a place in the forefront of righteousness. Twenty years had passed since she had been banished to Brandfort; ten years since the dark days in Soweto; three years since her husband had taken the oath of office as president of the new South Africa. Instead, she denied everything, dismissing those who had endured so much pain as people merely suffering from hallucinations and dementia. She had not asked for amnesty, and the TRC had no carrot and no stick for her. She dismissed her accusers as liars, lunatics and apartheid-era collaborators.

"Honestly, for me to have to sit here and answer such ridiculous allegations is great pain to me."

When darkness descended, Archbishop Tutu fell back on his last hope of redemption for her.

"I beg you, I beg you, I beg you, please. I speak as someone who has lived in this community. You are a great person and you don't know how your greatness would be enhanced if you were to say sorry, things went wrong, forgive me. I beg you."

The hearing room fell silent. Winnie turned to her lawyer, then switched on her mike.

"I am saying it is true, things went horribly wrong. I fully agree with that and for that part of those painful years when things went horribly wrong and we were aware of the fact that there were factors that led to that, for that I am deeply sorry."

The Truth Commission's final report contained a damning indictment of her.

"The Commission finds that those who opposed Madikizela-Mandela and the Mandela United Football Club, or dissented from them, were branded as informers, then hunted down and killed.

"The Commission finds Ms Winnie Madikizela-Mandela politically and morally accountable for the gross violations of human rights committed by the MUFC."

Nieuwoudt was denied amnesty in the Biko case. He refused to admit he killed the man and continued to insist it was an accident. If it was an accident, wrote the Commission, we have nothing to grant you amnesty for. Nieuwoudt was open to prosecution in a court of law, although it would be difficult to nail him on this one, since there was a twenty-year statute of limitations in manslaughter cases.

Gideon Nieuwoudt waited to face other days in other courts, alone and far from the spotlight of national interest. He might bring down a retired general or two, but they were past their prime anyway and the collateral damage would be minor.

Winnie was a seasoned fighter. Too many times opponents had swaggered into the neutral corner, waiting to hear her counted out, only to receive a stinging blow to the back of their own heads. On the day Nelson Mandela consigned her to history by marrying Graca Machel, Winnie attended an emotional funeral for the reburial of the remains of ANC guerilla fighters.

With voting in South Africa's second free elections coming up in June 1999, Winnie was the ANC's spearhead amongst the disaffected, who had not gained empowerment in the first five years of black rule. This constituency related well to her battle-scarred image. Her parting shot after each stop on the election trail was: "Vote for Thabo Mbeki. He is a much younger leader. He will get things done." Only Winnie would have the temerity to so nonchalantly dismiss a demi-god as her husband. The official Nelson Mandela biography recounts her love affairs with young men even after her husband's release from jail.

And the Truth Commission? The roots of the TRC are buried in the days of transition from apartheid. The Nationalist government was determined to protect its own and not lay itself open to Nuremberg-style trials by the new order. The ANC was keen not to provide a provocation that would leave parts of the old military and police forces with a clear motivation for not cooperating. The ANC also had its fair share of skeletons in the closet.

In essence, the Truth Commission sprang from an accommodation with evil and bore the strange fruits of that compromise. The commissioners struggled valiantly with the concept of truth, but the politicians and the country were less interested in truth and much more concerned with moving on. To that end the TRC accomplished its mission. It might not have revealed all the facts, but it provided the valve by which the pressures of political transition could be vented under a façade of decency.

Not a bad outcome when one considers a 1999 survey of the

public's opinion of the TRC. Sixty-one percent of blacks felt the TRC's decisions were fair, as opposed to 13% of white respondents who believe that. But, in any case, far more people were interested in what was happening on the cricket field. And here the news was sad. Makhaya Ntini was selected as the first black man to represent South Africa. In April 1999, he was convicted in a magistrate's court of rape and within hours dropped from the South African cricket squad for the summer's World Cup in England.

The final word goes to Peter Storey, who was Bishop of Soweto during Winnie's reign of terror. He made the following statement at Winnie's Truth Commission hearing: "One of the tragedies of life, sir, is it is possible to become like that which we hate most. Somebody once said, it is not enough to become politically liberated; we must also become human. This case is about becoming human again and recognising the inhumanities which some of us were capable of because of the times we used to live in."

# Parking Ticket

*By* Norma Kitson

I arrived in Zimbabwe in 1988 on a hot December day with my Bickerton bike and a cassette radio. David stayed behind in Oxford, finishing his term tutoring statistics and politics at Ruskin College, where he was an Emeritus Fellow. I had to be in Harare to take possession of the empty house we'd bought, there to wait months before our belongings would arrive by sea from the UK via South Africa. Knowing I would have to get around in a city with a poor bus service, I'd brought my fold-up bike and because of the silence I anticipated in the large, empty, hollow house, I also brought some tapes and the radio: two items I felt would help keep me sane in a situation of isolated waiting.

But Customs wouldn't have it. They said my bike was child-size and probably thought I wanted to sell it. They were equally worried about my cassette radio, and after hours of wrangling in the stuffy airport, they confiscated both.

When I eventually emerged into the reception area of the Harare Airport, it was to find that our only friend, whom we had met the previous year, had left, thinking I was not on the plane. All the other passengers had long since gone and the airport was empty of people.

I stood on the steps outside with my two suitcases, blinking in the harsh sunlight. I'd left England, mid-winter, with a splitting headache and a case of acute bronchitis. The plane trip, despite the antibiotics I was taking, had made me feel worse and now, after the argument with the stony-faced Customs officials, I was aching all over and quite at a loss to know what to do. A kindly porter directed me to the bank: I changed some English money and he put my bags into a taxi.

After an interminable ride in a rickety half-car with doors that didn't close properly, we arrived at the house. At the gate stood two very thin men and two skeletal dogs. All I could think about was drinking a glass of water and getting my pounding head down.

For two days I lay half-conscious on the single pallet bed—the only thing we'd bought from the previous owner. I was aware, now and then, of a gentle urging from one of the thin men to have a cup of tea and some mealiemeal. On the third day I began to feel a little better, had a bath, donned some creased clothes and began to look about me.

The two men—Tendai and Chipinge—had been employees of the previous owner of the house—the cook and gardener. They implored me to keep them on, but I said I couldn't do that until I had discussed it with David. We hadn't intended to employ domestics. But I said they could stay in the meantime. After all, the place they called home was the tiny, unceilinged, black-walled, dirty cold-water shack behind the house and I wasn't going to be responsible for throwing them out. We were in the middle of this discussion, and I was aware that all three of us—and the two dogs—were literally starving, when a car drove up.

Our lawyer's wife had come to check whether I had arrived and whether everything was all right at the house. She walked through the empty echoing rooms.

"You'll have to come and stay with us. You can't stay here. There's nothing here! Your shelves are all empty. What are you eating?"

I explained that I'd been ill and anyway was unable to visit the shops as my bike had been taken away and that I had to stay in the house.

"Look," she said. "I've got a meeting this morning. I'm going to send a car with a driver. Let him take you and do a big shop. Get some food in. Tomorrow I'll take you to get some things you'll need till your stuff arrives: sheets and spoons and things—and an iron," she said glancing at my creases. "You can't possibly live like this!"

The driver duly arrived and, promising Tendai and Chipinge that I would get food supplies for them and some clothing, still feeling rocky and clutching my list of staples, we left.

The car ran easily down Tunsgate but began to choke and jerk down Pendennis, then stopped. The driver got out, but when he started poking around in the boot I realised he knew nothing whatsoever about cars.

I sat on the grass verge nearby, my head in my hands, while he eventually discovered the engine and began tinkering about with its insides. The heat was overwhelming and there was no shade in sight. I sat, trying to think what to do, full of horror that perhaps the good woman who owned the car would think I'd been the cause, somehow, of its breaking down.

I sat there, the sun beating down, my head throbbing, the man tinkering.

A car pulled up beside me and a jolly-hockeysticks lady emerged. "Something wrong? You all right? Car broken down?"

I looked up and nodded. "It's borrowed," I said. "I've just arrived from England and I'm not well and I don't even know where the shops are." I must have sounded pathetic. Jolly Hockeysticks took over instantly.

"You jump in my car. I'll take you to some decent shops. The ones here are all over-priced anyway. And you," she pointed to the driver, "stop that and get that thing to a garage."

The driver looked at her helplessly.

Seeing some people walking in the road, she called to them: "Hey, you. Yes, you—Jim and you! You come and help push the Madam's car to the garage. Quick, now!"

She was instantly obeyed and the next moment had a crowd of people pushing the car off in what direction I never knew. I got into her car, gratefully sank into the fine leather seat while she efficiently whipped me from one shop to the next, telling me what brand of tea to buy, what brand of mealiemeal, what breakfast cereal. During the trip from one shop to another, she told me something about herself and her husband. She had been a nurse and had taken care of an elderly patient whose wife had died. He had a hearing problem and was a "rather crotchety old thing," as she put it.

"He's rich and needed someone to look after him and run his big house," she said. "Sometimes he even forgets we're married and thinks I'm a housekeeper or something! He keeps harping on about his first wife and how wonderful she was and what a good cook she was and how well she dressed. Well, that doesn't worry me much. I just get on with it." I listened to her through a mist of pain.

The shopping finished, she deposited me back home and said not to worry, she would go to the garage and see that the borrowed car was fixed and its driver dispatched back to the kind lawyer's wife.

The days passed. Tendai and Chipinge lost the grey look of starvation. The dogs gorged and began to look better and slowly my bron-

chitis cleared up and I began to feel better. Chipinge made a fire outside each day over which we cooked water and the three of us ate the
mealiemeal I bought, with rape and tomatoes that we got from a woman
selling at the roadside near the Northwood shops. There even came the
day when I could walk to those shops myself and re-stock on tea and
vegetables.

When David arrived a few weeks later, Chipinge had planted the
vegetable garden and the floors of the empty house shone with the wax
polish Tendai applied. He produced mounds of fried fritters, the tree in
the garden producing large hands of bananas every few days. The two
men were now proudly dressed in their new jeans and shirts. The swimming pool, fed with large doses of chlorine, gleamed. The dogs were
brushed and the lawn cut with the mower borrowed from next door,
and David agreed we could not abandon Tendai and Chipinge to a job-
less existence.

I told David about my rescue by Jolly Hockeysticks and how
efficient she had been, even if her methods were a bit high-handed and
reminiscent of the *ancien regime* in the way she had collared a span of
passing black pedestrians to do her bidding. He was nonplussed that
this could happen after eight years of black majority rule, but remarked
that it probably was just as well, otherwise what would have happened
to me! We decided to send her some flowers and a thank-you note.

Sitting on the patio one morning in our newly acquired garden
chairs, Jolly Hockeysticks drove up and stuck her head out of the car
window. We walked over and I introduced her to David.

"Want you both to lunch on Tuesday," she said handing us a card
with her address. "Can't stop. See you Tuesday. All right? About 12.30."

David and I discussed it.

"Look," he said. "From what you've said about her, I don't think
we ought to tell them about us. She's been kind. We'll just go and have
lunch and talk platitudes, OK?"

"What d'you mean?"

"Well, you know what it's like. We're new in town, so lots of
people have invited us and as soon as we get there they all want to
know why we've come to live here and where we've been and everything."

"So?"

"So I don't think we should mention anything about us to Jolly
Hockeysticks or her husband. It sounds as if they're Rhodies. Nor-

mally I wouldn't mind taking them on. But this lady was very kind to you, so I think we should just chat away and keep them happy."

"OK," I said.

On Tuesday we dressed in our best and arrived at the Jolly Hockeysticks' house. We were shown through an enormous lounge with three fireplaces and a sunken section swathed in dralon couches, out through French doors to a huge gleaming glitterstone patio. There a number of tables and chairs were laid out, each with a large umbrella and, sitting sipping cocktails, about twenty people. We were introduced and I noticed that they wore a selection of identifiably English clothes: Jaeger shirts, Reldan and Escada blouses, and fine wool skirts. But their raddled sunburned skins showed them to be indisputably southern Africans.

In the far corner of the patio, under his own umbrella, sat old Mr Hockeysticks alone, sipping a scotch. He nodded when we were introduced and then turned to his wife and said sharply: "Where's the ice? Eh?"

She scuttled off dutifully and we sat down, David over at a vacant chair near a group of men, and me between two middle-aged women in a semi-circle of about eight that included one thin, orange-haired man with a protruding stomach.

A long conversation ensued among the women—during which I kept bravely silent and sipped my soda—on how the country had "gone to pots since the Blacks took over," as one of them put it.

"You can't even buy salt anymore," one of them said.

"Yes, and all our good schools are full of them now," said another. "We had to send Peter to Johburg."

"And you can't even get olives or sardines," said the first. "And they've become so cheeky."

"And damned inefficient," said the weedy male. There was a general clicking and nodding of agreement among the ladies. There followed a number of examples of the horror that Zimbabwe had become since Independence in 1980.

I examined my fingernails, sipped my soda and looked longingly at David.

Old man Hockeysticks shouted out to the company at large that his wife made the best cheese scones of anyone in the world. "Then you'd have had a lunch to remember! On time too!" There were a few embarrassed murmurs as most of the guests realised he was referring to his dead first wife. Mrs Hockeysticks didn't turn a hair.

Then the topic at our end of the patio turned briefly to the virtues of England and London in particular—"home" as they called it, although I began to doubt any of them had ever been to overcrowded, polluted, racist England, where the sewers are breaking up in the major cities and we'd just left mad-cow's disease, poisonous water in the taps, salmonella chickens and eggs, fires and electrical failures in the underground stations, not to mention a season of vapid soap-theatre, deafening drug-infested disco terminals for the youth, a higher than ever unemployment rate and prisons over-crowded with rioting inmates. Beggars were sleeping in every doorway of the West End and under the famous London bridges, inflation was raging and the crime, drugs, murder and suicide rates were soaring.

"I always felt English flowers were so much prettier," one said, glancing at the bright beds of flowers. "And one could sort of rely on the local vicar."

"Yes," said another, "and what about all the wonderful theatre—Shakespeare an' all that."

"And Mrs. Thatcher's so well dressed and such a lovely woman," said a third. "She reminds me of the Queen."

"And what about that lovely Princess, Diana," said another. "I think she's beautiful. She's a bit tall, I do admit, but she is lovely. And such a good match for our Prince Charles. He's such a nice man!"

They nodded in agreement, and the lone man leaned towards me and said: "She's a bit of all right as far as I'm concerned," and took a long slug of his beer.

"And Vera Lynn," said another. "Home was so wonderful during the War."

There was a short silence while everyone swallowed that one. I took another sip of my soda. Then a little woman with purple lipstick sitting next to me asked: "Where you from?"

"Actually, we've been living in England," I said. "Isn't this a wonderful garden—so full of flowers."

"How long?" she asked.

"I was there twenty-two years. This sunny weather is magnificent, isn't it?" I tried desperately to turn the conversation away from dangerous ground. "It's very cold in England right now."

The woman flicked her hand at my arm. "Where were you before that? Your accent isn't English."

"We come from South Africa originally. Just look at that rose bush!"

"Was your husband with you in England?"

"Yes, mostly," I said.

She must know something, I thought. I paused, looked at her and said, "I'm sure I'd never be so successful at rose-growing. It's an art, don't you think?" I looked desperately at David, but he was in deep conversation with the men.

One of the women said, "Ooh! Don't tell me you've come out here to live after England. Is your husband on contract here?"

"No," I said. "We've just come to live."

Suddenly a crab-like claw with long red nails bit into my arm. Purple Lips turned on me, her mouth inches from my face and said in a loud voice, "I said, was your husband with you in England?"

"Some of the time."

"Well, where was he then?" She was almost shouting. I unhooked her nails from my arm and looked around. By now, a number of the guests were following our conversation and I saw old Mr Hockeysticks perk up.

"Where's the lunch, eh?" he shouted, looking heavenward.

I glanced across at David, but his face was closed. Oh, what-the-hell, I thought, I've tried. I've done all I can. I just don't know how to cope with this.

"Actually," I said. "My husband was in prison in Pretoria from 1964 to 1984. Anything less than ten years they call a 'parking ticket,' but he served the whole sentence. He was a member of the High Command of Umkhonto we Sizwe. That's the military wing of the African National Congress, you know."

There was a horrified silence. Everyone stopped talking and turned their faces to look first at me and then at David, Purple Lips with her mouth open. Mr Hockeysticks sat up and craned his neck to hear better. The silence continued. I took a sip at my empty glass and felt sweat running down my back. Eventually Purple Lips sat back gasping. Then one of the women made a rescue attempt:

"What an extraordinary coincidence," she said. "Do you know, I once knew someone in the ANC!"

There was a sudden buzz while everyone began remarking about how Black people weren't so bad. They were all natural dancers and so good at sport and very good at running and boxing and some of them were really quite educated these days, and it wasn't their fault, you know.

This started everyone off asking David what it was like in jail and how had he managed, and were they cruel and oh how awful, and what did you do for twenty whole years, and what was the worst part of it.

David obliged, as always, telling anecdotes that would amuse and put their minds at rest, easing their tensions.

Efficient as always, Mrs Hockeysticks soon broke up the conversation. "Come now, everyone! Lunch is served in the dining room."

As everyone rose and started trooping away, old Mr Hockeysticks stood up unsteadily, his face a mask of incredulity: "Twenty years," he said, "and for a parking offence!"

# Sister Hanh

*By* Ly Lan

The fish-egg tree is no longer there. But who cares about a fish-egg tree? And who cares about him? His name is Moi, it's both his first name and his last name, and it's also his home and homeland. He is Moi. Jack Miller has never been anybody.

"Moi!"

Yes, call out to him so that he's someone recognizable, someone having a past. So that all the chaos waking him every night is not merely nightmare and the dim figure in his dreams luring him back here is not just illusion.

"Moi!"

Call out to me! Why do you only stare, folks?

He looks at the adults and children gathered around him and suddenly feels frightened. It might all have been a lie, this past of his. But, no, how could all of it have been just a dream? Evening Market Alley, the fish-egg tree, Sister Hanh, Brother Beo—all of its stories imagined by a guy who is really Nobody? The looks he's receiving express just one thing: curiosity. Who is this black boy? Why is he here?

If he stands here long enough, a policeman might start to question him.

He walks away, his face showing bewilderment. Two little boys rush into their house, shutting the door behind them. He is not hurt anymore by such reactions. At the moment he is floating in an unreal world, asking himself a question that is of no real importance at all: Who is he?

"Moi!"

He keeps going, like a sleepwalker. Is the call he hears only in his imagination—the name and home he only made up?

"Moi!"

He stops and stares at the young man running toward him.

"Beo?"

Ah ha, it really is you? Yes, it is! And it's me. You! Me!

"Beo, you still recognize me?"

"Sure!"

Beo punches his shoulders, wipes away his tears. They embrace and walk down the alley together. People open doors to look at them. A woman says: "Just imagine! It turns out to be Moi."

Her child says, "What is Moi?"

Moi first appeared at Evening Market Alley sometime in the early 1970s. He and Beo began collecting the rotten vegetables Mrs. Bay threw away after market. They were both parentless and homeless. There were lots like them during the war.

In the afternoons they climbed the fish-egg tree, plucking its fruit for their lunch, then napping on the branches like monkeys. The fish-egg tree was in front of Sister Hanh's house. Sister Hanh was just a schoolgirl then, the only girl from the Alley in high school. The others had all quit school to become babysitters or domestic cleaners or clerks, until they got married.

When there was a wedding in the Alley, both adults and children gathered to share the newlyweds' happiness. Hanh would stand near the fish-egg tree, watching the bride in her rose-colored wedding dress shyly climb into the flower-strewn car. A romantic notion took root in Hanh's mind: One day a gentleman would come to ask for her hand, spirit her away from that winding dirty muddy alley, and take her to a place bright with happiness. She couldn't imagine what that man would look like, but she was sure he would be a genuine gentleman. She kept herself pretty and virginal in order to be worthy of such a man's love.

The bride was gone, and the people returned to their boring jobs. Beo and Moi collected the unexploded firecrackers to play with beneath the fish-egg tree.

"The bride and groom must have gone to the restaurant."

"No, they are going straight to the bridal chamber."

"You don't know anything. First they have to kowtow to the ancestral altar."

"Well, one day I'll get married myself."

"You? Marry?"

Hanh couldn't help bursting into laughter when she heard this debate. She was doing homework at her table by the window. The boys looked up at her. They loved Hanh better than anyone else in the Alley. She sometimes gave them food and always smiled at them. This meant a lot to two street boys, one of them black, who lived on rubbish.

"Sister Hanh, when will you get married?"

Hanh's cheeks burned with embarrassment, but the boys kept up their questioning:

"Will the groom arrive in a deluxe car?"

"And all your friends and relatives will be treated at the Grand Restaurant, won't they?"

"I wish I could be in the wedding party."

Something was smoldering in Hanh's heart. She said, "You will both be invited to my wedding party."

"Really?"

"At the Grand Restaurant?"

"Yes."

"But the guard won't let us in."

"You'll have my wedding invitation to show them."

"You promise, Sister Hanh? You promise you'll send us your wedding invitation?"

"I promise."

Beo has a pretty good business now at a corner of the crossroads not far from the Alley. He started out with bicycle repairs, later he managed to repair motorbikes, and now he can even renovate second-hand Hondas. Beo is as black as Moi because he stays out in the sun all day. The corner is his workshop as well as his home. But a street corner has no address. And, after Moi left for the USA, neither he nor Beo could read or write well enough to send letters to each other, so there has been no contact between them since.

Beo takes Moi to his "home." A small crowd has gathered there. Beo introduces his friend.

"My wife. My kids. Do you still speak Vietnamese?"

"Sure."

Beo laughs and declares in a loud voice: "This is my best friend, Jack Miller, American!"

The crowd regards Beo with awe, and Beo looks around at his neighbors proudly: Che, a barber whose shop is just a chair and a mirror hung from a tree trunk; Su, who sells used clothes on the sidewalk;

Thap, the fruit vendor. Kim Thoa sells cigarettes, old Chanh sells balloons, and their children sell lottery tickets or polish shoes or scavenge rubbish. They are all very honored to meet Moi. Once in a while they see foreigners in their huge shoes passing by this muddy corner. Their self-respect prompts them to make themselves as invisible as possible to avoid being turned into tourist snapshots of colorful foreign poverty.

But all of a sudden a foreigner, an American, comes and sits among them, a living embodiment of all the myths they've ever heard about America.

"Jack, where do you live? In New York or California? Is your house a one-hundred-story building?"

"What do you do in America, Jack? You must be very rich. Ky from our Alley is only a dishwasher in America, but he has dollars to send home every month."

"Jack, where are you staying? In a hotel? Fifty dollars a night? Wow, that can feed us for a whole month!"

Everyone looks at the American visitor with admiration.

"You come back here, stay in a hotel, eat in a restaurant, you're lucky, Jack!"

He asks them to call him Moi, but everyone objects. They want their friend to be Jack Miller—American. They've had enough of Su, Che, Beo. Who needs another Moi?

Beo's four-year-old says, "Uncle Jack, please take me to your hotel to see the soft bed."

The other kids noisily ask to go too. They want to pass through the automatic glass door.

Moi looks down at them with tears in his eyes.

"Then, we're off to the restaurant."

"Are we invited too?"

"Yes. All of you are invited."

"Five-star restaurant, Uncle Jack?"

"Five-star restaurant."

The whole corner is stirred up with excitement. Moi watches it all with a sad smile on his dark face.

The two rubbish boys Moi and Beo waited for the day they would get to eat at the Grand Restaurant. They longed as much as Hanh for the man who would come to make her a bride. At last he appeared: a gentleman with a good job, a senior-high-school teacher. Every time he came to take Hanh out on his Vespa, the children stood on both sides of the alley staring at their pretty virgin sister. She always smiled at them when they waved their dirty hands in greeting. Then they dived back into their dream in the narrow alley.

"He's quite handsome."

"And he loves Sister Hanh very much."

"He will marry Hanh and hold a party at the Grand Restaurant."

"And send us their wedding invitation."

But when would the wedding be? His parents came to see Hanh's parents. The wedding date was arranged. And the prospective bride and groom were making arrangements about the nuptial party.

Hanh said, "We're inviting Aunt Phuong, Uncle Tin, Beo, Moi...."

"Who are Beo and Moi?"

Hanh explained with her charming smile. Her fiancé stared back at her doubtfully, not knowing whether she was joking or going mad. But it was not a joking matter. He crossed the two boys' names off the list.

"My guests are respected people in society. What would they think if they were seated next to those rubbish boys?"

Hanh's voice was soft but not less decisive.

"If there were only two guests at my wedding, I would prefer that they be those two boys."

"You are mad."

"Those boys are the only ones who really want me to be happy."

"What about me? Don't I want to bring you happiness?"

"Then, please give me the pleasure of seeing those children treated as well as our other guests."

"You're crazy!"

She might indeed have been crazy. There were quarrels then every time they met. And always over the two rubbish boys! Beo and Moi didn't know anything about it. They were busy saving money to buy a silk doll for her wedding gift.

The five-star restaurant is crowded this evening. Mr. Miller hasn't booked a table in advance, so there is no room for his party. No problem, though. They rush off to another, floating restaurant illuminated by colored lights. The waiters are dressed neatly in white and wait on them politely and patiently. These strange customers noisily demand a second menu. The waiter brings it. Beo and his son excitedly study the bill of fare, but it's the same on both. Beo's wife proclaims without a glance at either menu: "I want chicken."

Kim Thoa prefers roast dove, then discovers seafood. Wow, there are swallow's nests too. Drinks? Of course, cola. No, I'd like fresh orange juice. They have imported wine? Fantastic!

The children jump up and down on their seats, screw their heads in all directions, stare at the customers at other tables. When the restaurant begins to slowly float down the Saigon River, the children all stand up on their chairs to see the brightly flickering lights of the hotels and restaurants on the riverbank. They embrace each other in glee, then turn to look at the other side of the river, trying to pick out the landscape of their Evening Market Alley. Then, along with the other customers, they cheer, drink and eat and shout and throw cans of beer into the river.

When the boat returns to its dock, the whole gang staggers out onto Nguyen Hue Boulevard, singing and laughing. They pay no attention to the angry glances of people on the street. Kim Thoa leans against Moi, her breast pressing hard against his arm. She sings all the way to the hotel. Once inside, the children immediately jump up and down on the bed and fight one another for the pillows. Then they race into the bathroom, turn on the hot water, climb into the bathtub and begin carrying on so noisily that the hotel maid comes round to complain.

At last Beo has to ask the children to go home. But go home where, they say? The corner at the Evening Market Alley?

"Please, Uncle Jack, let us stay here just for one night. I'll sleep on the floor by the foot of your bed," Beo's son begs.

Moi looks at them with moist eyes. His expression is always dull, half pain, half pity. Beo shoos all the children out to the elevator and says good night to Moi.

When Moi comes back to his room he finds Kim Thoa lying naked on the bed. A smell of some cheap, pungent perfume fills the air. She whispers, "Make love to me, Jack."

He laughs a quiet, ironic laugh. Kim Thoa repeats what she said again, this time more urgently: "Jack, love me."

He's no longer laughing, but stands watching her with his dark, expressionless face.

"Jack, do you look down on me?"

Jack collapses onto the bed like a puppet whose strings have been dropped.

"Why should I look down on you? We share the same fate. In America, I'm just a black boy, with no home, no parents, no education, no job, no future, nothing at all. I came back here to look for my childhood dream. I like you very much, Thoa. But I've already spent my last dollar."

Kim Thoa lies motionless, but her body is on fire with the wine in her blood. She looks in awe at the flowery curtains on the windows. The pink lamp shade on the bedside table, the pot of roses on top of the TV set, the fridge, the paintings on the wall—they're all exactly as in her dream. She takes Moi's hand. "Jack, don't make me stand in the street tonight. All my life I've dreamed of lying in the bed of a gentleman."

Moi touches her dark hair, then her cheek. "Then, sleep well," he says.

He closes his own eyes. Inside his head he sees the figures of a little black boy and his friend Beo—two rubbish boys of Evening Market Alley. After picking the fish-egg fruit for their lunch, they take a nap on its branches like two monkeys. The noise of a Vespa screaming out of the alley wakes them. They get down from the tree and crawl over to the window of Hanh's house. Sister Hanh is sitting inside, her head buried in her arms on top of the table where she does her home work, her face hidden by her long black hair.

The boys ask in almost a whisper, "Sister Hanh? When will your wedding be?"

Hanh looks up and pushes back her hair. Her eyes are red, but she manages to produce a smile on her pale face. She reaches out and places one hand on Beo's cheek and the other on Moi's.

"I don't know. But you both are sure to have an invitation."

# Dalit Literature:
# The Voice of the Downtrodden

*By* Razi Abedi

In today's world dominated by the culture of advertisement, even the miseries of the worker are glamorized. Two thousand years ago when Christ tried to ameliorate the misfortunes of the unprivileged, the shepherd's crook became the symbol of the Messiah's mission. Today bishops still honor this tradition by carrying a crook—made of gold.

All institutions ultimately serve vested interests. It is for this reason that the downtrodden of the earth have grown suspicious of all institutions and movements and insist on preserving their own identities. They do not want to be swallowed up by an ideology or a slogan. Such is the case with the movement called Dalit, which started in Western India in the 1960s.

Dalit is the literature of the Untouchables of Maharashtra, those who are looked down upon even by other workers. *Dalit* is Marathi for "the spurned." The term was first used for the Untouchables in 1930. It is a comprehensive expression which now includes Harijans (such as Mahars), Mangs, Mallas, Chambhars and Pulayas. Dalit is a protest literature against all forms of exploitation based on class, race, caste or occupation.

The Dalits are treated worse than animals. Their presence is usually banned from upper-class localities. Even then they are bound to hang clay pots from their necks so that they may not pollute the streets of the privileged by their spittle. They carry brooms tied to their bodies so that while passing through such "upper lanes" they can wipe away their footprints.

Arjum Dangle gives a harrowing picture of their wretchedness in a poem entitled "Chhavni Hilti Ha" ("The Cantonment Has Begun to

85

Shake").

> We fought with crows,
> Never even giving them the snot from our noses.
> As we dragged out the Upper Lane's dead cattle,
> Skinned it neatly
> And shared the meat among ourselves,
> They used to love us then.
> We warred with jackals—dogs—vultures—kites
> Because we ate their share.

Dalit has not yet been acknowledged as a literature in its own right, and no reference to it is found in the standard literary journals of India. But its reverberations are now being heard all around the globe. Like the stories of Prem Chand, it creates characters of great sympathy and humanity, humbly asking for their right to civic representation, but no moral or political organization has the courage to openly associate with them. Recently we have found them turning up in the odd literary story or what has come to be known as the "art film."

Dalit should not be confused with Marathi protest literature, because its subjects are very different. For example, the short story by Dr. Surendra Barlinge, chairman of the Sahitya Sanskrit Mandal, "Mepan Maze," deals with the topic of sex change, a subject that could interest only upper-class readers. Similarly, Padminiraje Patwardhan's story, "*Deepshikha,*" is about a beautiful talented girl, Brahamin by caste, who marries a civil servant.

No doubt these are stories that deal with genuine problems of modern life. But they are not the issues that interest Dalit writers. In their world women are casually stripped and molested, men brutally murdered, and this has been going on for centuries, generation after generation. These are Untouchables who invite death if they dare to quench their thirst from a common pond. Even the Brahamin's god is not their god. He does not accept their supplication. He is not even capable of feeling their misery. Keshav Meshram challenges this god in "One Day I Cursed That...God," in these words:

> Would you wipe the sweat from your bony body
> With your mother's ragged sari?
> Would you work as a pimp

To keep her in booze?
O, father, oh, god the father!
You could never do such things.
First you'd need a mother—
One no one honors,
One who toils in the dirt,
One who gives and gives of her love.

A homegrown movement of the Untouchables, Dalit is opposed to all notions of caste and class, but it also suspects the intellectuals of the left as well as Marxist ideologues who treat Marxism itself as a dogma rather than a science. Such people assume the role of Marxist pundits, and Untouchables cannot afford to trust pundits. The theoretical variety of revolutionaries cannot even imagine the predicament these wretched people live in. Namde Dhasal cries out:

This world's socialism,
This world's communism
And all those things of theirs,
We have put them to the test
And the implication is this—
Only our shadows can cover our own feet.

Their suffering is not just the suffering of the individual, and there is nothing romantic about it. Their problem is neither ideological nor philosophical. They do not seek poetic beauty. Similes, metaphors and symbols are not important.

The reality of their life is too hideously shocking, beyond the capacity of fantasy or imagination. Their tragedy is universal, trampling them down and disfiguring their humanity. Narayan Surve makes an ironical comment on the champions of revolution and their rhetoric in his poem, "Karl Marx:"

In my first strike Marx met me thus:
I was holding his banner high on my shoulder.
The other day he stood listening to my speech at the
gate, in the meeting—now we alone are the heroes of
history, of all the biographies too, henceforth...
He was the first to applaud, then

laughing boisterously
he put his hand on my shoulder and said:
"Are you a poet or what...
nice...very nice...
I too liked poetry
Goethe was my favorite."

Their bitterness is totally understandable. They have been subjected to the worst atrocities. A young man's thumb may be amputated just so that he does not become a better archer than a lad of the upper class.

These people see the class war that is going on at the global level as irrelevant to their cause. Class war is a long-term struggle. People like themselves have neither the time nor the patience to wait for the tide to turn. The verdict of history may come too late. Prabhakar Bangurde spurns such wishful thinking in his poem "Comrade:"

> Don't be in a hurry for revolution.
> You are still very small.
> Your ability to resist
> the atrocities, boycotts and rapes
> that go on every moment
> has become nil
> comrade.
> Tomorrow's sun is yet to rise
> sleep undisturbed until then...

This is their everyday experience that closely ties them to prevailing social conventions, justifying their appalling living conditions in the name of culture and tradition. They are particularly concerned about their daughters, who must be married according to strictly imposed custom and lead respectable and pious lives. This must be hard to swallow when they see that "they strip naked my mother, my sisters" and "my own daughter's virtue is looted in public, my eyes look on, my blood shakes." These are lines taken from a folksong.

But Dalit poetry is not merely protest. There are also the eternal emotions of love and sacrifice reverberating in it, as in this poem, "Mother," by Warman Nimbalkar:

> Dark, dark slender body—this was my mother.

Drudged in the woods for sticks from morning on.
All we brothers, sitting, waiting, watching for her.
And if she didn't sell the wood, all of us slept hungry.

And one day she died of hard work and left them wailing,
though not without leaving a sweetness behind her:

My eyes seek my mother,
I still grieve,
I see a thin vendor of wood.
I buy her sticks.

Consider this beautiful poem, "The City," by Daya Pawar. It begins like this:

One day someone dug up a twentieth century city
And ends on this observation.
Here's an interesting inscription:
"This water tap is open to all castes and religions."
What could it have meant:
That this society was divided?
That some were high while others were low?
Well, all right, then this city deserved burying—
Why did they call it the machine age?
Seems like the Stone Age in the twentieth century.

The Dalit are also burning with a desire for revenge. Their anger is reflected in, "You Wrote From Los Angeles," by Daya Pawar:

In the stores here, in hotels, about the streets,
Indians and curs are measured with the same Yard—stick.
"Niggers!" "Blacks!" This is the abuse they fling on me.
Reading all this, I felt so damn!
Now you've had a taste of what we've suffered
In this country from generation to generation.

But though it is the poetry of the oppressed, in it can be heard the echoes of a rebellious soul:

I'm the sea; I soar, I surge.
I move out to build your tombs.
The winds, storms, sky, earth.
Now all are mine.
In every inch of the rising struggle
I stand erect.

-J.V. Pawar: "I Have Become the Tide."

# Curses & Poetry

(from the novel)

*By* Anjana Basu

My first memories were not of my father and mother but of my grandmother. "You were always an ungrateful girl," Ma told me. "Other children remember their parents. Not you. You and my mother were so close that I used to be jealous." Now I can't really remember what Granny was like. "My mother was like a wax doll," I once heard Ma telling Maitreyi, her own granddaughter. "That was considered very beautiful in those days." Granny was the daughter of a relatively poor village landlord and, because of her looks, married into a family of comparative power and status. Her veiled sepia photograph hung in its oval frame in a place of honour at the head of the stairs. "But she's your mother," I argued. "Why is her picture hanging in my father's house? Where is my father's picture?" "Your father loved her very much," was my mother's curt answer. "He wanted her picture hung there."

She married at the age of eleven with more pomp and circumstance than anyone in her small village had ever seen, even though her father's small band of courtiers always predicted that she would marry well. "So fair, such large eyes, such smooth cheeks." She was as fair as an English wax doll and there actually was one of those rare commodities kept in a glass cabinet in the house, with the same rounded cheeks and endlessly patient eyes. Hansabati, they had named her, for the one white goose that paddled in continuous circles around the village pond. "You're as bad-tempered as that goose," they told her on the rare occasions when tears of rage welled up in those large black glass eyes. The goose was a double-edged comparison, both for its whiteness and for its temper. Actually, it wasn't a goose but what was called a *rajhans*. In English that made it something that was not quite a swan, so that she was not quite a Swan Princess, or so her tutor explained to her.

As far back as she cared to remember, she had had a tutor, to teach her English and fit her for her supposed high status in life. Because her father was a village landlord, her teacher was a round Babu with an accent not far removed from the Bengali he usually spoke. "A goose," he explained pompously, "is a large bhariety of dock. G-O-O-ESH-E." Still, from him she learned to gabble English after a fashion. The rest of the time, whenever she managed to escape from her ayah, she climbed the palm trees with the gardener's sons, or chased the goats in the field. Every time she returned from these excursions, the women of the house would gather to wail over her and smother her with plant extracts and buttermilk to make sure that the sun had not tarnished her complexion.

Then, one morning her mother brandished a photograph of a solemn-eyed boy in front of her. A solemn-eyed boy with a wide, sensitive mouth. "Your husband to be. The son of the landlord of Polashi." No one asked her whether she liked the picture. The two maids fell into ecstasies in front of it, exclaiming, "Ah ha, what eyes! What a young prince!" while her mother listened to their fulsome compliments with a pleased smile. Granny was not asked to say either yes or no; instead she was informed that from now on she would have to start performing *Shiv puja* for her husband's well being as part of her daily duties and that her palm-scaling days were over. The *Shiv puja* she could possibly accept, but it was hard to watch the palm fronds bucking like horses in a cool south breeze, their green necks combing the pale blue sky, and not want to scale them. Since she was obedient by nature, she stood by the pond and looked longingly up at the trees, but disciplined herself merely to look. No one would ever say that she was disobedient, not even the tutor who compared her to a goose.

Her prospective father-in-law came to survey her and a bustle of maids fell around her and dressed her in her best marigold muslin. Her mother bustled in with the pearl-headed pins that were to secure the elaborate coils of her hair, and discovered the little girl to be standing unnaturally still under her ministrations. So unnaturally still that she seemed to have turned into the wax doll that she resembled. "Is the petticoat string cutting into you?" Silence. "Is the blouse too tight?" Still silence: the white face was tight and still. Moved by a sudden impulse, the mother pulled out one of the ornate hairpins and discovered it was tipped with blood: in securing it, she had driven the spike into her daughter's scalp. "My mother was never like you," Ma told me every morning as she wound her hair into the tightly oiled plaits that I loathed with a passion. "Her mother drove that hairpin into her head and she never said a word." That one act of stoicism alone would have served to make Granny legendary to me. But Hansabati moved on from the hairpin ordeal to meet her father-in-law and speak to him in her curiously accented English in front of a whole room of encouraging women who hummed and sighed at her every word. What is your name? How old are you? Can you cook? She answered all the questions with precision and accuracy, looking at the red tips of her rouged toes as they peeked from under the gold border of her hem and occasionally at the curly tips of the leather slippers in front of her. They were very fine leather—much better than the ones her father wore. Her father-in-law had a big booming voice that seemed to echo under the rafters and cause the wounds in her scalp to start stinging afresh.

After a while the maid came, took her by the hand and led her out of the room. She was left stranded on a cool marble shelf in the antechamber and forbidden to move. "Good girl, sit here and I'll bring you some lemon water." She sat there swinging her legs and watching her red toes swish through her marigold skirts, wondering what was going to happen next. She sat there until the shadows slanted upwards and the light began to thicken. The marble shelf had a window to it and she could see the deserted courtyard where a fat grey pigeon ran bowing and bubbling after his sleek pink-footed wives. The pigeon suddenly started and rose into the air in a clap of wings, followed belatedly by the rest. She saw one of her father's subjects run across the courtyard. Then there was silence again and the pigeons returned. The marble under her began to feel uncomfortable. She shifted uneasily and thought of pulling out the hairpins and letting her plaits snake down. She even had one hand up to pull out a pin, when the maid came back full of her own self-importance. "What on earth are you doing? Come, they're calling you."

She was lifted down from the shelf like a doll and led back into her father's meeting room. There she was placed in front of the same gold-embroidered slippers she had talked to all morning. The booming voice boomed again. After she had adjusted to the echo, she realized that it was welcoming her to his home as his new daughter-in-law. Almost simultaneously, she could hear the conch shells, as booming as the voice, being blown from the puja room. Dutifully, because she knew it was expected of her, she bent down and touched those curly leather-tipped slippers. Then the maid propelled her towards her mother and father, and she touched their feet too. When Hansabati glanced up, she saw her mother had tears in her eyes and she wanted to hug her, but all those days of training held her in check. "Go to the prayer room," her mother bade her, "and touch the god's feet. Then go to your room."

The *pandit* was standing unctuously by the Krishna image, clutching the small silver pot of holy water. He sprinkled her with it after she rose from the floor, and as the cool drops touched her cheeks she realized how thirsty she was. Gathering up her skirts, she sprinted out of the room on her maid's wail of dismay, scattering the hated pearl hairpins behind her, and ran to the water pot in the kitchen. The water splashed over her marigold and gold finery, tangling it with her legs, and she deliberately tipped the pot over even more to feel the coolness. The maids had to strip the wet sari off her and hang it out to dry immediately, worrying whether the brocade would tarnish, but whether it did or not was not passed down to Hansabati's descendants. For them she remained a model of stoicism, the legendary example of grace under pressure.

Very gradually, the course of her days changed so that she had little time to watch the goose paddling around the pond. Her days began with prayers for the length of her future husband's life, progressed to the designing of *alpana* patterns with coloured rice powder, moved to the niceties of cooking, and ended with the interminable afternoon English lesson. Every afternoon, as the light thickened in the windows, her tutor's snores grated on her ears while she patiently scrawled compositions on The Cow or The Cat. And at sunset, the maids came to comb out her hair on the breezy terrace while her mother instructed her on the different types of hairstyles appropriate for young brides and showed her the various kinds of hair ornaments. "You will be going to a more sophisticated family, so you should be aware of these things."

"Do they have a big house?"

"Yes, a very big house."

"Do they have horses like we do? And a phaeton?"

"More. They have motor cars!" The maids gasped and clutched at each other in awe whenever they heard such things. "Think what a lucky girl you are, to have been chosen out of so many!"

Once she asked, her young voice as clear as the ring of bell metal ware over the babble of adult conversation, "Why did they choose me?"

and set the maids gabbling and bubbling like a flock of upset pigeons. "What a question! When she's so fair, so white!" "Who can boast a complexion like that, even in Calcutta?"

"It's a great honour to us," said her mother severely," that you have been chosen. You should accept that fact and not ask unnecessary questions." Vanity was not part of Hansabati's nature—the fact that she had a skin as white as the goose's feathers did not seem to her to be such a great advantage. "There must have been other girls," she protested, "girls from Calcutta. Why me?"

"Are you unhappy because you've been chosen?"

"Not unhappy exactly..." The trouble was, she didn't know what to answer. The idea of marriage to the boy in the picture still seemed a remote possibility indeed: even the ceremony in front of the curly-toed shoes had passed like a dream. Living anywhere else except in this rambling shabby house was beyond her imagination because the farthest boundaries of her life were the *sal* trees on the edge of her father's land that marked the beginning of the forest. Beyond those trees, she had been told, ran a railroad track where the fearsome iron *railgharry* belched smoke and rattled and chugged to Calcutta. On days when the wind was in the right direction she had even heard the iron monster scream. But she had never been able to persuade their grandly named coachman to drive her in that direction to show her this wonder. In the ten years of her life she had been nowhere and seen nothing. She tried to explain some of this to her mother, but her mother failed to understand. "Where would you possibly go?" she asked. "Where does a correctly bred girl go? I have never been anywhere except my father's house and here. And, oh yes, your father took me once to Calcutta. But that was all."

Perhaps her mother had once been her age and had also wondered where she was being sent to, but from the immaculate red-and-white-bordered look of her, that seemed difficult to imagine. And her mother had never been the sort of child who rode the flying palm fronds when the wind was blowing hot and strong from the south. That was something Hansabati had apparently inherited from her father. Between herself and her mother was a gap as wide as the one between the house and the faraway *sal* trees. Oh, they coexisted in harmony as the house and the trees did, with fair weather days and days when no one could tell which way the wind blew but, for all that, the gap was there. It was because of the gap that her mother had driven the hairpins into her head, meaning well all the while. It was because of the gap that she found the *alpana* patterns so hard to bear, the monotonous meticulous curves of the green mango, the sinuous shape of Lakshmi's feet. There was duty between herself and her mother, but no love at all. Her mother had raised her for ten years in the hope that she would be a credit to the family and find herself a niche in a good man's house. Questions of distance and time and space were ones her mother was not equipped to answer, and she reacted to them with impatience. "Don't fret," Hansabati's maid told her, as she fanned her in the silence of her room at night. "Nothing but good will come of this. It is a girl's duty to get married."

The oval daguerreotype of the wide-mouthed boy stood next to her bed, and she found herself staring at it often. Did he have a pet goose in Calcutta? Did he climb trees or tear his clothes or play cricket? Was that wide mouth capable of laughter? Beyond the fact that he was the Rai Bahadur's son, no one seemed to have anything to say about him. Her mother's maids stitched yards and yards of cloth into *kurtas* for him or little bags for her to carry her betel nut box in. The flashing needles dug patterns of green parrots out of the off-white silk. "Country patterns," said her mother, "simple ones, since we cannot pretend to their sophistication. However, the craftsmanship will show through." Her mother had chosen the maids carefully for their skill at needlework and their ability to tie hair or devise original garlands out of available flowers. She was busily choosing one to send to Calcutta with Hansabati.

The Ray Bahadur sent his *pandit* to confer with Hansabati's father's *pandit* and, between the two of them, a suitable date and time was found for the wedding. Hansabati only discovered that the date had been set because she patiently and charmingly wheedled it out of the maids. The house and the village grew even busier. Boxes and boxes of things came in and out of the courtyard. The village jeweller set up permanent shop on the terrace with his little low table, red tablecloth and skeins of silk. Pearls were marshalled deftly onto his needle and strung in moonlit rows: pearls for necklaces, chokers, bracelets and bangles. There were so many of them that it was a wonder the pigeons did not mistake them for a new kind of seed and swallow them by accident—she was terrified that would actually happen and destroy all the poor jeweller's work. All her mother's chains and chokers acquired new elaborate brocade tassels that prickled at the nape of her neck whenever she tried them on. Her father never had time to smile at her—he was busy organizing the selling of crops, the collection of rents, all to raise money for the dowry that had been asked of him.

"Was it a very big dowry?" she asked her maid, shyly.

"No, not very big, but quite big. It's an honour child, a great honour. They could have asked for five times as much." Even if they hadn't, the amount seemed to have upset everyone in the house because day and night they talked money and possessions and nothing else. A great hall was built in one of the fields to house extra members of the groom's party. The cook summoned his brothers and cousins from their villages so they could support him in producing the wedding feast.

And then everyone turned round and began to concentrate even more fiercely on Hansabati. Her skin was rubbed with flour and buttermilk and steeped in pomegranate juice until it was even more waxen than before. The tailor arrived with new bodices and blouses with elbow-length sleeves and lace ruffles. She had new petticoats, new hair ribbons, new gloves—so many new things that she was afraid to look into the mirror in case she found a new person there confronting her. Don't walk, don't sit, don't move, from all around came a flurry of contradictory instructions. Her mother and the maids seemed to be suffering from perennially lost tempers, her English lessons had been stopped, and the Brahmin governess expected her to memorise a new recipe every day before she did anything else.

When the wedding day finally arrived, the groom's party was late and Hansabati's father was surrounded by a host of murmuring guests who were ready to offer their condolences and point out that such an ambitious marriage was bound to end in downfall: After all, how could a humble village landlord hope to compete with a Rai Bahadur? One or two were already busily pushing their own sons forward when the conch shells blew.

In the dream of confusion that was the wedding, she remembered the sharp, sudden malice of those faces, the way they fell when the conch shells blew, the glitter of eyes resenting her father's good fortune. "No matter what you do," she said later in life, "you'll never be able to please everybody. And there'll always be people who will be glad to see you fail." She taught that to her elder daughter, who learnt the lesson better than the younger one. Despite the knife-edged envy in those faces, she was carried by her uncles seven times around the fire, with the end of her gorgeous red and gold sari attached to the robe of someone who was probably not much taller than herself. Her groom's face was so covered in tassels that all she could recognize of it was the wide mouth, and that mouth did not smile even once.

The wedding night, draped in a mass of tuberoses, was filled with an assortment of in-laws. Hansabati slept on the bed with her mother and mother-in-law while the groom shared a mattress on the floor with the two fathers. By then she had seen her husband's face, caught a fleeting glimpse of it when she exchanged garlands with him, uncertain of her balance on the small square of wood beneath her. Then her uncles had mercifully put her down and the maids had led away, teasing her about what was to come.

Her new in-laws snored, she noted, as she lay wakeful far into the night, watching the moon rise and spill its light over the edge of the bed. And then she was aware of a quiet furtive rustle on the floor, and the moonlight spilled into a pair of wide eyes peering anxiously over the side of the bed.

# The Long Journey

*By* Vasanthi Victor

Kamala wipes the tears from her eyes. She cannot help it. It is in her nature to cry whether she is actually sitting in a theater watching the film or only recalling it, as she is now. *Devdas* is her all-time favorite. The old black-and-white classic reeling through her mind one tearful scene after another makes her weep every time. She takes a quick peek at Shyam seated beside her. Fortunately he is asleep. They are an old couple and so well-versed in each other that even if she did try to hide her tears during a film, which she has begun to do of late during a particularly poignant scene, he would still turn to look at her, having anticipated just such a response. She sighs—there are so few hidden corners of the heart—and peeks at him again. He looks dishevelled and rumpled as he sits, swaying. They are travelling on the Deccan Queen in the second-class compartment—reserved berths, so they can sleep comfortably. He will be on the upper berth and she on the lower. It is not the first time they have travelled together, not the first time they have used these sleeping arrangements.

How was it that first time...? They were making the trip from Baroda to Bombay with her parents, who had come to escort the new bride and groom back to their home and had taken seats on the berth across the aisle from them. Shyam had said, Let me lie with you.

What! What will my parents think?

I don't care what they think. We are married now.

But how could she lie with a man in full view of her parents? She shook her head no, though it did seem strange to lie alone after almost a month of marriage. Still, she would not hear of it. He had given her a miffed look, clearly put out, and climbed to the upper berth. When she tried to say something to him, he refused to look at her, had turned his back and soon was asleep.

Dust and grime sweeps in through the open window next to her, settling on the floor and the dark-green vinyl seats. Stale, stagnant air, peculiar to Indian Railways, clings to her hair and clothes. She brushes herself and rearranges her saree in an effort to shake it off.

But it clings nonetheless. Getting up carefully so as to maintain her balance, she walks down the aisle at a slant against the movement of the speeding train and navigates her way to the restroom. In the crowded passageway she steps over extended legs and then unwittingly onto a bundle on the floor. The bundle moves. She immediately removes her offending foot with an apology, but the mother of the sleeping bundle stares up at her accusingly. Some young men standing near the exits watch her as she approaches the toilet. How can they stand the odour? When she comes out again, re-arranging her saree, they have gone back to watching the Deccan Plateau rushing past. Meanwhile, the toilet smell follows her back down the aisle as she again steps around the bundle on the floor.

Shyam is still asleep. His head moves from side to side with the rhythm of the train. The slippers have fallen from his feet. From a bag under his legs she picks up a magazine and flips through its pages. Out of the corner of her eye she glimpses the furtive looks being exchanged between a middle-aged man and a young girl seated across the passageway, occupying single seats. She continues to watch them and decides there is something illicit going on. A woman who appears to be the man's wife lies dozing on the extended seat near him, and two children share the bunk above her. Kamala decides the girl must be someone's maid or relative. He has not yet made a move. He is waiting for an opportune moment.

She glances at the wife lying innocently asleep. Wake up! she thinks, but who can hear thoughts? She turns her attention back to the magazine on her lap, blindly reading the words, the lines of the page merging into one. Eventually she begins to nod and dozes off like Shyam and the other passengers.

A long time ago, back in her childhood, her aunt—the one with long black hair, shining eyes and dark skin, skin so dark she could not possibly be related to Kamala's own family—has come to send them off. Everyone is sitting and talking in a loud chatter, the aunt among them, and suddenly the train jerks into motion. No one heard the whistle!

I must get off.

Don't go, Auntie, Kamala says.

Silly girl, I must.

Kamala tries to hold her back as Auntie moves hastily to the exit, crying, Let me go!

Auntie, please don't go! Please don't...

But Auntie pulls her arm free and jumps. The moving train has almost passed the platform, but somehow she lands safely on her feet. Kamala's mother begins to scold her: What on earth possessed you to act like that? You could have hurt yourself. Naughty girl! But watching the receding shape of her aunt, Kamala pays no attention and waves despondently....

And as she waves she thinks about Devdas, the tragic hero who gradually, scene by scene, becomes an alcoholic. A wayward youth, he has rejected his childhood sweetheart and left the village where he grew up in order to live in the big city. And there he does what other young men do who live alone—he falls into bad company. As he sinks deeper and deeper into alcoholism, a dancing girl looks after him. She does everything in her power to help him, but he eventually leaves her too, longing for his lost love....

Someone jostles her and, against her will, she pries her eyes open. What...?

Shyam pokes at her arm. Almost mealtime, he says. Wake up. See, some people are eating already.

As she comes awake she asks automatically, Do you want the puris we packed?

No. I'll wait for the tiffin-carrier. We should be getting it soon at the next station.

But she reaches for the bag under the seat and, unwrapping the package she finds there, mutters, These *puris* are good. Taste really good with the *sabji*.

No. We should be stopping soon.

What about your stomach? You know you have a weak stomach.

But he shakes his head in the negative.

Have this *moosambi*, then.

She offers the orange fruit. He takes it and begins peeling the skin off. When he bites into it, it drips all over his shirt and she scolds him for making a mess. Just like a child you are, she says.

Don't bother me, all right? See, I am eating my *moosambi*.

The people across the aisle from them smile. And, playing to them, he says, Right? This is how you eat a *moosambi*. Yes, yes, they nod in

101

assent. Kamala does not look up. Tearing open the *puri* with her right hand, she scoops the potato *sabji* and places in her mouth. Shyam watches her with interest, so she offers to share. But he does not want to appear greedy in front of his newfound friends. I will wait. It will only spoil my appetite.

When the train comes to a halt at the next station, there's a mad rush of people entering and exiting. The tiffin-carrier, stainless-steel trays piled in one hand, clambers into the carriage, balancing the trays expertly. At the window a hawker with a snack tray cries above the din, selling his wares from the outside.

How much is it? Shyam yells back.

Saab, teen rupaiya.

Nahi, nahi. Chal.

The snack is cold, not fresh, he tells Kamala. But the hawker belligerently calls: *Bilkul* fresh. *Dake.* Sensing an argument, Kamala pulls Shyam away from the window and cajoles: See, the tiffin-carrier is coming our way. The hot tray dropped unceremoniously into his hands by the carrier is piping hot, but Shyam digs into it with relish. The curries have spilled out of their round steel containers, but Shyam exclaims, They have mango pickle!

Don't eat the pickle, it will be too spicy for your stomach.

You leave my stomach alone. Why can't a man have his meal in peace!

She pays no attention to his rebuke and continues with her own eating. When he is almost done he calls out to the *chaiwalla*. The *chaiwalla* is alert and quick on his feet. He comes at once and hands her a thick steamy glass of tea. With the tea in her hand, she gestures to her husband: Does he want any? But Shyam shakes his head no. The glass is hot in her hand and it spills a little as the train jerks forward again. The passengers still hobnobbing outside somehow scramble to get back on. The young men from the doorway near the restrooms clamber aboard, laughing together. Comfortably sipping *chai*, Kamala watches the station slip in slow motion from sight. As the commotion of its leaving subsides, the people inside the cabin settle down to eat and soon care about nothing else. Sipping more *chai*, she sees the middle-aged man talking to his wife. The girl has moved from her earlier spot and is now seated farther away. Like the others, she is eating with her hand, her head bent over her food. The man's children are also awake and his wife, feeding one, murmurs:

Take, take.

Shyam gets up to wash his hands at the washbasin at the other end of the carriage. When he returns he smiles at Kamala. Want to play cards? he asks.

All right.

He invites anyone who is interested to join them, but they shake their heads. But after a few hands the same few who had just declined to play are gradually drawn into the game. Before long an enthusiastic session is in full swing. Finding herself surrounded entirely by men, Kamala excuses herself. They hardly miss her as she becomes the spectator, watching her husband play. Eventually she loses all interest in the game and reverts to watching the middle-aged man and the girl, who has resumed her earlier position near him. The man's wife has retired for the night, sleeping with the sari *palloo* covering her head. Except for the card players, everyone in Kamala's own and the adjoining cabin are making preparations to sleep. She pulls up her legs and curls herself into a comfortable position. The card players lower their voices, and a hush descends on the cabin. One by one, the lights wink off. The middle-aged man rubs his shoulder against the girl. She feigns sleep.

Kamala wonders if the girl has already been spoilt. Someone—an uncle, a family friend—could have made passes, or worse. It happens all the time. Sooner or later, a girl like her, from a poor family judging from her clothes, gets spoilt. *Bechari!* Still, no point in conjuring up useless thoughts, is there?

Shyam asks, Kamala, are you ready to sleep?

No, no. Continue playing if you want.

But he has already turned to the others. What do you say, friends? Shall we call it a night?

Yes, yes. No use keeping the missus up. Shyam responds, Any way, it was a good game. Someone lying down nearby shushes them. Goodnight, Shyam whispers with his fingers to his mouth. Then he asks Kamala if she needs anything before climbing into the upper berth. Slouching down into the vinyl, she murmurs, Turn off the light.

Though it is quiet now, she cannot sleep. In the dark she imagines bedbugs are on the crawl. She sits up straight and searches for any sign of them, then slouches down again. The Deccan Queen chugs along, rocking and swaying in a desultory fashion. Kamala can hear a few snores already and wonders if some of them are her husband's. Swaying to the rhythm, she begins to drift off herself....

Her parents would be proud. A granddaughter in America! And, Kamala, you are going too, they would say if they were still alive. But right from the start she has been uneasy, and long before it came time to board the train she felt full of apprehension about the trip. Shyam tried to reassure her before they left Baroda. It is official now, Kamala, he said. The documents are prepared. We must leave in a few months or the visa will expire. And what about Rita? She will be waiting for us.... Besides, think of all the fun you will have with your grandchildren.

She paid no attention to his words. Instead she thought about the photos Rita had sent from New York. The snaps showed them all smiling happily. The photos were taken in different locales and in the many different seasons of the New World. In one they were bundled up because of the cold, Rita and the baby both. All around them was white with snow. Though Kamala peered hard at the photo she could barely make out the baby's tiny face in all the heavy clothing he was wrapped in. How could she, she asked herself, live in such a cold place? She had only to look at that poor baby. He looked so pale, his skin, she imagined, turning white! She has always been such a warm-blooded creature, a woman accustomed to heat beating down on her. So brown she'd grown over the years. Living in such a cold place she'd have to be wrapped up like that baby. How could she, of all people, bear to walk with her feet covered? In Baroda, she went barefoot. Her saree flew freely about her as she went about her daily routine. In New York (Rita, bless her soul, had always been a good daughter) she wouldn't even be mistress of her own house. What would she do with herself?

She told Shyam her bones would ache with cold. The sun could not shine in such a cold place. Imagine me, she said, bundled up forever. But Shyam, turning a deaf ear, brushed aside her concerns. You will be fine Kamala, he said. Anyway, your place belongs with me, and I have agreed to go to live with our daughter and her family. When we leave here, after we arrive in Bombay, we'll drive to the airport and catch our plane. We'll fly in a jumbo jet. Rita, he said, will take good care of us. See! She has already booked our tickets. Who else is there to look out for us in our old age? Come down to earth, Kamala, he said.

Suddenly sitting up, she looks about her. Where am I?

Then she slaps at the bedbugs, twisting this way and that, trying to find a more comfortable position. The girl she saw earlier, now crouched on the floor, is sleeping with her head on her knees, rocking with the motion of the train. The man must certainly think she is asleep because his hand has crept up under her skirt. The girl suddenly becomes very still but doesn't raise her head or move at all. A little later she begins to rock again, lifts her head and glances at him shyly. He gets up and heads for the restroom. When he comes back the girl tries to move closer to him, but when he looks around he sees Kamala. Their eyes meet then he looks up at his wife, who is sleeping in the berth above him. He doesn't seem to care if a strange old woman sees him.

Kamala silently calls him louse. Louse, louse. Doesn't he care that he's being watched? And that girl, letting herself be used like that. What kind of people travel in these trains anyway? Shyam should have booked seats in a first-class coach. But then she remembers how there weren't any sleepers available.... Stop! she tells the bedbugs, stop biting me.

In the morning the cool air and the jolt of the train coming to a stop wake her. Shyam is bright and cheerful when he finds her already awake as he comes down from his perch.

Did you sleep well? he asks.

The bedbugs kept me awake. Don't they ever bite you?

I slept fine. Did you want a cup of *chai*, I am going to get one.

Maybe later. I have to brush my teeth and freshen up.

Come with me outside, then, and use the washbasin on the platform.

So, wrapping herself up and adjusting her hair, she steps out into the cool morning air.

There are people asleep on the benches and the cold floor of the station. Such people, she thinks bending down to rinse her brush and wash her face at the faucet, pass their whole lives in these places.

They find there will be a minor delay and decide to stretch their legs a bit. From nowhere a beggar woman accosts them: *Amma, mai gharib hoo. Mujhe paisa dede.* She has one child on her hip and, pushing forth another, she repeats the words till Shyam, annoyed, fishes out some change from his pocket and drops it in her cupped hands. The woman thanks them both, touching her hand to her forehead as the child at her hip stares up at them with big black eyes.

When they return to the train the young men are at the same spot by the exit doors they occupied yesterday, smoking Charminars and Luckys. Kamala walks past the man with the roving hands. His wife is sitting next to him, now wide-awake. Kamala glares at him as she passes, but he ignores her, staring out the window. His wife begins to rearrange her saree and comb her hair, apparently without a care in the world.

As they sit down on their seat, the card-players wish them good morning.

Good Morning! Shyam replies. Good Morning. Have you had some tea? Very good tea here.

No, Sir. We are only now getting up. Where are you going? To Bombay? they ask.

Yes.

All of us here are headed there as well. Whereabouts do you live in Bombay?

No, no. We live in Baroda. At least, we used to. My wife and I are flying to New York. Our daughter has invited us to come and live with her. We are grandparents now, you see. And he beams proudly.

To New York! How lucky to be travelling abroad, they say. You must be rich.

Shyam, still beaming says, Hardly rich. Lucky, yes, that I agree. Isn't that right, Kamala?

She responds with a wan smile.

The card players begin discussing the ups and downs of life in a city like Bombay. How, with the cost of living going up and up, a person should consider himself fortunate just to own a flat. Flats are so tiny and so hard to find that one can barely manage a sneeze in one of them. In between, someone tries to get their address in New York, but Kamala nudges her husband. Surprisingly, he comes up with an excuse not to give it, though she is convinced it is she who has averted a disaster. What if a relative of this stranger suddenly lands on Rita's doorstep? Just like that, out of the blue. It could happen, perhaps it happens all the time, one just never knows these days. She congratulates herself...she has stopped him just in time.

Look, look, she says suddenly. Do you see this station?

As the train creeps slowly past a non-descript platform in the middle of nowhere, Shyam asks, What about it?

It's like the one in *Devdas*, she says excitedly.

Devdas? What are you talking about? And he looks at her carefully.

But she is back in the emotional scenes of the old black-and-white classic playing in her mind: Devdas passing from town to town, wandering by rail. He comes back to the town where his childhood sweetheart still lives. She is married now to a widower with two grown children, is well respected and leading a comfortable family life. Devdas is sick and perhaps already dying, his liver abused by years of drinking. He finds a rickshaw driver to ferry him through the night in a worsening downpour. Unable to continue on, the driver abandons him as Devdas in a delirium calls his sweetheart's name.

In the morning people begin to gather around the tree where he has been found lying atop the cement platform. As they mutter among themselves about his identity, a servant from his sweetheart's household overhears them. He tells his mistress, There's a man lying in front our house uttering your name. Who is he? she asks. Devdas, or some such, the neighbors are saying. The sweetheart runs in anguish out of the house, her stepchildren following. They try to prevent her from reaching the crowd gathered outside. Shut the gates, shut the gates! they call to the sentry. She reaches the main gate just as it closes and she collapses on the railing, sobbing. Outside, Devdas breathes his last, miserable to the end.

Kamala wipes a tear from her eye. Dilip Kumar played the hero, and what was the name of the actress who played his true love? She can't remember. But it doesn't matter...they don't make pictures like that anymore. She sighs and shakes her head.

All around her, people are beginning to gather together their belongings and are busy tidying up themselves and their children. With the end of each passing mile they begin to shake off the lethargy of the trip and look forward to their destinations. Shyam tells her excitedly, We are drawing closer...the end of our yatra. Somebody from across the aisle reaches out to shake his hand as if they were old friends. Kamala looks around for the girl, but it is hard to find her in the crush. Suddenly she spots her. The middle-aged man is trying to slip a note to her, but the girl is hesitant. He tries to force it on her, stepping very close, but she makes no attempt to take it from him. Louse! Kamala hisses, pulling her saree tightly around her and adjusting her hair. Shyam turns to ask what is the matter? She smiles and shakes her head.

The train has slowed to a crawl, and from somewhere a whistle blows. Coolies wrapped in red turbans swing on to the sides and clamber inside. Then there is a loud babble of voices, some of them annoyed and some confused. She hears the crunch of brakes and the last sudden shriek of the train as it finally comes to a halt.

# The Big Lie

*By* Viktor Car

### Pristina

Yesterday I found myself staring in amazement at the front page of the *Toronto Star* where I saw a photograph of the very same barracks where I spent five months back in 1986. I had been conscripted into the Yugoslav Army—my home state of Croatia was then part of Yugoslavia—and sent to Pristina. By some cosmic poetic justice, the very place where I once suffered hellish mistreatment and Kafkaesque denouncement is in flames, fulfilling my prediction thirteen years ago that the only way to stop the chain reaction of Balkan tragedies, with Serbs at the epicenter of each conflict, would be by military force.

### Albanians

Kosovo means the "place of crows." Hilly landscapes, barren meadows, poor villages, skinny cows that stand in black mud and stare back at you like humans. Poverty is everywhere—barefoot children, horse-drawn carriages, people in worn-out clothes, muddy streets.

Being a Croat and an intellectual was not a popular profile in 1986. I was part of a so-called "squad of the punished." We worked twelve hours a day, carrying 120-pound bags of rice or potatoes, barrels of oil, beans, cans of beef. We unloaded wagons from dawn to dusk, walking in a slow procession, our eyes cast down on the heels of the man in front. In the evening four or five of us snuck out to the village store to buy some good Albanian brandy, and then drank it sitting on a plank resting across a couple of concrete blocks over a black dirt floor, occasionally chatting with the passing locals. I wore the Serbian uniform, by then a worn-out piece of green burlap, the clothes of a laborer. It was evident back then that nothing good was in the offing. The Serbian authorities were treating the Kosovar Albanian majority with relentless harshness. Often I heard from the Albanians, "It's easy for you Croats, you are part of the West. But us, who will ever know what happened here?"

Their kids were barefoot, skinny, big-eyed and openhearted. Sometimes through the barbed wire we'd give them money to bring us brandy, and they always brought back the exact change. I gave them baksheesh for the candy, or cans of food. The locals appreciated these gifts, and sometimes in the village store they'd insist on buying us beer, little as they could afford it.

On Sundays I got to walk the village streets, along with women in shawls watching over their remarkably subdued children. The soil was black but the vegetation sparse, a barren land of poverty. The streets I walked were cobblestoned, lined with brick wall fences, making me feel as if I were walking in a maze. The silence was eerie, as if in anticipation.

Our squad shared a dormitory with three officers' drivers. Conscripts like us, but clean, they were tall good-looking guys who drove the colonels and generals around in army-issue Fiats. The drivers were well fed, well informed and hated having to share the same dormitory with smelly scum like us. They were Serbs, two from Belgrade, one from Novi Sad. There was an incident once—some Albanian kids threw a stone at one of the army Fiats in which Dragan, the one from Novi Sad, was waiting for his colonel. Dragan complained to the colonel and the next day all drivers were issued pistols and ordered to shoot at kids who threw stones at them.

From those very same barracks that I saw burning on the front page of the *Star* I used to slide through a hole in the barbed wire to sneak into Pristina. Returning to the barracks, drunk, on a dark Sunday evening, bending down to squeeze through that same opening in the barbed wire, I heard a dry metal click, the sound of old M-48 rifle being repositioned. I lay down on the ground, knowing that a Serbian guard, a shepherd from eastern Serbia, was on duty.

"Is that you Mirche? It is me, Viktor. Don't shoot"

No reply.

"It's me, Viktor. Don't shoot."

Still no reply. Then his voice out of the darkness: "Come on in."

But something seemed fishy, and I remembered some talk I had overheard among the guards about weekend passes for those who shot intruders. I crawled back through the hole, walked around to the other side of the camp and found another hole in the fence.

Later Mirche admitted to me that the sergeant had promised to let him go home for the weekend if he shot me. Mirche desperately missed the roast lamb they made back in his village close to the Bulgarian border, and he would do anything to go home again.

Later on, when I was accused of being a spy for the West, Mirche testified that he had seen me reading *Time* and *Beaux Arts*, and that the night I came back drunk from a pub frequented by Albanian separatists he would have shot me like a stray dog if he could. He also said I was a chauvinistic Croatian and that I was guilty of ridiculing the Serbian nation. Mirche was eighteen at the time, I was twenty-seven.

I had a Serbian friend in Kosovo, a farmboy with the most wonderful sense of humor, warm as a woolen blanket. We spent numerous mornings together, routed out of our beds at 4:30 only to then wait till 6:30 to hoist the flag and have breakfast. We spent the time telling each other jokes. He was a pure soul and a faithful friend. When I was in prison he brought my letters, phoned my father, and it is to him that I owe my ultimate release.

Leaving Pristina by train I spoke for several hours with an old Albanian man who remembered World War II. He asked where I was from. Croatia, I said, and added, "This situation with the Serbs is no good." He shrugged, his tired but clear eyes laced with wrinkles, his skin brown from the wind and sun. He didn't say a word about what would happen in Kosovo. Instead he spoke about German uniforms with hand-sewn buttons, two loops over every button on the uniform, practically untearable.

"Ah," he sighed, "I wore a jacket stripped off a dead German soldier until 1955, God bless him."

*Krusevac, Serbia*

In November, 1986 I was transferred from Pristina to Krusevac, in central Serbia. There I tutored the commander's daughter in math and literature. She got good marks in school, and I was fed nicely and allowed to stay late in the local pubs.

I enjoyed the cuisine, all those roasted peppers filled with white goat cheese, and finely chopped salads. Serbian hospitality went beyond the ordinary Western sense of "hospitality." I spent numerous evenings with the CO's family, talking about Croatia, a world they knew nothing about.

There in Krusevac I also befriended a Serbian veterinarian my age who was also a conscript. He had studied in Belgrade, and some of his colleagues lived in Krusevac. Often we would visit them and be treated to excellent Serbian cuisine with copious amounts of wine. During our endless discussions there was always one common thread— Kosovo was sacred Serbian land and Albanians would have to be killed or expelled. As blunt as that, the only solution being to "cleanse" their religious cradle. I heard this from illiterate conscripts and from intellectuals, from young hotheads and from old babushkas with soft warm eyes. I heard it from my own Serbian relatives.

Some of my Serbian friends who had studied in Belgrade were familiar with articles I had published in the Zagreb University magazine that was also distributed in Belgrade. They liked my wit and anticommunism. I even met one fellow who kept clippings of the articles. They liked to discuss my ideas and would get very exercised over my inability to see their own point of view.

Sometimes, when the plum brandy was flowing freely, I thought they'd surely rise up and skin me for being a seditious Croat. But I was part Serb myself, and an intellectual, and so worth converting.

Sometimes I tried to point out what the world would be like if we all claimed the right to lands taken from us six centuries ago, but I never got anywhere with that argument. Instead, I was reminded that Croats would have to pay for their genocide of Serbs during the Second World War.

In Krusevac, central Serbia, where young people dressed in the latest Italian fashions (they had no hopes of ever owning any other significant investments), I met a young woman and was invited to her house for dinner. Her father was one of the new capitalist entrepreneurs. He owned a fancy house and enjoyed excellent food—roasted peppers, eggs filled with paste of parsley, diced ham, French mustard, fine meats—meticulous Serbian cuisine that required lots of slicing and dicing, their way of expressing respect and appreciation to their guests. Later, over good coffee and brandy, the conversation got heated. They were impressed with my knowledge of Serbian history and literature, and surprised that I personally knew a couple of Belgrade writers who were big names at the time. I said that the younger generation of Serbian writers (by which I meant Serbian Jews like Danilo Kish and David Albahari) was quite progressive. I meant it as a compliment. The young woman responded:

"But, of course, we are superior to Croats in every way."

On such occasions you try to remain calm and civil, talk quietly and slowly, and leave in peace. After all, the meal had been excellent and these fine people had even cracked open some Croatian wine for me. So I smiled, begged their pardon and said, "What exactly do you mean by 'superior,' my dear?"

And then I heard it all: Serbian history, Serbian victories, Serbian superiority, a people chosen by heaven itself. Walking back to barracks later that evening I felt scared, scared that the war would start before I had a chance to get the hell out of there.

## My Seriban Relatives

My mother is half-Serbian, and I have relatives in Serbia. Some of those aunts kept buying me books and encyclopedias, including *Le Petit Larousse* in Serbian, Francophiles that they were. I visited them every other summer. Culturally and by nationality I was a Croat, not a Serb. My aunt in Belgrade taught history at a local college. She was determined to teach me the "truth" about Serbia: its sacred myths, the illusions about Serbian grandeur and its lost territories and inherent superiority. Half-truths and distortions of historical facts in the most blatant form, these were essentially the principles of the Nazis, also a superior race with the God-given right to dominate others.

I liked my Serbian relatives—an emotional lot, madly Slavic, refined and vulgar. I loved their crazy dirty jokes, their openness in expressing their feelings. If you were a friend they'd give their life for you. I still dream about them—my granny, the raspberries, the watermelons and the incredible warmth they gave me and their own children. I think about my friends from Belgrade University, smart, funny, well-read people. Yet, their inability to see things fairly and objectively, to accept other nations as their equal, made the present-day tragedy inevitable. Despite a virtually common language, their mentality was totally opposite to my own. All those dear funny people, not just the bloodthirsty thugs among them, fell for the idea of a Greater Serbia at the expense of their neighbors. Even back then it was painfully obvious to me that the Serbian military would sooner or later have to be eliminated.

Today, with bombs falling all over Serbia, I think about the gentle faces of those old people as they spoke about how all Albanians would have to be killed. Many an evening I spent trying to suggest to them that this is the modern world, that we don't have to kill to prove our worth, that personal value now is in our ability to produce, to manage, to work, that there is no example in the modern world of genocide paying off. But they always fell back on history, what the Turks did to them in 1389 and for six centuries afterward. And they would say, "We may not know how to work like you Croats, but we can fight."

The distortion of reality became particularly absurd when the Serbian military started instigating one war after another in that region. When their army attacked Croatia, my Belgrade aunt phoned me. I told her that we were being bombarded by Serbs and had to take cover in shelters. She dismissed what I said as Croatian propaganda. She said that it was not happening.

## In the End

What happened next is now history: the wars, the exiles, the pain of friends lost, the tears of silent despair, the poverty and madness, the emigration, my forecasts coming true to a painful detail.

I saw a Serbian woman on TV, in a shelter, saying that she couldn't believe this was happening at the end of the millennium. My words exactly, murmured in a shelter in Zagreb some eight years ago as we cursed the West for doing nothing to help us. We died while Austrians skied their Alps and in Switzerland the production of soft cheese went on as usual.

I am sick from it all now, sitting broken in this little room, half a world away. Cynic that I am, closer to Beckett than to Brecht, bitter and resigned, disgusted with this world and what it has done to me, I nevertheless feel like sending a thank-you note to the White House for the effort finally being made, for the understanding finally of what must be done. It's so unlike 1991, when we sat in those basements during Serbian air raids, so unlike the Bosnian war and its quarter of a million dead, so unlike the repeated appeasement of the killers and the policy of looking the other way typical of the previous French and British governments.

What is happening now is 500,000 corpses overdue. Unfortunately, we hear scarcely a voice from the Serbian opposition denouncing the leadership for ruining their country, for turning them into the pariah of Europe. And, in all frankness, it is not just the leadership who are at fault; it is the Serbs themselves, the people who accepted the mass psychosis of the Big Lie, of historical defeats remembered as victories and the myth of superiority.

# Diary of a Street Kid

*By* Fanuel Jongwe

*25 September 1993*

Yesterday evening was hell-hot. A bad day. Someone stole, or the Municipal Refuse and Cleansing Department men burned, the cardboard I usually slept on. Insomnia. I spent the long hot vermin-infested night rolling on the dusty ground under the Rezende Street North Parkade where poor punters—men and women—bet their pittances away every day, but on Sunday I had trouble with the fat guard in the railway station waiting room.

Maki was arrested by a member of the Special Constabulary. He was caught sniffing thinners in the alley between a cloth shop in Robson Manyika Street and the Central Police Station building.

Collected $4.23 today. Bought bread and a tomato.

*29 September 1993*

Woke up late to an empty day. Feeling really hungry—hungry as five Somalis. The refuse-collecting trucks had already left with the trash and our food when I was frightened out of my late-morning slumber by the blare of a bus horn. The Power Sales accounts manager, whose car I usually guard, did not come to work, so no money, no food, no nothing—absolutely nothing today.

*1 October 1993*

A scuffle over a newly arrived Zimtours Land Rover with the big boys at the National Gallery Car Park. "This is our territory, our area of operation," one of them told me through a gap where his front teeth were missing.

Am writing this at noon. Painfully tired and my body is shaking with hunger. I have been feeling dizzy and my vision is blurred. Nearly crashed into a speeding Medical Air Rescue Services ambulance while trying to cross Union Avenue. Harare is turning a blind eye on me. Everyone is engrossed in his own business.

It's evening now. Dusk has descended like a giant's eyelid closing. Neon signs are blinking advertisements. Street lamps are glaring down upon the busy streets. A fruitless day. For the first time in my life in the Hararean streets, I have spent the whole day on an empty rumbling stomach. How I wish everything was edible.

I remember the story—I still find hard to believe—of hungry Chinese blokes who cooked and ate their boots when their food reserves ran dry during the Long March. I have no boots to roast and eat like the Chinese did, but a pair of dry cracked feet.

*2 October 1993*

Feeling drowsy. I am afraid of sleeping. I might fall asleep forever like Dostoyevsky's Beggar Boy. Grandmother used to threaten me when I refused to eat supper: "If you don't eat, you'll die in your sleep."

*7:00 p.m.*

Saved at last from the brink of the abyss. A brilliant tourist couple on a late evening stroll saw me trembling with hunger, pitied me and bought me a chicken—a full chicken, intact in its Chicken Inn pack. A Christmas feast on an October evening. Feeling strong again. Yes, tourists have "hearts of gold."

# The Transformation of Sleepy Hollow

*By* Richard Czujko

A small crowd is gathered around a sunken arena about the size of a boxing ring, listening to a three-piece band render ragged versions of old reggae and rock favorites. The dreadlocked Rastafarians are using a primitive amplifier and the drummer is a girl barely in her teens, but they play with enthusiasm.

A pickup truck eases to a stop under the oak trees less than a hundred yards away. Revivalist gospel music begins to blare from a loudspeaker. A second crowd gathers around the pickup, but even though the truck's loudspeaker has more volume than the band's amplifier, the band remains more popular with the onlookers. Significantly, there are no whites amongst the crowds.

This is a Saturday-morning scene in Freedom Square, Pietermaritzburg, a five-hectare open area in the centre of the city located about a hundred kilometers inland from the port city of Durban. A decade ago it was a very different place with a different name.

Pietermaritzburg is a colonial city caught between pre- and post-apartheid cultures. Founded in 1838 by Dutch Voortrekkers seeking to escape British rule, it ironically developed into a British garrison town and became renowned as a Victorian enclave in the Zulu heartland. Its sedate colonial lifestyle gave rise to the nickname "Sleepy Hollow," and Tom Sharpe in *Riotous Assembly*, a satirical novel about apartheid South Africa, rather unkindly dismisses Pietermaritzburg (which he abbreviated to Piemburg), as a "tiny town that seems to have died and been embalmed."

But in the last decade the character of this colonial outpost has undergone a dramatic change.

The city centre was carefully laid out to cater to the Eurocentric tastes of the white settlers. The black majority was confined to townships on the outskirts of the city, and the substantial Indian and mixed-race community was likewise restricted to designated areas. Blacks and Indians could not legally own property within the city limits. When I arrived in Pietermaritzburg nearly twenty years ago, most blacks did not even venture into the city. The shops reflected exclusively middle-class white tastes: bookshops, dress shops, hobby shops.

Then, in 1990 Nelson Mandela was released from prison and the expectations of the black majority were raised. There were mass marches and demonstrations that paralleled the collective action that had led to the downfall of communism in Eastern Europe.

Two incidents in particular during this period roused Pietermaritzburg from its long slumber. In 1992 there was a mass demonstration by mini-bus taxis that brought the city to a standstill, an awesome parade of several hundred sixteen-seater mini-buses whose work stoppage paralysed business and terrified pedestrians and motorists while the police were off pursuing renegade taxis elsewhere.

The second incident occurred soon after the murder of the South African Communist Party leader Chris Hani at the hands of a white expatriate in 1993. Hani had been tipped as a possible successor to Nelson Mandela and had enormous support from the black population. A rally was organised after the murder, and thousands of blacks gathered in the city centre. Freedom Square became a mass of very angry people. A considerable amount of damage was caused and most businesses had to close.

After the elections of 1994 brought the African National Congress to power, the city entered a new phase of cultural change and a consolidation of black African influence. There was now no longer any need for people to demonstrate: democracy had been achieved.

Then still known as Market Square, the area is an appropriate site for political gatherings, flanked as it was by buildings symbolic of the apartheid regime. On one side is the multi-storied provincial government building. Facing it directly across the square is the municipal administration building. The third side is occupied by the Voortrekker Museum, dedicated to the Dutch pioneers. The fourth side is dominated by the library and city hall.

At the end of the 1980s, the Square was basically a parking lot and bus terminus. The only notable activities that took place there were occasional people's markets and the annual Pancake Race on Shrove Tuesday, a quaint Eurocentric tradition sponsored by city businesses.

The sunken arena in which the Rastafarian band was playing that Saturday morning used to be a giant chessboard with life-size chess pieces. Those chessmen have long since vanished and the pancake race has been discontinued. Now the square is typically filled with freelance vendors. Even the former apartheid National Party was obliged to recognise the special political significance of the Square during last year's general election campaign. The party's youthful leader made a rousing speech from the back of a pickup truck there, but he failed to attract more than a few curious onlookers.

The bus service was another symbol of the old Pietermaritzburg, but it became uneconomical and was terminated. In its place came the mini-bus taxis whose drivers are so feared for their aggressive road manners and disregard for public safety. The taxis are not just conveyors of passengers, they are extensions of their drivers' personalities, with sophisticated sound systems and exotically printed slogans on their windshields, from the intimidating "Warrior," "Bullet" and "Burning Spear," to the gentler "Mr. Loverman," "Smooth Operator" and "Wishmaster," to the honest "Just Plain Ruthless."

Just as the city's streets have become more representative of Africa, so too have the businesses. The change began in the 1980s with the establishment of informal traders on the sidewalks, a novelty then to most white residents. Gradually, more sidewalk vendors appeared, selling everything from cheap imitations of famous-brand sneakers and clothing to locally produced wooden artwork. Many of these business people are immigrants, legal and illegal, from West and Central Africa. Meanwhile, the shops on the Square also underwent a transformation as many white-owned businesses withdrew from the city and relocated to the suburbs—a common phenomenon all over South Africa as fewer and fewer whites frequent the city centres.

Some of the vacated shops have become African hair salons, with names like "Ghanaian Unisex Hairstylist" and "Papa's Hair Salon." The liberalisation of the laws gave rise to escort agencies, sex shops and gambling casinos. Then the casinos were declared illegal and closed down. In their places loan companies sprang up, offering cash with no strings attached.

Despite frequent complaints (invariably from whites) that the city centre is dying, the truth is that the character of Pietermaritzburg has simply changed to reflect the interests and tastes of the community as a whole rather than just those of a minority.

The transition from apartheid to democracy has been difficult, but people generally have adapted well and are keen to get on with the job of making a living. This is evident by the current lack of support for mass gatherings and protest marches. Organisers are lucky to muster a hundred people. The reasons for the demonstrations have changed too: Protests against apartheid have now become demonstrations against unemployment.

Perhaps the most significant indication of the city's power shift is the relocation of the prestigious Victoria Club from the city centre to an affluent suburb where it has merged with the equally exclusive Country Club. The Victoria Club was the symbol of the colonial regime par excellence. Membership was by invitation only, and women were required to use a side entrance right up into the 1980s. Declining numbers and crime were cited as the main reasons for the club's difficulties. Now the once-proud Victoria Club building has been cut up into business rentals. One of the more prominent tenants is yet another loan company, promising cash "sharp sharp."

# The Ngong Hills

*By* Rasik Shah

There were three of them in the cab of the jeep. The vehicle was what they called a boxbody, the back having been enclosed. Ramesh used it to make deliveries during the week. The shop made no deliveries on Sundays except for "urgent" orders—meaning simply that the customer was of long standing and had good credit.

Ramesh usually had two men, called "turnboys," with him. These were full-time employees of the business, beasts of burden who carried two-hundred-pound gunny sacks of flour or sugar on their backs, one bag at a time, the bags held secure by holding onto the sack's "ears," arms extended backwards from raised elbows, legs hobbling from warehouse to vehicle. When offloading at the retail shops in Pumwani, Majengo or Shauri Moyo, one man stood the sacks up at the edge of the platform and then helped load the other man. They took turns loading and carrying, causing Ramesh to wonder if this was the reason they were called turnboys.

Shauri Moyo was one of the "locations" where the city's black population lived. Shauri meant "matter" in Swahili, as in *"shauri ngani,"* "what is the matter?" *"Moyo,"* he found out years later meant, "heart." "A matter of the heart." Shauri Moyo was not a place he would have associated with matters of heart. It was where the poor of the city lived. To its north were the mud and wattle houses of Pumwani and Majengo. The railway line to Mombasa cut across Shauri Moyo. On the south side of the line were ugly industrial installations, oil tanks of Shell and Caltex, flourmills, shoe factories. Chimneys spewed out thick black smoke all day.

The three of them, Ramesh and his buddies, had decided to go to the Ngong Hills this Sunday afternoon. Ramesh had completed Form VI just two months earlier. The results had come in from the Overseas

Examination Board in Cambridge, England only a week ago. Ramesh had failed his science subjects. If he had passed, the family would have sent him to Britain or India for a professional degree. His buddy Narinder, sitting between him and Amichand in the jeep's cab, had just scraped through all his own subjects and had already started classes at the Asian Teachers' Training School.

The red jeep had just reached the unpaved leg of the climb up the first of the seven Ngong Hills in the range overlooking the hot Rift Valley to the west. The jeep would have to manage this hill all the way to the top in four-wheel drive, for they were getting close to the summit, eight thousand feet above sea level. The sky was pale blue, with a scattering of white clouds sailing over the horizon. Ramesh leaned back from the steering wheel and took in the scene. These hills, he thought, were a majestic dividing line: the hot, dry plains of the great Rift Valley to the west, the lush highlands in the north. In the south and east was acacia country, arid and thorny, rolling all the way down to the coast. The Maasai roamed with their livestock in the plains below, sharing the land with lion and giraffe, buffalo and bushbuck. The Kikuyu used to farm the best part of the highlands, now occupied by the white settlers. What a splendid country it seems from up here, he said to himself, looking at Nairobi, a couple thousand feet below. The strife there—Mau Mau, arrogant settlers, repressive elders—seemed very distant.

At the Maasai Store in Ngong Village they had brought three big bottles of Tusker and some chips. Amichand had stayed in the vehicle, although he was the one who had dished out the money. Amichand always had money. He had been helping out in, and was now virtually running, his father's wholesale produce store for more than two years, having failed the Cambridge School Leaving Certificate Exam at the end of Form IV. He remained in the jeep because he was afraid he would be recognized by the Maasai Store people who were his father's old customers. All three of them could be in trouble then if word about the beer got out.

Ramesh had been in a foul mood all afternoon.

"Motabhai is being difficult, eh?" said Narinder in Hindi. Narinder, being Punjabi, did not speak Gujarati, though he understood it well enough. Motabhai itself was a Gujarati word, though, a term of respect for "Elder Brother." There were times the three of them used words from five different languages during a short exchange.

"He refused to give me the jeep's keys. In the end I took them from his coat pocket and just took off. He was so startled he couldn't say anything. It has been a bad day. In the morning I got into an argument with a customer in the shop. This fellow said he had given me a five-shilling note for the miserable three cigarettes he was buying. He hadn't paid a cent. He was going on about the colour bar—*calaa ba*."

"*Calaa baaa*," repeated Narinder, contorting his face.

"I told him to go away, but he just stood there accusing all the *wahindi* of practising *calaa ba*. Speaking of colour bar, the other day I met Tom Mboya at Tirlochan's father's tailor shop. Mboya's office is next door. He does not have a phone of his own, so he uses theirs. I tell you, that fellow is a born leader."

"Tirlochan's going to India to study medicine," said Narinder.

"He got a letter of recommendation from Tom Mboya," said Ramesh.

"Too bad he can't get one of those scholarships Mboya is organizing for African students going to study in America. Tirlochan's dad can barely afford to send him to study in poor India," Narinder said with a sigh. "Maybe one day we will learn to call all people who are born and live in Africa just plain Africans and be done with these stupid division of African, European and Asian."

"Talking about colour bar, you know what Tom Mboya did the other day? He got together with a couple of other African and Indian leaders and tried to have dinner at Safari Hotel."

"Who were the Indians?" asked Narinder.

"Chuni Madan, the new Asian member of Legco...."

"What's Legco?" asked Amichand.

"It's short for the Legislative Council. Didn't they teach you anything in Eastleigh Secondary? Anyway, the other Indian was the editor of the *Daily Chronicle*. They all walked into the restaurant at Safari Hotel. They went in and sat down at a table. The African waiter called out the European manager, who politely asked them to leave."

"And what did they do?"

They asked why they were being asked to leave. The manager pointed at the sign they have in all European restaurants and cinemas: THE MANAGEMENT RESERVES THE RIGHT OF ADMISSION.

"In South Africa they are more direct. The signs say 'Coolies, Blacks, Coloureds and dogs not allowed in.'"

"Well, in the end the manager called the police and they were forced to leave. The next day the *Daily Chronicle* printed a big head-line about the colour bar at Safari Hotel."

Amichand wanted to know how many Asian members Legco had.

"There are three elected Asian members and five African elected members. The Asian seats are divided; one is reserved for a Muslim member, the other two for non-Muslims. Europeans have eleven elected members."

"The British know how to divide and rule," said Narinder.

"Hey, look at that cute Maasai girl."

Amichand was pointing at a lithe, young woman walking with her arm around a big gourd balanced on the side of her hip.

"You will have to be born again and be in the right Morani age group to get any attention from her," Narinder said.

The girl had a series of tight bead necklaces strung around her long neck and strings of bead around her waist, just above the hips. Her hair was in braids glued with a mix of red ochre. Her features were angular.

"Look how red everything is. The red jeep on the red tracks of the unpaved road and the girl wearing the red ochre *suka*," Amichand said with enthusiasm.

"And if you think you can invite her to join us we will soon have red blood sprouting from a Maasai spear. Get the idea out of your head," said Narinder.

Ramesh laughed and took three Clipper cigarettes from the pack on the dashboard and passed two to Narinder, who pressed in the lighter. The road was getting steep now and he had to switch to first gear.

"Remember the time we picked up the Wakamba women near Machakos? They kept saying they wanted to go to the *'raiki'* and we couldn't figure out what the hell they meant," said Amichand.

"You were getting pretty friendly with one of them?"

"I've figured out what they meant by *raiki*. It's a lake. There is a small one further along the road to Nyandurwa."

"They would have come along with us if we had anywhere to go."

"We are the wrong colour in the wrong country."

The lighter popped up from its socket. Ramesh lit his cigarette and passed the lighter to Narinder. They were getting close to the top of the first of the seven Ngong Hills and the gradient was getting steeper. A vista of the sun-baked plains of the Rift Valley opened up to their right as the road curved to the left. The ridge they were on dropped precipitously down. They could see the dry, burnt plain below stretching to the horizon. Far away, past Mount Longonut, they could see a streak of blue. That had to be Lake Naivasha, thought Ramesh.

Although the sun was shining, there had been a shower earlier and some of the hollows on the meandering road were waterlogged. As they approached the next dip in the road they saw a Ford Cortina stuck in a water-filled hollow. The rear wheels rotated furiously, churning out mud, the vehicle refusing to budge forward.

"Looks like *wazungu*," Narinder said.

"Don't feel like helping them after what that bastard settler said when we were dropping off the British soldiers at Gilgil."

"'Since when have you started a transport business?'" Narinder imitated the settler's gruff voice, managing to rub in the insult Ramesh had felt at the time.

Ramesh recalled how he had stopped to let out the soldiers after giving them a lift from Naivasha. As he yanked down the rear door plank to let them out, a settler's car pulled up behind with bright headlights beaming into the jeep's box. A red-faced, paunchy man in khaki shirt and shorts came marching out of the car shouting, "What the hell is going on here?" his revolver slinging from the sagging belt on his shorts.

The man walked to the front of the jeep, took a look at Narinder and Amichand and then turned to Ramesh. Ramesh was frightened by the tone the man had taken and managed to stammer that he had just given a lift to the soldiers. The settler then spat out, "Since when have you started a transportation business?" and marched back to his car and drove off. The young Scottish soldiers from the Black Watch unit were in Kenya as part of the British effort to fight the Mau Mau. A state of emergency had been declared in Kenya for some years now. The soldiers apologized for the settler's behaviour.

They had to stop a short distance behind the Cortina. There was no way of passing it, and it was too risky to try and wedge their way around the furrowed track. The grassy bank was too high and the space between it and the Cortina too narrow. The Cortina's driver and passengers had gotten out of their vehicle to examine the situation. They were two young white men and a girl in a gray flannel skirt and white blouse. She had long blonde hair done in a thick braid hanging down to her waist.

"Let's see what happened," Amichand said.

The driver got back into the vehicle, and the girl and the other man took up positions behind the Cortina. The driver put the vehicle into gear and started revving up the engine. The rear wheels turned, but the vehicle stayed in the same spot. Mud spluttered everywhere. Soon the girl and the man were covered all over with it. They stopped pushing and the girl stepped back a few yards. Suddenly the driver revved the engine again. Rear wheels spun, spraying two parallel streaks of mud on the girl's skirt and blouse, her neck and her cheek. She yelled and tried to duck out of the way. Then she began laughing. She stopped for a moment, then bent over double with laughter, at the same time trying to brush some of the mud off with her hand. The driver got out of the car, took a look at his companions and then both men joined in the hilarity.

The girl pulled a big cake of wet mud off her skirt and threw it at the driver, splattering his shirt. They were now running in circles around the car like escaped lunatics. Then the girl lost her footing and fell into the watery furrow on the road. The men continued to laugh helplessly as they pulled her up. As she got up Ramesh noticed her braid was now caked with mud.

"At this rate we will never get out here, but the show is great," said Narinder.

The girl and the two young men laughed and ran around for what seemed a long time and finally, exhausted, they collapsed onto the front of the car and lay sunning themselves. At that point Ramesh got out of the jeep and walked towards them.

"Do you ever want to get out of here?"

"No," said the girl, "never," and she started laughing again.

The mirth on her muddy face lifted Ramesh's gloomy spirits.

"I can try pushing up the rear." He was pointing at the back of the Cortina, but was still looking at the girl. At that moment she seemed the most stunning young woman he had ever seen. Her features were hard to make out through the caked mud, but he loved her just as she was, covered in mud and laughter.

"You are visitors from Europe?"

"Yeah, all of us. Joe here is my cousin in Kenya, and Philip is also my cousin, from London. I am Felicity," she said between more bouts of laughter.

"My name is Ramesh."

She put out her hand, then started to withdraw it. "It's wet and muddy."

"Never mind." He took her hand and shook it vigorously. They laughed. Her hand felt warm and inviting and he shook it over and over again. Then he said, "Okay, I will push you out of that hole."

He walked back to the jeep.

"They are having fun," said Amichand.

"They know how to live," said Ramesh.

He started the engine, engaged the four-wheel drive and roared up to the back of the Cortina. Then he slowed down and edged along until he made contact with the rear bumper. Felicity was watching from the back seat of the Cortina, directing him. As the jeep was about to touch the bumper, she put up both hands and began shaking them wildly. The Cortina's driver, the fellow called Joe, revved the engine, and the jeep pushed the car out of the mud, up the little slope and on to the dry tracks again. As the Cortina continued along on its own power, Felicity waved a two-handed good-bye, punctuating it with several kisses blown their way.

"Yes, they know how to live," said Amichand.

They followed the Cortina to the top of the first hill and parked further up on the little plateau to the right side of the summit facing the burning valley below. The sun was lighting up the whole of the plain in gold, broken only by the shadow of a range of hills far away. Mount Longonut stood in the centre, its jagged extremities reminiscent of volcanic ferocity. And yet, at the moment the mountain seemed lonely, strange and desolate.

Ramesh opened the door on his side and stuck his legs out.

"Let's have the beer."

Narinder had stepped out of the vehicle to watch the Cortina and now came back to report that the occupants had gotten out of the car and were carrying the girl up to the top of the summit. Ramesh stuck his head out of the jeep to look. There she was, perched on the seat formed by the joined hands of the young men on either side of her. He accepted the bottle of Tusker that Amichand had opened for him and took a long swig.

Ramesh was silent for a long time. He wanted, he thought, the simplest of things. He worked hard. All he expected from life was what most people in the world somehow got, even if they were poor. He didn't mind hard work, but needed some personal freedom, some opportunity to enjoy things. Play some sport, go to dances, make friends, meet women. Simple things, yet somehow not possible.

He said quietly, "Look at us. We've got nowhere to go for fun. The swimming pools and the restaurants are closed to us. There are no girls for us to take out. The *wazungu* won't even look at us. This girl who talked to us is different because she is a visitor from England. Our own Indian girls are not allowed to go out at all. The Africans live in their traditional ways and stick with their own people. The only women we can have anything to do with are the malayas—those prostitutes in Eastleigh. Other people play tennis on beautiful club lawns, even go water-skiing at the Nairobi damn. Not for us, no, it just ain't available."

"Well, there are dances at the Goan Institute, and a friend of mine has got in sometimes," said Amichand.

"Only if he is taken as a special guest by some Goan friend."

"London is the place. We've got to get out of here," Ramesh said, thinking how he would have to face the wrath of his elder brother on returning home.

The air up there on the hilltop was crisp, the soil red and the grass bright green. Down on the plains below, hot air shimmered and created double images. In the distance lone Mount Longonut loomed again. Its dark, ragged edges seemed forbidding as they were silhouetted against the dipping sun. He could make out the elliptical lines of the crater at the top of the volcano. There had been some rumbling there not so long ago. The prediction was that there could be a major eruption.

It would be hot and uncomfortable when they got down to the plains again.

"Or, maybe, just maybe," Amichand offered hesitantly, "Ghana. It is the only free black country. At least then we would still be in Africa."

"Dream on. What the hell do you know about Ghana? Do you know what language they speak there? Whether they would let in people like you and me?"

"And what do you think you can do in London?" said Amichand, "Work as a waiter—if they let you in at all, that is?"

Narinder felt the bitterness in the air and said nothing.

# Snapshot

*By* Miroslav Kirin

They told me to tell this story. To describe the photograph with me, Darko (that's my name), in it. As if I were, after all that I've gone through, able to give a reasonable account of anything. It's been a long time since I left my village, my country doesn't exist any more, and in this no-longer-existing country lives my older brother. His name is Micho. Recalling that he lives in Croatia, and I in Serbia, is painful for me. But perhaps I don't actually live in Serbia. I do live somewhere, one has to, be it Bosnia, Canada, Germany. It doesn't matter. Life is miserable no matter what. If I were dead I wouldn't be able to tell you this. Or perhaps I would. When it comes to writing, words can come out of the mouth of a dead man, and they never tell lies. So perhaps I actually am dead. But I am still able to tell my story.

Maybe I shouldn't bother you with the particulars concerning the fact that my brother lives in one country, I in another. It's a very common situation. There are many more terrible stories. One of them might be yours. Families split up, the husband takes one path, the wife and kids take another. If a man and wife come to an understanding, which is, you must admit, pretty difficult, they stay together, sharing the same burdensome path together. The story of a family is like the story of a nation. The house, following that simile, is a kind of state. They both follow familiar patterns of misfortune.

Well, Micho never loved Mother, for she was a hard drinker. He used to drink too, but he couldn't bear to see her doing it. I myself loved her, I believe I did, or at least I thought she was trying to protect me from my abusive father who used to, because of my roguish behavior, thrash me and forbid me to leave the yard. Micho was older and was allowed to do anything he liked. He knew how to talk to Father, he could always find the right words. My own words only enraged him. Words so easily depart from the meanings we assign to them, playing devilish tricks on us. What I am going to tell you now may be still a little too hard for me to say but...all right. There's no way out: My father...perhaps, my father is not my real father. My mother might have got pregnant by somebody else. These things happen. And I got the consequence of it, a father who doesn't love me. I don't know why I'm even wondering about this, probably because I yearn on some level to be miserable. The deeper I sink, the better I feel.

You see now what words are for? You may as well cover me with tar, the whole world is pitch dark anyway. Feathers swirl in the air where snowflakes used to fall. I'm all alone in a strange world, with no name and no mother of my own. Perhaps she died from alcohol. Maybe she was killed in the war. I haven't seen her, and I've been everywhere, a displaced person. Horrid rumours have reached me. I don't believe them, they are too atrocious.

Mistakes are possible. And possibility brings hope. Even when it is no longer possible. If a friend of mine was killed, that doesn't mean that my friend actually died. Someone's friend died, yes, but not mine. God forbid. I can be deeply moved, for a while, and then I forget. Who can bear to remember all that suffering?

My guess is that Mother is probably still alive, I just don't know where she is. Which makes her dead in a way, because she's not with me. If she were here I could at least take care of her, all thin and shriveled, her face covered by a long black veil. Instead, it is the world which takes care of me, passing out packets of humanitarian aid, asking me to report every month to their blue office. They tell me to be patient. I can't go anywhere anyway. I'm chained to my calamity.

It all boils down to the same wretched thing. Sometimes the world is a monotonous wasteland, sometimes a flat tyre gushing human blood. You set out to find your fortune. Each encounter brings you closer to a conclusion, but they all look alike, and you fail to recognize yourself in any of them. You have to reach the edge to realize you can't go any further. After that you just go into free-fall and disappear.

If I were a believer I would set out to look for the lost God. Something would draw me onward, some bright vision. But I have never learned how to pray. I do know how to raise three fingers, which was a way to show some kind of loyalty to my comrades, but I still don't know the meaning of the gesture. They were all doing it, so I did too, and the houses vanished in flames.

I'm so lonesome I could cry. All I do is sit in my shack with one window and one door. Sometimes I take a walk. I can't tell if I'm already half-blind, if I'm losing my sense of smell, if my body parts are withering away. I turned thirty yesterday. I remembered just before I went to bed. But there was nothing I could do about it. Get up and pour myself a shot? I switched off the light and watched the well-lit guard post outside my shack until I fell asleep. During the night I woke up a few times. No one was lying next to me. Not even a cat escaping from the frosty night. At one point I thought I spotted someone peering in at me. Then there was a knocking on the door, but when I sat up in bed the knocking stopped. Eventually I fell asleep and I dreamed about my village, but it could have been any village.

I don't trust myself, never mind anyone else. In my village, Slana, no one went to church. The building just stood there amidst a godless people, to no purpose. The only day it was attended was on Ascension Day when the lime trees are in bloom. When ice-cream vendors reappear. When merry tunes are played. We thought, what's the use of going to church when life is so good? You need God when things get tough—if you're lucky enough to know the code words with which to address Him. If you don't, you're out of luck. The village was ethnically mixed. The Orthodox thought: If we go to church, what will our Catholic neighbours think of us? There's no Catholic church in the village except for the chapel in the cemetery. It wouldn't be fair if Orthodox could go to church and Catholics couldn't. So no one went. Out of solidarity. Out of brotherly love.

And then, under cover of darkness, they blew this place up. Just because it's ours, not theirs. And then we burnt down each other's houses and slaughtered each other's families. I have no idea whether anyone's living in Slana right now. Some news does reach me, but I don't know who's sending it. I've lost confidence in words. I know what they are capable of doing. I deeply regret what I've done, but what's the use of my remorse? Who can I ask for forgiveness? I know well enough that my neighbours will never absolve me. It wasn't me who burnt down Vesna's house, but I doubt she would even talk to me now. I don't know who did it, but it could have been me. Down deep we're all the same, us Croats. This is what they think. I guess it's true, because I think it of them as well.

Perhaps there is a God, but after all that has befallen upon us, should we care? Perhaps things might have been different, but they weren't. Life goes on. Frankly, I no longer know what I've done or haven't done, so how can anyone believe what I say? And my disintegration has only just begun. I talk nonsense, my hands tremble. Sometimes I forget the way back to my shack. I spend entire afternoons walking about aimlessly, through the neighbourhood, trying to retrace my way down blind alleys. In the twilight I end up again at the door of my shack. My name is there, and it matches the name on my ID. A sense of guilt lingers, but what is guilt but a sense of togetherness in time of darkness.

What else should I say? Oh yes, you were interested in that snapshot. I don't actually have it. You see, Teach, Miro's father, made only one print, and I saw it only once. It's rather difficult for me to remember clearly, but I'll try.

Miro, Teach's son, was a little older than me. I lived some three hundred yards from the school in a one-storey house made of wood and brick. We played together, so I guess we were friends. True, many times I embarrassed him. What did I do? I played all sorts of pranks, took my clothes off in front of the girls, told them lascivious stories, made them blush.

Even now I can't understand why. Perhaps it was a need to extend the borders of my ordinary world. The image of my father hovers like a ghost through all memories of my childhood. I had to lie often, invent stuff in order not to be thrashed by him. I wanted to please that little god. Tell him what he wanted to hear. And then, once the walls of my imagination had been breached, I invented all sorts of stories for any ear willing to listen and bear witness to my falsehoods.

One day I told Miro about a naked couple I had seen in the meadow just a few hundred yards from the school. He said I was a liar, because he knew that I lied at every opportunity. Maybe he was right and I did lie that time. Everything's mixed up now.

After he moved to Petrinja we no longer saw each other save for a few brief encounters. I guess we weren't such good friends after all. Real friendship endures all hardships, doesn't admit defeat. I know exactly what he's going to say when he sees the ruins of the school where he spent the best years of his childhood. His response is already burnt into my memory. I have to live with it, day in, day out. He'll hate me. I was there when it happened. I feel responsible for all those burnt-down houses. But what good is my remorse.

Let me finish the story of that snapshot. In the end you're all alone, cornered like a rat. Well, it happened one sunny summer day, probably around noon. Everything is bright in that snapshot, our features submerged in a brilliant haze. The two of us are squatting next to each other in the middle of the schoolyard. There's a wooden shack behind us. The grass seems to have melted into the whiteness of the ground. A hen is standing at the edge of the image, silhouetted against the pale brown boards of the shack. Miro's hair is neatly combed, unlike my own, which is rumpled, his blond curls glued onto his forehead. His face is quiet, looks reserved with a hint of irony breaking through the surface of his well-behaved demeanor. Miro is wearing a white, yellowish short-sleeved T-shirt with a small pocket on the left side of his chest, shorts and yellow plastic sandals. He's watching me stare at his father's camera: my broad smile, teeth obscured by the shade of my upper lip, my grin on the verge of bursting into mocking laughter, or worse even. My lop-ears are of the kind one sees at carnivals. My eyes are narrowed in a broad smile. I'm wearing an old navy T-shirt that belonged to my brother Micho and long—probably my father's—trousers cut to fit by my mother, a fabric of indeterminate colour extending down to my sandals. I am hugging my knees and stretching my neck so that all the veins there have become prominent.

That's it: the snapshot. But what puzzles me is this: what are you going to do with it? Will it somehow help you to make up for your own losses? This is the end of the world, and we're both here together. Would you rather go back and start all over again?

Look at me, friend. This is where you'll find your answer.

# Singing in the Wind

*By* Keith Smith

Carnival Tuesday evening, from the vantage point of the tray of the Laventille Rhythm Section truck, I am looking across at Roger George, much higher than me on the tip-top of his own Charlie's Roots' truck.

Or rather, I am listening to him and it seems to me that he is singing for me alone, not that he has any idea that I am there, only that down below people are moving around in a swirl of Minshall red going about their business, buying corn soup and bread and shark, beer and soda water, pausing to pee, the band standing still, as always, at this enforced Memorial Park pit-stop so the Minshalites, perforce, are occupied doing their human things on the ground while, perversely, this Minshalite is deep into the divine playing out on high.

All yuh ever hear Roger George sing? Well, I am hearing him this Tuesday evening, and I, who have made it my business to hear him sing whenever there is the opportunity, find myself stunned for the umpteenth time by the variety and range that this 26-year-old brings to his craft: as gruff as Satchmo would have it, and so high that hearing him, David Rudder, who is sharing the truck with him (is Charlie's Roots' truck, after all), playfully asks of this married man: "Yuh ent have no balls?"

Between Satchmo and the high falsetto that you'd expect only from a eunuch (thanks, David), George's voice covers all the bases and he is singing his original but Beanieman-inspired chant, only, of course, Beanieman never sang anything quite like this: George singing lead as if he was not one but all of three singers.

Indeed, he catches me because I find myself looking to see who really is singing atop that Charlie's Roots' truck because, look! Roots also has not only David, who alone is more than enough, but KV Charles, who alone is a star, and Kerwyn Trotman, who could carry the whole damn show if all of them were to get sick.

But this evening, this moment, whether by accident or design, it is Roger's show, and show off he does, singing and scatting, doing all kinds of wonderfully impossible things with that voice, and I fancy (we are outside the hospital you see) that the sick are pulling themselves up to peer out of their windows to see and hear; and as for the dead, well, the only reason they don't wake up is because the mortuary is quite across on the Belmont Circular Road so they out of earshot, poor things!

Now, the prelude finished, George presses into the song proper and it is "Man A Bad Man" and I tell you and I warn you that after you hear George sing that song you don't need to hear Bud sing it again; which is a helluva conclusion to come to because there is also something divine about Bud's voice, only that in sharing voice when God reached Roger he was distracted by the need to reach out and save a drowning child, so that he hand slip and George end up with his and five other people's share.

So that, friends, was one of the transcendental Carnival moments for me; but before I leave I want to leave you with a few others in, as you'll see, no particular order.

Gypsy is singing. The last night of Spektakula's calypso season. A good but not full house. The song: "Lift Yourself Up." The style: Soulful. The Groove: Just right. And the crowd doesn't really want him to go so he asks the willing Wayne Bruno to bear with him ("is the last night, after all; what the hell!"), and this man who has just been deposed as the reigning king gives this kingly performance, so relaxed and so unperturbed, caressing each cadence; and I relate because both of us, I know, grew up with the blues and what Mr. Peters is here doing, this Carnival Saturday night, is chasing not his own (Gypsy is a nationally entrenched entertainer so the crown is neither here nor there) but other people's blues away.

And I am proud of him and thank God for giving us such an all-reaching talent as this one, and later I make it my business to go round the back to thank the old "Gyp" for all that he has given us.

Dimanche Gras night and I am home watching it on the television. Nothing moves me until the very last item, which is David Rudder with "High Mas."

As usual David Michael is making magic, but neither I nor the audience stage-side knows what a double whammy he has in store for us until he jumps off the stage and heads into the North Stand, where he continues singing and singing and singing as if he's never going to stop.

Man, the lights go up and David Michael is still singing so that TTT "in one of the most ill-advised departures in local entertainment history" returns to the studio (to hell with deadline schedules, I would have said had I been the programme director, all yuh ent see magic going on here?). Which just shows, of course, why nobody in their right mind would ever make me programme director of anything. And I literally dive across the bed to turn on the radio where David is still singing and I know what he is doing, which is spitting defiance at his and "High Mas's" critics; only, David is incapable of spitting on or spitting at anybody, so what he is doing is not spitting but singing defiance, threading the song with other music from his great repertoire.

Calypso Music! Yes! Yes! Yes! Miss Elsie's son is standing up, once again, for Kaiso's children and when he is finished I flop down on the bed, sweating, as if like him I had just ran a musical marathon.

Carnival Tuesday night and finally Minshall's red sea is sweeping stagewards, but instead of waves there is this raging rhythm. The Laventille Rhythm Section has been becalmed for hours as the band has been kept waiting.

But now, like men possessed, they fall upon their instruments and I seem to be standing still, but all that is illusion because, in reality, I am being swept along by these singing irons and I don't know how but I find myself singing this wordless melody and I think: "Buh, boy, Keith yuh singing in tongues."

And I laugh this kind of a manic laugh and jump high in the air on my old pinched-nerve foot, coming down to look at how many, 10, 12? pairs of black hands and one pale, because one of the Salloum boys had asked to join us and we haul him aboard and his playing helps to give the band a zing!

And I think all yuh think is only black man have rhythm, and somehow the thought pleases me and I hear myself, sober as a Carnival judge, laughing and singing in the darkening night into the Savannah wind.

135

# The Lost Village
## (Lang Lo)

*By* Le Van Thao

*Translated by* Ly Lan

It was a sunny afternoon. I was sitting in a provincial bus station waiting for a ride to Saigon. The man sharing the narrow shade with me beneath a small tree was a lieutenant colonel—at least, I thought that was what he was; I didn't know much about military ranks. He was in his middle fifties with gray hair, a thoughtful look, and a painfully constricted face. He was holding on tight to his briefcase, but his luggage was laid on the ground by his feet. His uniform was quite worn, seemed too large for him, and was buttoned at the neck as well as at the wrists. Both of us were wet with sweat.

Our bus was already there, but it could be a long time before it was ready to leave, so I was just waiting patiently. Other passengers were quietly reading newspapers and smoking. Children were running about playing or eating. Women were chatting noisily in groups. The colonel was neither eating nor reading. Every once in a while he looked at his watch and then glanced around excitedly as if he were impatiently waiting for something. The sun shone more and more fiercely. The bus station was crowded with passengers coming and going, peddlers hawking their wares, conductors shouting and laughing, policemen whistling, a cacophony of noise mixed with unbreathable dirty air, heat and sewer smells.

"Too noisy!" the colonel said.

"That's how a bus station is," I replied.

A group of new passengers arrived, carrying all kinds of farmer's tools and other things. They appeared to be villagers from the remote countryside and included men, women and children, all led by an old man of seventy, with white hair, a wrinkled face but sturdy limbs. The old man walked into the bus station ahead of the rest, looked at the row of buses parked there, then turned to his people to tell them something.

The colonel gave them an indifferent look, then checked his watch. All of a sudden he seemed to remember something. He turned and stared hard at the old man, his forehead furrowing, then stood up. Holding his briefcase close to his chest, he hurried toward the old man, leaving his luggage untended at my feet.

The group of farmers walked into the waiting room, arranged their possessions on the floor and sat down around them. They wiped the sweat from their faces and began talking to one another quietly, with many pauses along the way. The old man came in too, after shouting something to somebody outside. I spotted the colonel mingling among the farmers then sitting by the old man's side. They were conversing earnestly, but it was so noisy that I could only hear a little of what they were saying as I approached with the colonel's luggage.

"Are you Mr. Tam Dau from village T?" the colonel shouted.

"What?" the old man shouted back.

"I wanted to know…. I once stayed in your village."

"What? Speak up. I'm half deaf."

"I said that a long time ago, twenty years ago, I stayed in your village."

"There is no more village. It's in the river now."

"What? In the river?"

"Drowned. Nothing amazing about it. The river bank collapsed."

"All of it? No house was spared?"

"All of it. Not a single house." Then the old man added in a strange voice, "We are the last of the villagers whose houses fell into the river…. What? How could houses just fall into the river like that? They just did, just as they were. With a lot of noise over several days and nights. That's how Nature is."

Just then a group of tourists arrived at the bus depot, well-dressed people with cameras hanging from their necks, talking loudly in foreign languages. Their arrival made me lose track of the old man's and the colonel's conversation. When I looked back at the farmers again I now saw them in all their poverty: how thin, weak, and pale they were in their worn-out clothing. You couldn't even call what the children were wearing "clothes."

The old man and the colonel were still sitting side by side, their voices more subdued now.

"Strange!" the colonel said, clicking his tongue.

"What's strange?"

"The way the river bank collapsed. I knew when I was there it was eroding, but I didn't realize it would happen so quickly. Please tell me the whole story, from the beginning."

"Which beginning?" The old man laughed. He was obviously someone who took delight in telling stories. "As I've already said, there was no beginning and no end. It was going on day and night. That's how it was. It was strange to watch. Especially in the rainy season when the river flowed fiercely. One night we heard screams for help from every direction. When we came with torches we saw that Hai Non's kitchen had collapsed. The pigpen had fallen into the river with the pig still inside. Then Nam Mung's house started falling down. He couldn't get out. He was kneeling on the floor inside and shouting.

"Another time, a group of young men were drinking together. The house they were in was halfway into the river already, but they didn't care. When we heard a big VROOM! we all ran to see the house floating in the middle of the river and the young men swimming away from it like rats."

The colonel asked softly, "Everyone was all right?"

"What?"

"I was just asking if anybody drowned."

"Yes, some did," the old man said. "Hai Suong, a widow whose husband and sons all died in the war. She lived with her twelve-year-old adopted granddaughter in a small hut on the river's edge. But she spent her time looking for food rather than taking care of her house. One night, hearing the 'VROOM!' we lit torches and ran over there. But we found no hut and no people. We couldn't find their bodies either. It was pitiful."

The old man turned to ask the man sitting next to him, "Chin Man, do you remember when Aunt Hai Suong's hut fell into the river? Wasn't it pitiful?"

Chin Man was repairing a basket. He said, "Yes. Pitiful."

"Wasn't there any plan?" the colonel asked.

"What?"

"I was asking if the government didn't have any plan to move the village."

"Move it where? You don't realize, we villagers are very poor. We work day and night just to earn enough to eat. The little that's left over we put into our houses. 'Move once, starve three years.' We didn't have any money to move, and nowhere to move to. Besides, our ancestors' graves were there. So, we had to let Nature do its work."

The colonel hung his head in silence. The old man turned toward me. "Isn't it so, young man? We can't interfere with Nature's work, can we? But do you understand this story of how a river can destroy an entire village?"

I said I did not understand. I had heard about it happening, but this was the first time I had heard it firsthand. I asked the old man, "What about your own house?"

"My house? Well, I had nothing to worry about. My sons and daughters had already moved out. The house was just a small hut waiting for its turn to fall into the river. That night I was smoking a cigarette. All of a sudden I heard the river strongly under the floorboards. It was midnight. I lit another cigarette and waited till the hut started to shake. Then it floated along the river like a blade of water hyacinth. I kept smoking while the hut floated past the bank near where my friend lived. Then I climbed onto the sampan, untied it from the hut's side and paddled to the bank quite easily."

This was so comical, I decided the old man must have made some of it up. But the colonel's face had become dark. The old man turned toward him again. "You said you visited our village once. Whose house did you stay at?"

"I was just passing by. I was on a mission during the war. My boat was sunk when I was crossing the river. I swam to a house.... Do you know a Miss Hue?"

"A girl?"

"Well, she would be a middle-aged woman now. This was twenty years ago. Please try to remember. Her house was at the end of the village. There was a big tree in front."

"I'm trying." The old man asked the man fixing the basket, "Do you remember a Miss Hue, Chin Man? A girl twenty years ago, but now a grown woman. No? Well, it was a long time ago. Houses were always being washed away. It's not easy to remember."

Then he asked the other villagers, "Any of you remember a Miss Hue? Try to remember. Someone here is looking for her."

A woman said, "Didn't Miss Hue run an inn? Soldiers stayed there."

The man fixing the basket said, "Soldiers stayed in every house in the village."

The colonel said, "She didn't run an inn. She wove mattresses."

"Then, I don't know. Soldiers used to stay in lots of houses in our village." The old man tried to comfort the colonel. "Keep looking for her. You'll find her one day."

The colonel replied sadly, "I planned to come back, but I was very busy. Besides, I didn't expect the village to be washed away so soon."

"Nobody expected it. It's Nature's way." The old man stared at the buses lined up in front of him. "It's fate that our village was destroyed. There was nothing we could have done to prevent it. So, now we have to move, but it's okay. We're moving south, where the land is big and people are few. Still, we don't know how we'll survive there. We used to live by a river flowing rapidly day and night. Now we're moving to a dry land where heat burns the grass."

The man fixing the basket said, "It's all part of our homeland. The people there will not let us starve."

Children had gathered to listen to the story but found none of it very interesting. They asked the colonel, "You've been in the army for a long time? You look very old."

The colonel tried to smile, but the effort only made more wrinkles appear on his face. "Yes, I'm old. But once I was young. I once swam across the river to your village."

Someone announced that the buses were getting ready to move.

Everyone became excited. Children called to one another. Grown-ups checked their belongings. Women hugged their babies. The old man began walking around giving orders. "Look out for your things! See to your hoes and spades! You'll need them as soon as you arrive in the new land. Who left this net here? You don't want fish anymore?"

Then he said to the colonel, "I'll say good-bye now. Since you once stayed in our village, you are considered one of us. Please come to see us again in our new home when you have the chance."

"But where is your new village? Which province? Which district?"

"Who knows? We haven't gotten there yet. We'll decide what to name it when we do. It's somewhere in Vietnam, anyway."

They went off with their heavy luggage. The colonel stood bewilderedly for a moment, then ran after the old man. "There was no house left in village? Gone completely? Oh, God! I meant to come back so many times, but I just wasn't able. I was..."

"Don't blame yourself," the old man said. "We all have things we must attend to."

"But where can I find Miss Hue?"

"What?"

"I stayed with her for only a few days. I left without saying anything. Twenty years have passed without any word from her."

"'Join us together, then separate us.' That's Nature's way."

"But what can I do?"

"Nothing. Good-bye."

The buses started up. The old man got on the last one and waved to the colonel. The colonel raised his hand to wave back. By the time the dust cleared, the buses had already disappeared into the distance. The colonel stood watching for a moment, then came to where I was standing and picked up his luggage. After that he didn't say anything until we arrived in Saigon. He just sat quietly staring at the road ahead.

# Snapshots of Elsewhere

*By* Raymond Ramcharitar

Of all the adjectives that could elbow their way into a definition of New York City, "elsewhere" is probably too reticent to make its way to the front of that line. Garish, graphic, vulgar, vile, fucking fun—you get the picture. And yet in this reading it remains there, hovering, vorpal feet barely touching the ground.

So start on the ground. In the city, day one, exhausted. The exhaustion is long, malevolent: the susurrus of a disease of the mind. You who already feel constrained in your small island, weary of the endless, meaningless struggles to reconcile grinning, opulent evil and unassailable poverty with the fineness of your nature—effete, helpless against the rush for the trough. The suspicion that the fineness is just weakness. All this put away for ten days. Curious feeling of relief. You try not to think of the obvious: the order, the freedom, the hugeness of the city. The contrast, most of all, with the smallness, restraint, chaos of an island.

At the Trump Plaza at Columbus Circle. The buildings go up vertiginously for miles. The wide streets, the people, the surreal variety of humanity—sooty-faced bums, busy working girls in Prada pumps and black tiny backpacks, cops, old ladies, black men, old, young, seething with rage. Wall Street types in $900 Versace suits and an air of impregnable smugness and contentment. Masters of the universe in the center of the universe. You think of this as you record this last image—nine hundred dollars, mouthing the words, is all I brought with me. Exchange rates.

Wandering around the city brings little joy. Looking into uptown windows adds to the feeling of removal. Outside looking in. Meeting your own insubstantial reflection. You are your own Virgil. In the bolge of Greenwich Village the world becomes funky, fierce, the faces young, pierced: studded septa, ringed eyebrows, wild clothes, impenetrable ice-blue irises cold-burning through you. This used to be the arty part of town, till the stockbrokers from below Canal St arrived waving money and put a price on funk. Now 19-year-olds off the bus from Minnesota pay $900 for a broom closet in Manhattan. You think this and stop. Why think on it? What reason could you have? Who wants to hear it? Walk through the rush dazed, flickering.

Things strike you at unguarded moments. "The president is a lying sack of shit." Christopher Caldwell, columnist in one of the weekly papers talking about Bill Clinton. A few pages in, a cartoon showing the president butt-fucking Uncle Sam. *The president is a lying sack of shit*. Can they *say* that?

You resist the urge to hold up your images of home against the picture that surrounds you, but they come anyway. And there, in the middle of those pictures, aware you belong in neither, the city becomes elsewhere. Linear narrative, rather than an encompassing, unquestioned paradigm, an extension of linear theocratic dialectics, is a single—and rather pedestrian—choice among many here. Choose one interpretation, or two or ten. Hear Armond White, a film critic for *The New York Press*: "Playing a transfusion-addicted underground hero who defeats a nefarious corporate-like breed of bloodsuckers makes a handy political allegory of dependence and resistance."

The film is a futuristic shoot-'em-up, Wesley Snipes taking out the bad guys with extreme prejudice—the Green Corner synopsis. The wonder is the energy and depth given to something so inane. In Trinidad the very word "review" or even "critic" elicits an involuntary snarl of contempt from almost every editor you've ever worked with. The act of criticism is inevitably personal, never detached. Each statement is part of a sublimated dialogue of the collective voiced by the individual about the world we live in. No wonder we despise it.

In *The Village Voice Literary Supplement*: an interview with Irvine Welsh, former heroin junkie responsible for *Trainspotting*. His latest book, *Filth*, depicts a policeman orally sodomising an underage girl. Reading in Barnes & Noble at Union Square. Attended, among others, by a red-faced woman with short curly hair, untidy but comely, who still manages to look maternal in corporate battle gear—navy pinstripe skirt suit. "...dos fockin cunts..." Nobody around you is offended. Astounding, the capacity for vulgarity, the range. Or perhaps not. The voices are so eloquent, but so shallow, narcissistic, nihilistic. Does anyone actually listen?

Richard Foreman is a playwright who has staked out "ontology," a little known transit system between Freud and the behaviourists, and the Greeks. His plays are dense, illogical, surreal, impenetrable. Winner of several awards. His *Angelface* in a small space in the Village. A pale girl in a pale pink dress who might be an angel. A young handsome man in black, another woman, a door, another man, other people. The dialogue is hopeless, unyielding, but strangely soothing. These are our choices: oblivion or an endless night of despair.

The city by night in the Village is a river running, past evening and without a damn for time of day—if narrative genres change, so do lives; if lives change, time changes. It's all relative.

At the Royale Theatre, 45th and Broadway, *Art*, by Yasmina Reza, French play, gadfly literariness. A huge hit. Wednesday matinee. Me and a thousand other tourists. Packed theatre. Fifty bucks a pop—after discount. Clean, smart, slick. It's all relative.

Comedy club on MacDougal St. College kids in the front row. The headline comic, Italian man, short, vicious, bored, is on.

"So where're you kids from?"

"Jamaica."

Smooth black face, expensive sport coat. Wide grin. White girl at the side. You do not know what to make of yourself for noticing this. It all has to do with fitting in, you rationalise later, staking a claim. Join the party. Fuck a blonde.

"Jamaica, huh? You know what a West Indian is? A black guy with a job." Everyone laughs. I laugh.

*The New York Times*, September 18, 1998. Page one (below the fold). Headline: "For Affluent Blacks, Harlem's Pull is Strong." "Black professionals are snatching up 5,000-square-foot brownstones off avenues named for black leaders.... What started as a flood of young African American lawyers, doctors, professors and bankers moving back into Harlem and other historically black neighborhoods seems now to have reached flood stage.... Howard Sanders had...a degree from Harvard Business School, a position with a high-powered Manhattan investment firm and an apartment on Central Park West.... 'I don't want to live next to a white family,' Mr Sanders, 32, said. 'I have effectively integrated. I've gone to predominantly white schools. I work in a white firm, and I can live anywhere I want. It really is psychologically soothing for me to be back in Harlem.'"

"I don't want to live next to a white family...." You reread it several times over several days. Expressed in the sedulous *Times* stylebook prose, it doesn't sound terrifying, you suppose.

"Anybody else here from the West Indies?" The comic is trying to find his stride. Not in the mood to be a good sport. Sit quietly. An Indian girl sitting at a table with a white man smiles and waves at him. "Where you from?"

"Trinidad." She sounds very happy.

"You know what a Trinidadian is? A black man with two jobs." Laughter.

Perhaps the most pleasant ritual in American urban life is a coffee shop breakfast. Old place in Park Slope, Brooklyn. The New Purity Cafe. Community bulletin board in the vestibule. Formica tables, four-person booths. The day's *Times*. Old waitresses, thick legs, short skirts, blue veins showing through the skin, watery blue eyes. Calling you "Honey." Not like the busy, contemptuous Manhattanite *maedchen* waiting tables with one eye on the tip, the other on the road opportunity might walk by on. Ready to slam your two-over-easy-with-ham in your face at the slightest. (What was the line from Cummings? "They kill like you would take a piss".)

But Brooklyn. Relaxed, cool mornings. The good that came from the spillover of all the New York-obsessed white kids who would skip meals for a Manhattan address. Brooklyn Heights, Carroll Gardens, Cobble Hill, Park Slope. Mainly white, black yuppie, starter yuppie, low crime, coffee shops, bookstores. East of Flatbush Avenue it's all hair salons, cheap Chinese takeouts, grime, dealers, dangerous-looking black young men, dangerous-looking cops.

There's no bookstore past Grand Army Plaza, where Park Slope meets the Brooklyn Museum. Plenty of beeper shops and nail salons and accents. Trinidadian, Jamaican, some ineluctable, all harsh, the first world's Third World. This is exactly the America they wanted: no civic responsibility, no thought for the apparatus of the state that preserves the order they feed from and shit in, the order that makes it possible to exist here in extravagant squalor, breeding, feeding. Cockroaches. Further evolution unnecessary. Remain in this form until nature loses patience.

The week after Labor Day. Reported a few months ago, or maybe just overheard somewhere: Some West Indians complained they'd been bilked of $300–400 for Labor Day *Mas'* costumes. They couldn't go to the police because they were illegals. Three hundred dollars is a month's rent for these people. For Carnival. Carnival? This Labor Day a freak storm hit the parade, the last gasp of one of the early hurricanes. They partied through it.

Pockets of chaos exist as entropy in any huge system. Large numbers lessen the value of each unit. Economies of scale. Who pays for all this and how? The Strand bookstore. Hardcovers, brand new, half off the cover price. It is astounding to you that a business could actually be in existence for your benefit. Somehow, you feel this is all a mistake that you could be given such variety, such consideration. You run out laughing with the bounty. You realise this, and your mind returns home.

Final day. Four a.m. Awake. In the airport, still bleary-eyed. The line to the Bwee counter snakes outside the cordons. You are the only one with two normal-sized bags. Everyone else carries four, five, seven cases, boxes, huge, heavy, taped up. Tune out. Shut off. The last image, the girl in front of you in the white two-piece gangsta bitch number with the synthetic leather platforms with the barb wire tattoo on her arm turns toward you: "Fock, dreeaaddd, look at all these mudder cunt suitcase nah." Over and out.

The pilot's voice—bored, red, irritating—"'Proaching the east coast of Trinidad, 70 miles out." Then the beaches come up, the trees, long, neat swathes of road. Surprisingly, shockingly soothing. The carpets of green, the delight in the thousands of grades of it seen from above as you sit calmly, patiently; the descent into order. From above, it looks almost real, the rectangles of cultivated land, gravel, the roads, out over the west coast, the Caroni pouring its shit into the Gulf, the water brown, dirty yellow, widening from the mouth of the river into the omnivorous sea. Over the Swamp, over bulbous, surly green clumps resting in pools of black, evil fluid; deadly still, a kind of ugly perfect symmetry about it, like a black Zen water garden. Perfect, beautiful, home.

# The Burden of Grace

*By* Vasilis Afxentiou

Alicia Novapovic, neophyte stuffer of fish, one-time assistant to her marine-taxidermist father in a coastal city of Yugoslavia that in better days enjoyed a booming trade with the entire globe, lowered her thoroughly blue eyes and tossed her worldly possessions onboard the skiff. When Alexi Novapovic was killed—a stray bullet tinkling through the iced window pane one flurrying March morning—and left her with nothing more than the proprietorship of a well-kept shop that was do-ing no business at all in that war-ravaged country, Alicia was forced to take her courage into her own thirteen-year-old hands and forge it into her destiny.

A zephyr tousled her solemn young thoughts and tufted straw hair as she lifted the oars into their tholes.

Swallows once flew here instead of incendiary shells. Back then her father and she turned dead, empty-eyed fish into handsome, life-like trophies for customers to hang on their walls for friends to admire, and eventually ignore. She had mulled over the many other things grown-ups neglected, failed to learn from the dull stares of their angled prizes, and refused to entrust her young life into their wardship.

She gave a hefty shove to the deserted wooden quay and rowed till she was well offshore. Then she turned and looked back, savouring the crisp outstretched splendour surrounding her aunt's slumped and patched red roof. She would never see that house again—just like the mother who vanished one day on her way to her teaching job at the municipal orphans' school. The pristine break of day was balmy and bright and promised a good voyage, so she put everything else behind her. She undid the gaskets and unfurled the mainsail, drew it up the wooden mast, pulled the halyard taut and lashed it to a cleat.

"Now, the proof of the pudding," she said. She took a hefty whiff of iodine, her boyish bust bulging.

The canvas fluttered a bit and she pushed the tiller out to trim it. The bag swelled in the salty breeze. The skiff leaped forward, hissing as it skimmed the gentle brew like a gull's wing through the air. She secured the tiller, walked the starboard side to the foredeck and rigged the jib. The boat cleaved the sleek bay in two, tacking into the draft. Bit by bit the cove receded and melded into the checkerboard of golden-brown fields in the distance. The prospect ahead spanned forty kilometers of sparkling Adriatic, its conclusion lapping the sandy shores of northern Greece.

The small boat pranced onward, banging on the ripening crests, lifting the coruscating spray into dozens of little morning rainbows.

But Alicia's lack of maritime seasoning soon began to tell. One minute she was lowering the sail—the next beating the waves.

She craned her neck and blinked the streamers off her eyes, only to catch glimpses of her boat floating away, one sail ballooned out with the force of the gale behind it. She drew her lanky legs in, hoping to escape a subterfuge of currents below. She pivoted to face north, away from the lash of the wind. Before her churned sky and sea, fusing into a cobalt unity. "What happened to—?"

Then the world flashed and crackled just a few meters away.

In due time she understood that she was underwater, tumbling, her mouth full of brine, unable to tell which way was up. She flayed, semaphoring haphazardly. Squeeze your nose, Alicia, and blow.... Her father had been so vexed with himself that day for not having told her sooner.

Ears popped and orientation returned. The depths receded and a turbulent, platinum twilight took their place. Surfacing, she retched and drew in oxygen through clenched, smarting jaws. She wanted to cry, but the tall battering waves would not allow her the luxury. She needed her father to counsel her, her mother to impart her woman's strength...and her life to live, seize it and shake it and tap it dry.

Raindrops fell. Just a few fat ripe ones at first. Then torrents. She lapped the rain from her lips and nose, slurping it down.

Around her fish, countless, surfaced to drink from the shower, brushing and tickling the soles of her feet.

I must get away, she thought as something like a giant cake of soap bumped against her. Behind her, splattering fins moiled and lathered the waters. "It takes several minutes to die, and it is a lingering death," her father once told her. "A manifold of deaths, being eaten alive." Better a quick bullet, amply more merciful.

She released the air from her lungs and allowed herself to sink. God, please, the next breath...let it be the last.

But then her understudy broke the surface with her and began to mimic her silly paddling. Two jasper eyes studied her own as she scanned the sea around her.

"No sharks!" Not with him—her—around. For the mammary glands quavered in full bloom.

"Jjaaarh! Jjaaarh!"

"Yes, I love you too."

It sniffed and nibbled her, fascinated by the soaked strands of her hair.

"Lost my permanent."

She timidly scratched the velvety epidermis behind its nape around the breathing orifice. Her companion cuddled closer.

"Just like Alicia, the back always itches."

It watched her, intently listening to the sounds she made. But only mournful calls emerged when it tried to imitate her. She laid her lightning-singed cheek against its smooth flank and listened to its heartbeat. But when she dipped her head into the cool water, it raised a blustery protest.

"Aren't we the den mother! Do you know that you're a cetacean?" She needed to talk, and the dolphin was keen on listening. "You are intelligent and kind...."

As she prattled she drew her hand over the powerful back and grasped the dorsal fin. "When you were born all the adults helped to lift you upward to the surface to whiff your first scent of life. It was gracious of you to do the same for me. Thank you...Grace."

She was grateful for the day's end. The sun's glare and the hours of being dragged through the sea were killing. Her parched throat was almost closed. And water was everywhere.

She dipped her tongue into the stream and swallowed. Then she managed to pull herself to a half-prone straddle of the mammal. To her wonderment, the dolphin shimmied and flexed its muscles to distribute the weight evenly. Alicia nestled closer to its warm body, her exposed backside still taking the brunt of the frosty waves.

Hours passed like winters. Grace jolted her to wakefulness several times to keep her from sliding off. The stars were all out now, the

North Star flickering high ahead. Alicia blinked back at it, fighting drowsiness.

"You're travelling into the current, heading for—"

"Jjaaarh."

"Nobody'll believe—"

She swallowed with difficulty.

"Why aren't you minding your young ones?" she tried to say, but it came out like a neigh. "You left them behind, chased away those sharks, to save—who? A runaway."

She felt a great bitterness but also a greater love than her years should have allowed.

"Why, Sea Mother, why?"

Then something familiar came suddenly back to her.

"Mother's not running away! She's hiding the orphans, and no one must know. To protect them from the land sharks." Her light-headedness bubbled up into a croaking titter. "And fish now will feast themselves on Alicia?"

"Jjaaarh, jjeeer."

"Dear heart, I can't make it. Too weak...dehydrated. I'm dead weight, Grace. I can't see for thirst, I can't hold on without—"

She let go her grip. As she slipped off, the dolphin came to a dead stop. This time it did not protest but remained solemnly still.

Alicia sank.

And drank. Sank and drank. The dolphin rolled over. They broke the surface together, and now Alicia could drink and breathe as well and even make out a spray of twinkling lights, and bobbing close by the half-draped skiff she thought she'd never see again. Her nose and eyes ran together, but the dolphin remained serenely supine as she hauled her charge hungrily to the other tit.

"Jjiiih, jjiiih."

Alicia suckled, sobbed, suckled and cried some more. And to her amazement, the sounds she made sounded exactly like the dolphin's own.

# Spectacles

(from *The Price of a Dynasty*)

*By* Anjana Basu

It was a small insertion in *The Statesman*. They gave it an inch on the bottom right-hand corner of the middle right-hand page. FREE-DOM FIGHTER'S SPECTACLES BROKEN. Underneath it said: *Yesterday, Padma Bhushan Moitra's spectacles, housed in the Moitra Museum in Amnaguri, North Bengal, were damaged through sheer carelessness on the part of a sweeper. Padma Bhushan Moitra was a noted freedom fighter, as well as Minister of Culture under the Gandhi Government.*

Spectacles. That was one of the first things they told me about Padma Bhushan Moitra. How he'd stand there like a monolith, letting the light glint on his spectacles like a miniature interrogator's spotlight. They were thick round lenses rimmed in gold or silver wire, depending on whether he wanted to be discreet or ostentatious. I believe he had them made by Lawrence & Mayo.

I am looking at him now the way you would look through a pair of spectacles, but the way a shortsighted person looks at things, holding them close to her nose to catch the details. I am not a historian, by the way, so my interest has no basis in scholarly research. Nor am I even a relative. But I was once almost a relative. I ran around with Padma Bhushan Moitra's grandson for eight years. At the end of that time the relationship fell apart, and it fell apart because Padma Bhushan Moitra cast such a long shadow. I saw the spectacles once on a rare trip to North Bengal. Shubho was still talking to me in those days. He took me reverently to the museum and almost made me cover my head before I crossed the threshold—after all, I was the family daughter-in-law who was visiting my revered elder's place of pilgrimage. We were met by the small dusty curator who quivered with awe when he saw

Shubho.

He conveyed us to an equally dusty, dirty glass case.

The glass was so furred with dirt that you could barely see the outline of something inside. The board next to it probably said something about the history of the spectacles, but I had no time to read it. Shubho had me by the arm and was demanding a flat-on-the-floor obeisance to the spectacles. For a moment, I couldn't take in what he was saying. When I did I found myself stretched flat-out on the dusty floor. The habit of obedience dies hard in a woman, even in a so-called Anglicised woman.

I got up, shook the dust from my clothes and bit down on my feelings. "You believe in ancestor worship," I said to Shubho, "the way the Chinese did." He didn't understand what I was saying, but he had read about such things in those books that he bought so compulsively, so he laughed. "You say such things, *yaar*...how about a cuddle?" And he engulfed me in front of the scandalised curator. "That's bad manners," I told him, after I had extricated myself into the sunlight. "How could you do that?"

"My grandfather wouldn't mind," he said. "In fact, he'd probably enjoy it." I had a momentary vision of eyes behind those spectacles, peering out through the fog of dirt. Beady, hot eyes, exactly like Shubho's. "It was my grandfather's ambition," he was saying, "to sleep with three women at once. So he went to Geneva for this operation...you know, glands, *yaar*...but somehow it bumbooed him. He died."

I didn't pay attention to what he said then, though later it was to echo in my mind. I was too hot and shaken and embarrassed—so embarrassed that I didn't even dare look at the curator. What I needed at that moment was to prove that I was respectable, a worthy almost-granddaughter-in-law to the man in whose honour the museum had been built.

Disillusionment about that worthiness was to come later, but then I just shook Shubho off and went back to read what was written on the board beside the spectacles. There was the date of a birth and the date of a death. There was also a long list of meritorious public works, of awards and the names of children and grandchildren. "He wore those very glasses when he came here to open this museum," the curator quavered at me. He had inaugurated the museum wearing those spectacles. Of course, the curator was wrong—the museum had been inaugurated after Padma Bhushan Moitra's death, but I didn't know that then.

I left the museum and Amnaguri that afternoon. Shubho drove to Badogra and escorted me possessively onto the flight. The airhostess smiled at him with a shade more warmth than was required, silly bitch. In those days he was short and square, a cross between a teddy bear and a brick wall. He still had all his teeth and he looked like a German navvy with Roger Moore's forehead. People liked him when they saw him, women smiled at him. Take him, I said to her silently in my head, daring her to, wondering whether I would mind if she did. I did mind when it had happened in the past. Possibly it was Shubho's ambition as well to sleep with three women at once and one of these days he was going to achieve it, with or without glands. The only thing I knew for certain was that he expected me to be one of those three women. If you could call that a commitment to a relationship.

Mrinalini would probably have died for a commitment like that; perhaps once I might have thought it meant something too. Instead, I fastened my seatbelt, sank back into my seat and when the plane took off watched Shubho become a small speck in the glass of the porthole. Then the image ran with water droplets, and for no reason at all, I was reminded of the lenses in the dirty glass case. I hadn't heard about the glands and the three-woman thing before. Perhaps Shubho wasn't serious about it—perhaps it was just excitement caused by the fact that he was about to do something forbidden like humiliate me in front of the curator. His behavior certainly didn't improve our relationship, and it made me feel soiled.

I made up my mind that I would ask Shanto about what Shubho told me the moment I got home, because Shanto never said things for effect. And I did, that evening, half an hour after I arrived. Even over a bad line I could hear Shanto was shocked. "My brother told you that?"

"Why? Wasn't I supposed to know?"

"Yes, but well, not till much later...."

"Why the secrecy?" I asked, my voice reduced to a tired croak, the day beginning to catch up with me.

"He was afraid you wouldn't marry him.... Look, you've accepted most things about our family. You know what we're like.... Hello, hello, are you there?"

"Yes," I said, "I'm still here."

"You sound like you're coming down with a cold or something. Why don't you go to bed with a nice hot cup of soup? My brother's arriving in a few days.... We can talk things over.... I'll call you tomorrow...."

At the climax of his life, at seventy, Padma Bhushan Moitra was found dead in his bed as the result of the combined attentions of three whores and a host of goat-gland-bearing Swiss doctors. The servant, tiptoeing blindfold in with bed tea at seven and finding no relieving hand to lighten the tray, unveiled his eyes, discovered the corpse and alerted the police. A fleet of severe black cars flashed their red-sirened way to the chalet and erupted into official blue-coated men. The Chief of Police was confronted by the butler wringing his hands. "Sir, sir, such an unfortunate...."

The Chief shrugged himself out of his fur-lined coat. "Where's the body?"

"This way, sir. I assure you we haven't touched a thing.... Oh dear, so unfortunate...." The butler's voice trailed away as he opened the door.

The first thing the Chief noticed was the smell—an almost tangible stale greasiness, oozing coldly on the air. "Open those windows!" he snapped. The butler scuttled toward the windows, carefully averting his eyes from the bed. Cold sunlight sliced into the room and glinted on a pair of gold-framed spectacles. A cuckoo clock hiccuped eight with an ironical whir. It was a wide, well-gilt room carpeted in simulated mink. The rumpled bed was the biggest thing in it. On the marble bedside table bristled a black millipede. "See what that is," the Chief ordered his subordinates. "Be careful."

There was a tense pause. Then, "It's eyelashes, sir."

"Eyelashes?"

"Yes, sir. You know, those false ones women use."

The body was half out of the bed, lolling face downwards. They straightened it carefully. The pillows were smeared with Vaseline. The Police Chief found the half-empty jar under the bed. While the forensic experts carried out their examination, he went into the adjoining bathroom and discovered dollops of pulped lipstick-smeared tissue.

No one could exactly state the time of death. The experts surmised that it was between midnight and two-thirty. To them it was a matter of grave embarrassment, given the fact that he was, after all, an Indian Minister of State, no matter how dubious or how internationally unimportant.

"It will be very difficult explaining this to the press," said the Chief.

"But is there a need to explain?" said his colleague. "He is old, he died of heart failure."

"The Indian Government will be bound to ask questions. This is not an easy matter. The forensic department has assembled four different types of hair...."

"A blonde, brunette and a redhead?"

"Swiss doctors are matters to be ashamed of, comrade. It is a well-known fact that before this happened he had implants. I am told it was in all the Indian papers."

"Was it the goat or the monkey?"

"The goat."

"It obviously worked." The Police Chief sighed and perambulated once around the bedroom, his hobnails scuffing the mink. "It is very serious. The body bears evidence of at least three sets of teeth, traces of scarlet nail polish."

"Three women! He was ambitious!"

"And he was also a Minister of State."

"Come on, *mon ami*, cheer up. We must issue a statement for the papers. I will help you write it."

India mourns the passing of Padma Bhushan Moitra. The 70-year-old Minister of State for Culture passed away peacefully in his Swiss hideaway yesterday. Doctors said the cause was a sudden heart attack. Padma Bhushan's family was informed.

In Amnaguri, his eldest son glared at the telegram and wondered what to do about it. "Someone's got to go to Switzerland, I suppose."

"Why bother?" asked his wife. "Tell them to send you the ashes in a copper urn and have a public scattering ceremony by the dam. It'll be good for your elections."

She had other things to do. Straight after the telegram she went into the Austrian woman's room and unlocked a brassbound chest. From its camphor interior she dragged out a bulky coat, releasing a flight of moths from the folds of the Russian leopard. They flapped dementedly around the room like bad memories and finally roosted in the cracks of the shutters. The coat was almost bald. "Thank goodness he didn't give it to one of his women," she sighed.

His second son received the news at the factory and went running to tell his wife. "Damn, I suppose they'll have taken everything out of

Amal's wife's cupboard by the time we get there."

"But you did remove the emeralds when she left, didn't you?" he asked her worriedly. "Because if you didn't, Hari's bound to give them to his wife."

The third son took himself quietly down to the country liquor shop and was not heard of for the day.

As I far as I was concerned, Padma Bhushan's pornographic death wasn't how the whole thing began for me, even though it might have been how the whole thing began for Shubho, since his world fell apart when his grandfather died. He came back from Amnaguri to boast about his grandfather's death as if it were some great achievement, while I was looking for an explanation or consolation for being associated with a family like that. Shubho told it like the start of a Mickey Spillane or a James Hadley Chase—all we needed was for a gun-toting blonde to walk in and rake the room with flashes of machine-gun fire and leave dead cops all over the place. The way they related the death to me was deliberately obscene—let's show poor little Nandini exactly what kind of family she's getting herself in to. If I had been older and wiser I would probably have seen it as a cry for help—Shubho wanted attention from me and decided the best way to get it was to scandalise me. But he never realised that my story with him didn't begin with a death in Geneva. Nor did it begin as a kind of negotiation—though for members of the Moitra family life itself was a negotiation and there was no deal that could not be won and no person who could not be bought over. My story with Shubho began with the exit of a girl called Mrinalini from his life.

One fine day—why do writers always use that "one fine day" business? I don't know whether the day was fine or not—Mrinalini stormed into Shanto and Shubho's house in a flurry of red sari and temper. She was in her usual state of untidiness, her petticoat sticking out a palm's breadth below her, with cheap plastic slippers flopping underneath. Today, they were red plastic to match. "Where is he?" she stormed as soon as she cleared the door.

"Who?" Shanto asked, knowing perfectly well.

"Shubho!" She was so angry, she was panting and her corals danced in a pattern of coils on her breast.

"Sit down, sit down," he said patting a chair. Whenever Shanto saw her he wondered what his brother saw in her. She was so dark and fussy. Bits and pieces of her escaped all over the place, her hair straying out of its bun, her petticoat out from under the sari, and she was forever trying to herd those bits and pieces back into place and never quite succeeding.

"I waited for him an hour and a half," she fumed, rearranging herself unsuccessfully.

"Where is he?"

Since the age of five, Shubho had thought he was a Casanova. Well, no, five might be a bit of an exaggeration. He was seduced by the maid at thirteen, that I know for sure, since according to Shanto, they all were. Of course, if you are Padma Bhushan Moitra's grandson, I suppose it was inevitable.

Shanto and Shubho grew up with their eyes glued to keyholes, and Shubho was always snuffing around Grandpa's heels. When they were four and five, they would sit on the edge of the courtyard and watch the pretty starlet whores leaving grandfather's room in the morning. They called them the *devika ranis*, after an actress who was all the rage for her beauty and scandalous love life. Because Shubho had a year's advantage, he liked to act more knowing. "Look, look, see, that one's more swollen here," he would say, fumbling at his chest. Or, "That one's nose is like Sati Auntie's dog's. Grandpa can't have liked her."

Shanto told me that he consoled himself with the fact that their mother never liked Shubho. She always preferred himself. Shanto was the one who got to rub oil into her legs when she sunned herself on the terrace in her bikini. Shubho, on the other hand, brought her flowers from the roadside and got slapped because the mud stained her dress. He brought her water in a glass, and some of it always slopped over onto her hand.

"Where is he?" Mrinalini asked Shanto again. She was obviously getting fed up by his glassy-eyed silence.

"Have some tea," he said and got up to make it for her.

Shanto never said that he had loved his mother. It wasn't possible after what she did to them. All he said was that she loved him better, which probably made him more balanced in his attitude towards women. Shubho always ill-treated women and expected them to keep on loving him, despite it. In a way, he was getting back at them for all his mother's slaps.

Shanto gave Mrinalini her tea with a squeeze of lemon in it, and he served it in the chipped Satsuma cups that he found in the Thieves Market. The tea and Satsuma combination obviously did something for her morale, because she relaxed into the chair. "I wouldn't be so angry," she confessed, "if I hadn't bunked two lectures. I can't afford to keep bunking lectures for your brother."

"Who asked you to?" Shanto said.

A stray hair dropped into her cup. She fished it out with a finger. Looking at her, Shanto found it hard to believe that she and Shubho were an item. Everyone cooed indulgently about them in Presidency. Shubho's friends told Shanto how the two held hands in deserted classrooms or were discovered clinched on the dusty library floor. Someone compared them once to bullock-cart wheels; two round forms rolling side by side. Shanto didn't think they belonged together. He thought she was just part of Shubho's Casanova image. De Sade was Shubho's role model, of course, I knew that now without Shanto having to tell me. In Shanto's head his brother was the man who got all the women and made them run. Shubho could take away a worker's daughter if he wanted without raising a storm in the tea estate. Padma Bhushan carried on the same way till the time of his death. Not that Shubho had the grandfather's style. All he had was the chip their mother had left him with and the bad habits he had learned from their father. At sixteen Shanto caught him mixing cocktails of rum and vodka to see how they tasted. "It's the alcoholic's blood," he told Shanto proudly and forced some down his throat. They were both very sick that night, and the next day their House Master sent them down for being drunk.

Shanto had a thousand and one stories like those about his brother, and he was sure Mrinalini didn't know half of them—he did his best to make sure that I was enlightened too. Mrinalini was the sort who'd get drunk on a glass of orange squash if you let her. The first time they all went out together Shubho brought her a glass of orange juice and told her there was gin in it. They'd gone to this restaurant with a view of the river; it had plate glass windows lined with high red-leather stools that were jammed together. It was very popular with courting couples in those days. You could sit and kitchy-coo for hours over two cups of coffee or a Limca. Anyway, Mrinalini squealed so loud when she heard about the gin in the orange juice that all the courting couples unglued their heads and turned to look at them. Then, after she'd taken a few sips, she started to teeter on the stool until it tilted. Shubho was a little slow to catch her, so she crashed on the floor and burst into tears in a welter of orange juice. At that point, the male of one of the courting couples stalked over to them and said angrily, "You don't behave like that in here. This is a decent place." Mrinalini cried harder at that. Shanto offered her his handkerchief, but she didn't seem to see it.

After a while Shubho picked her up and dusted her down. "You wait here," he said to his brother. "I'll put her in a cab home."

Shanto waited until he couldn't look another Limca in the face. Then he paid the bill and went home. Shubho staggered in somewhere around midnight. "Don't make a big deal of it," he told Shanto irritably when he saw him glaring. "I had to see her home, didn't I? And soothe her up a bit."

"You needn't have asked me to wait. And why on earth did you have to give her that gin?"

Shubho paused in the midst of pulling his singlet over his head. "Who said there was any gin in it? I gave her straight orange squash. If she's such an idiot that she gets drunk on orange squash…."

Mrinalini got out of her chair. "I'm going to put the cup in the kitchen," she announced. "Shall I take yours?" And she did without waiting for an answer. After a while Shanto heard noises from his brother's room and went to investigate. Mrinalini was going through his drawers. She pulled out a pair of pajamas streaked with grey and made a face at them.

"You'd better put them back," Shanto warned her. "Shubho hates people prying into his things."

"These need washing," she said. "I'm going to take them to the washerman's."

She rolled an eye over him. "Do you have something that needs washing too? Give it to me."

Her hair cascaded over her eye and she pushed it back impatiently. The other problem with Mrinalini was that she was always trying to take care of the two brothers, pushing her way into places where she was not always welcome. When their father was in town she would sit at his feet, rubbing oil into them for hours on end "What on earth does that girl want?" he asked once after she'd spent the day ordering the servant around the house. "If you're going to marry her, Shubho, I'd advise you not to. She's not our class." What their class was, was debatable. Mrinalini, if untidy, was at least decent. As far as Shanto could tell, she didn't have a history of alcohol and *devika ranis*. But she didn't have enough money either; she wore plastic slippers and Shanto didn't like the possessive gleam in her eye, as if she were already a daughter-in-law of the Moitra family.

"I don't need anything, thanks," Shanto said. "My brother is the dirty member of the family. Perhaps he'll be glad if you keep him clean."

She flopped onto her knees and pulled out a few more pieces of dirty underwear. Everything Shubho wore next to his skin was a uniform shade of grey. As she shook out a pair of underpants, Shanto saw rusty stains caked on them. He thought they were blood at first, then something about the pattern caught his eye: the unmistakable print of a lower lip.

Mrinalini was looking at him with an expression that he thought was embarrassment. "Don't worry," Shanto smiled, trying to put some warmth into it. "I won't tell anyone."

The tears welled up in her eyes and bled down her cheeks. She dropped the pants, buried her face in her hands and rocked back and forth. Like everything else about her, she was an untidy crier.

"What's the matter?" Shanto asked. "Look, I won't tell anyone...."

She mumbled something into the palms of her hands. Shanto had to bend forward to catch it.

"How could he do this to me?"

Shanto heard a scuffling in the other room and dashed off to investigate. Between rooms he reached an inevitable conclusion: The lipstick stains were not Mrinalini's. He found Shubho standing in the drawing room looking distinctly rumpled. He opened his mouth to say something, but Shanto rushed in. "Where on earth have you been? You were supposed to meet Mrinalini at the college steps. She's in your room."

"What did you let her in there for?" Shubho said angrily.

"Where were you, anyway?"

"That's none of your business."

"Well, Mrinalini's in there crying her eyes out, so you'd better make your alibi a good one. And who's been leaving lipstick stains on your underpants?"

Shanto had his hand on the door handle when he said that. Very slowly, Shubho turned to look at him. "Who told you that? Have you been spying again?"

Shanto began to back away. "Mrinalini was taking a couple of your things to the dhobi's. She's the one who found it...."

Shubho cursed and swung out of the room.

Shanto heard a high babble of voices in the next room and decided he was best out of the place. He took a tram to visit a friend in Gariahat. When he came back Mrinalini was gone and Shubho was sprawled on his bed in his shabby navy dressing gown. His grin stretched from ear to ear. "I sent three of your vests to the dhobi with Mrinalini," he said. The bed was a mess of rumpled sheets and the room stank.

"I don't know how you get away with it," Shanto said.

"It's the philandering blood."

"You mind telling me exactly where you were this afternoon?"

"Amit and I went for a stroll by the river. He had some good hash. It didn't seem worthwhile rushing back. In any case, I got my screw for the day."

"How about the lipstick stains."

Shubho shrugged. "I told you, she and I have a no-strings relationship."

"You may think so, but does she?"

"She wants to marry me. Don't forget that."

"I'm not forgetting anything. But, considering you've been going around with her for almost six years, isn't it time you came to some conclusion?"

Shanto was itching to get out of the room. On summer days you could smell Shubho, rank and ripe in a good south wind. It got so bad, Shanto had to stay downwind of him, otherwise his asthma played up. He wasn't like that in Amnaguri, only in Calcutta when the two of them were together. Shanto thought it had something to do with the German in them, which made him extra careful when it came to his personal hygiene. Shubho thought it was just macho.

"You know Baba doesn't approve of her," Shubho said finally.

"But you can't just go around with a girl for six years and then drop her. She expects you to marry her. Why is she taking care of the washing otherwise?"

Shubho heaved himself over so that his dressing gown gaped and his stomach heaved and billowed like a pregnant whale. "I'll take care of that, little brother. I'll take care of that."

# A Feast of Crows

*By* KC Chase

Ander eyed the silver-slick Identacard as it danced across the seller's lean fingers. His gaze roamed greedily across the twining salamander coils of the double helix that flowed across the card's pristine surface. Quite of its own volition, his tongue slid delicately to the cusp of his lips and peeped out, pink and wet as a boiled sweet.

"Do ya or don't ya?" the seller's voice, harsh and crumbly, jattered through the dank air. "Ya know the penalty, risky-risky."

Bright black eyes flashing in the gloom of the storeroom, the seller tipped his sharp chin at Ander with a crocodile's canny smile. "It's late for second thoughts. Credit or geddit." One brown thumb jerked in the direction of the door to illustrate.

Ander shook his head violently. "No, I want it. I know the penalties for…. I want it...please."

Shrugging indifferently at Ander's sudden passion, the seller's hand produced a bancskan, magician's fingers nimbly thumbing the matte black module to life.

"Ya know the price...."

Trembling, Ander fumbled his own bancskan from his pocket and grasped its butt in his sweaty palm until he was able to force his hand to stillness and allow the two tiny displays to come into contact. A bare whisper of sound issued from the devices, a soft green glow flashing as the credit transfer was approved, draining the lion's share of his life savings into the seller's account.

Back in the fresh air, Ander caught a whiff of enviro-scent peaches and thought it the most wonderfully inviting aroma he had ever smelled. His expression of dazed wonder melted years off his appearance. In the 20th century he would have passed for twenty-four years old. In the shimmering glass-front window of a Health Shake shoppe his reflection gazed wetly back. Typically handsome, of average height and weight, he was a standard prototype variant. Darkly tousled hair and moderately athletic build, his parents had chosen well. His shade-3 ice-blue eyes glittered with sudden moisture. "Long-Timer again...." he told the wind, and laughed.

A small group of business people, splendid in their colorful plumage, crushed past him on the sidewalk, forcing him to step out of the way. Their bright-eyed gaiety and obvious health for once didn't sting him. He was one of them now. A card-carrying member of society once again.

Not a Short-Timer. Not a liability.

He had time to spare...and time again...or so it would seem to anyone viewing his Identacard. His birthday, his 438th, had been wiped from the system by the ratty little life-dealer.

During the thousand years before Ander's birth, the genetic slipstream had been forever altered. Biochemists had tapped the wellspring of continuing youth in the form of a single chromosome that could be artificially replaced and replaced again, lasting each human a span of close to five hundred years, each year enjoyed in perfect health. A single critical fragment of genetic code could be duped by the constant infusion of a nutritional supplement—duped into preserving the human algorithm in the blush of youth. It wasn't "forever," but it was Time.

But now, while Ander might actually only have a maximum of sixty years of youthful perfection remaining before complete cellular breakdown, his Identacard boasted that he had only just passed his second century.

No longer an outcast.

It wasn't the law that prevented an aging Ander from the full benefits of citizenship. The law didn't go to any lengths to protect or prosecute Short-Timers; it simply looked the other way. But who would want to enter contract-love or marriage with someone who might only have a few decades left? Why would a company invest in a short-time employee, wasting valuable time training someone on his way out the door? And what could be more embarrassing than to have a Short-Timer shuffle off the mortal coil in a flurry of convulsions during a board meeting or merger deal. The final breakdown wasn't pretty.

The Civil Rights Act of 2690 provided that Short-Timers could not be passed over for hire or promotion or dismissed without cause, but in the last three weeks before his "planned retirement" (planned by who? Ander had thought bitterly on more than one occasion), he had often felt the fearful glances of his co-workers, as if he had caught something that might be contagious. After 157 years of service, he was neatly and quietly pushed out of his job. Better for everyone this way. More efficient. Disposable humans. Best if used before 400 years.

They had met two weeks earlier at a small cafe overlooking a nature-node park. A dazzling sunny day with enviro-scented air ripe with the tang of new-mown grass. The scent lent a charming nostalgia to the day. The previous day's enviro-scent was pineapple, and Ander had spent the entire day with a crushing headache from its cloying sweetness. Buoyed by the sunshine and the scent of grass, he had stopped at the cafe for a Health Shake, taking a seat on the breezy deck over-looking the precisely manicured grounds. The measured spaces be-tween the trees were filled with prototype variants of all sizes, shapes and colors, both male and female, the only commonality being their ages, concealed on carefully-tucked-away Identacards as they moved between the trees, sporting their activist signs and chanting slogans in unison: a sanctioned Short-Timer rights rally. He had considered at-tending, a kernel of fear and hope lodged in his belly like a granite pellet. Just a quick stop to get a Health Shake and he would join the other Short-Timers, make a difference. The cafe's deck was crowded. The rally was a spectacle for these people, like a car wreck, you couldn't help but look.

Not us. Certainly not us.

Twenty minutes into the sludgy sweetness of the Health Shake, his body trapped by the plastic contours of the deck chair, he heard a voice nearby. "Look at them all.... So many.... Did you know there were so many?"

Ander turned and smiled and was rewarded with a matching ex-pression, perfectly shaped pearls. Not a standard prototype. Something more exotic hinting at family money or political connections. Burgundy hair, soft river of wine in a casual twist laid across slim olive-tanned shoulders. Wide dark eyes with thick-fringe lashes streaked with gold. "Nova. Nova 4591 Dresden." She extended a delicate hand. Ander set down his Health Shake and brushed the cool beads of condensation onto his napkin before accepting it in his own. "Ander 4508 McCaffe." He glanced around the crowded deck, then indicated the empty chair at his table. "Sit down?"

She smiled, sinking a dimple deep into the flawless skin of her cheek. "Love to. Zero-eight? I know that one…. Isn't that Scotland?" Her Health Shake nestled next to his on the table. Ander's noted her own flavor choice: Rose Synergy. He wondered if his Spice Stamina seemed posturing. "Scotland, that's right. I don't know 91."

"No one does. New Vargo. Just recolonized."

She stuck out her tongue, and they both laughed together. Recolonization—another way to make a chunk of a resource-poor country look new again. Burn out some old colonists, new flag, new government, new re-tax programs and tougher requirements for residence and birth permits.

A comfortable silence fell between them as they watched the rally. "So many..." she said again, softly.

They had known each other scarcely five minutes, but in a few moments she would ask. She would produce her own Identacard and smile sweetly, ask him for another meeting, something with food or entertainment involved where she, as asker, would pay...assuming his Identacard met with her approval. Blood types would be compared, IQs exchanged. Assuming he wasn't defective or a Short-Timer, things could move forward. One of her lovely hands slipped into her purse, her expression confident. But her expression abruptly changed as a thin wail spiked above the lunchtime conversation, shredding the pre-recorded bird song.

"Over there!"

A tall prototype variant, blond-green, stood at the railing, pointing across the nature-node to a frenetic cluster of Short-Timers. Many of the other lunchtime patrons rose from their seats to gawk. Ander's jaw tightened as his eyes located the cause of the disturbance. A short figure surrounded by other Short-Timers had come to his or her end. Tough to judge the sex from this distance. Light-skinned, dressed in a snowy-white jumper, the figure was having some kind of convulsion, writhing on the pristine turf of the nature-node. Limbs flailed as the body sunfished and shook, its cellular construction breaking down at the most basic levels. The other Short-Timers watched in silent sympathy. Nothing to do, nothing could be done. There was nothing now but the cleanup. Faux birdcalls once more claimed the air.

"Exactly," the tall variant said, strutting back to his chair. "And they want more rights? They want better jobs when *that* is what is going to happen and who knows when?" A few patrons nodded agreement. A woman's cultivated voice carried above the whisper of conversations. "So unsightly. It's not as if there aren't facilities. They have places to go. Running about in the streets, going out like animals in gutters. Dreadful."

Ander worked at unclenching his fists beneath the table, rubbing them against the soft fabric of his pants until they were only hands again. Across the table Nova's dark eyes filled with a kind of sadness that hurt his head to look at. He should say something. He should say the right thing. "It's...a fact of life."

"Doesn't make it any easier to watch. Have you...?" she faltered, her gaze fixed on the sunset of her Health Shake.

"No, never anyone close to me."

She shook her head. "Can you imagine...?"

He felt bitterness swelling in his mouth, thick and chalky. Charming, her ersatz sympathy. She had plenty of time left herself.

"What's the point?" She rose to her feet and fumbled with the strap of her purse. "I'm late."

His mouth became fluid again. "Wait. I'm sorry. It's a terrible thing to have happen at a first meeting. Will you see me again?"

She hesitated. Protocol had not been followed. Without the exchange of Identacards, she would be taking a risk. "Yes. All right." Her eyes were bright with pleasure as she scribbled some numbers for him and then left the cafe.

After two weeks, Nova was still unable to broach the subject of Identacards. They had followed all the other requisite rituals. She had treated him to holo shows piped into her luxurious loft straight from Broadway theaters and had ordered unpronounceable delicacies for them to eat. For his part, he had procured lab-grown trinkets and genetically altered hothouse blooms to match her hair and complexion, insuring that each item was delivered at her workplace or when she was among her friends or family. The mating dance was, by all accounts, going well but for a growing seed of discomfort between them whenever Time was mentioned.

The Broadway holo was a romance, two lovers thwarted only by the selfish desires of the ingénue's Short-Time mother. The mother's death scene was played to grisly perfection. From across the vast desert of the designer sofa he felt Nova stiffen as the actress twitched in her final throes. Nova slipped her hand into his. He could feel her eyes on him in the semidarkness of the flickering holo scene. And he could feel the questions.

Tell me. Show me. Reassure me. His jaw tightened.

In the ebony-tile landscape of his bathroom he confronted his reflection, his even white teeth and taut skin. His shade-3 ice-blue eyes were clear and bright. The reflection offered him a glossy magazine smile. He returned it. Things were better now that he was no longer a Short-Timer. He could go to Nova free of fear. Let her ask. Let her ask aloud for the card, and he would show it. He could also work again, and at the top of his field. He would buy a better, more expensive loft and order dinners and holos, and soon he would execute contract-love with Nova. Twenty years, sixty years, plenty of Time.

The mood fountain's misty violet light painted Nova's heart-shaped face with celestial colors. They exchanged Identacards to the fountain's liquid, gurgling accompaniment. Ander watched her fingers slide across the surface of his card, almost caress it, until the moment dragged on so long that he wanted to ask for it back.

Then she flung her arms around him, firm and warm. Her breath whispered against his neck. He could feel the bubbling of joyous laughter inside her chest. It was she who had orchestrated their first meeting and therefore it was her choice whether to initiate a request for contract love. She would do so. He was sure of it. He put the card carefully back into his wallet. Her silken, olive hands laced through his. "I can have the paperwork ready by this afternoon."

"I have a business meeting."

"Another?" she pouted.

"Promotion."

"We'll celebrate afterward. For both occasions. I'll make the arrangements.

Transmit your guest list?"

"Tomorrow," he promised.

Contract love brought with it permits for more spacious living arrangements. Ander purchased a comfortable flat in a prestigious area just across from the metro. The whiz of transport tubes was all but inaudible through their walls, and from their windows they could look across a large nature-node preserve complete with holo wildlife and artificial bird song.

After work they curled up on the sofa, Nova's back socketed gently against his chest, arms twined and fingers laced. The catchy music and flashing logos of the evening news flowed through the flat. A standard prototype, only her stiff-styled lemon locks to distinguish her from other protos, ran cheerfully through the evening's fare: an illegal-birth ring, a recolonization in the Alaskan territories, the standard run of congressional sex scandals, all issued without distinction from the pretty newscaster's perfect mouth as Ander's thoughts wandered to the next day's work.

His attention returned only when he felt Nova's delicate shiver, her flesh tingling against the skin of his arms. The newscaster's expression altered effortlessly from muted shock to unspoken disapproval as the visual cut away to live vid of a man in a dark suit surrounded by an entourage of EnForce officers. As the man was marched up the wide stairway at Central Justice by his blank-faced escort, the voice-over reported, "Horror and shock are the reactions of employers, family and contract spouse as Dylin 4123 Barrett is brought to justice. A Short-Timer of 461 documented years, 4123 Barrett purchased a forged Indentacard on the black market which reduced his indicated his age to 200 years." During the anchor's calculated pause, Ander heard Nova suck her breath in distress. Meanwhile, the vid followed Barrett's progress into the Justice Chamber.

"His true age concealed, 4123 Barrett willfully sought employment, defrauding the Taslon Corporation of thousands of credits of training and wages. Displaying no regard for his fellow citizens or any sense of human decency, 4123 Barrett contracted love with a woman of only 186 years, forcing himself into her life and the lives of her family members. 4123 Barrett, found guilty of one count of Felony Identa-Forgery and six counts of Malicious Fraud, has reaped a nightmare of pain and suffering for those around him."

They watched in silence as the vid displayed a woman in Center grays administering the sentence to Barrett as he lay helpless in full restraints. The injection took only seconds. Barrett's face, a bleach-white smear on the vid, became instantly flushed crimson as convulsions shook his body. His eyes bulged from their sockets, his mouth gaping open in a silent scream. His fingers scrabbling vainly at the smooth armrests, he let out a final ragged hiss and died.

Ander punched the off button before the anchor could launch into her wrap-up.

It was Nova who broke the silence. "Horrible. Just horrible."

He did not trust himself to speak. His mouth was dry, the tart flavor of fear on his tongue. He felt what she felt. They were one now, caught in a nightmare together.

She faced him with wide doe-black eyes, a hectic color in her cheeks. "What he did to her, his contract spouse. How could someone betray another person like that?"

"Her?" he heard himself say, his voice hard and accusatory. "What about him? He still had Life, and the Justice Center took it. There was still Time left for him."

The space between them suddenly yawned like a chasm. He hated her, hated her for the Time she had left.

"But he took what wasn't his. He was a Short-Timer. He should have...."

"...Should have just checked into a Retirement Facility and died quietly? He had forty years left. Forty! So much Time."

But she didn't seem to hear. "What will she do," she said, twisting her hands around each other. "My god, what will she do?"

He got up, walked over to the window and pressed his forehead against the cool surface. His shade-3 ice-blue eyes did not see the holos of flamebirds dancing in the nature-node across the street.

He was at his job when they came for him. An EnForce officer in immaculate dress uniform accompanied by a woman in anonymous Center grays. He saw them through the transparent office walls. Neat, economical people striding down the hallway, brusquely waving away his secretary, they rode the floor-trac to his office door. His body pulsed with the desperate instinct for fight or flight. Instead, he sat quietly waiting for his judgment. His Time had run out. Fifty years, was all he could think. I could have had fifty more years.

The EnForce officer's finely chiseled features bespoke privilege and good family connections. His tailored genes were expressed in rich mahogany skin tones and startling silver-white eyes.

"Ander 4508 McCaffe?"

He croaked an affirmative. Why aren't there more of them? An army of EnForce to take me down like a rabid criminal. Where are the newscams, he wondered, his eyes drawn to the shiny sidearm at the

EnForce officer's hip. The Center woman made a clucking sound and stepped forward. Crouched down in his chair, the desk his last line of defense, he waited for her to put the restraints on him. Her cool fingers stroked his shirtsleeve as his hands lay open and helpless on his lap. They simply would not turn into fists. His body would not obey his command to grab a chair and smash it against them. He sat imprisoned in his flesh, waiting like a condemned animal. The EnForce officer's full lips parted, his pale eyes betraying nothing. "If you will please come with us. I'm afraid there has been an accident."

The funeral procession wound slowly through the nature-node. Mourners moved ceremoniously through the trees, their footsteps swiftly erased as the fat blades of simugrass sprung back to attention. The gleaming container that held Nova's ashes stood on a dais in the center of the small park as the mourners arranged themselves beneath a dark pavilion. Ander had stopped trying to put names to faces.

His tone ringing with pious feeling, the minister began the eulogy. His voice trembled with emotion as he described Nova's unkind fate.

Ander was sitting in the front row with no one to give him comfort, his grief represented only by the presence of his co-workers. Avoiding the phalanx of Nova's friends, relatives and colleagues, he kept his focus on the dais.

The minister extolled Nova's exemplary work ethic and the importance of ComTrend's work in metro business. Then his voice rose in a slow-rising anger that became contagious throughout the assembly as he began to speak about Nova's co-worker, Reynold 4452 Fairweather. A Short-Timer in the process of his planned retirement, Reynold had come to work that day with a briefcase packed with two shiny full-auto handguns and seven boxes of ammunition. He started his fateful day's work by walking through the building blowing neat holes in his co-workers. He killed or wounded everyone in his path on his way to his supervisor's corner office. Undaunted by Nova's presence there, he shot her twice in the chest before pumping twelve rounds into the supervisor. Then he reloaded and fired several shots at the computer terminal before turning the gun on himself.

Ander sat quietly, his eyes fixed on the dais as the mourners rose and began to cluster around the food tables under the pavilion, picking at the buffet like a flock of dark-feathered birds over carrion. He remained motionless as a stone amidst the munching and guzzling, the youthful bodies moving in ever-shifting, sinuous groups, exchanging pleasantries and knowing glances. They either imagined him deaf or so completely in shock that he could not hear them.

"Simply terrible."

"What will he do now?"

"What can he do?"

"Such a nice man. How could this happen to him?"

The enviro-scent of lavender mixed with the smells of the different kinds of food turned his stomach, hemming him in from every direction. It was too much to bear. He would climb up on his chair, startle the complacency from their faces and send them winging across the nature-node in panic. His cries would echo throughout the city. He would not wait meekly for his turn to be cut from the herd. He would not accept his fate complacent and accepting. But as tears coursed down his cheeks, they seemed to seal his lips shut with their salt, and he merely sat silently rebuking his beloved...for running out of Time.

# Jesus Christ Lord of Hosts
# Discovers Southern California

*By* Holly Day

Jesus is standing in the soft shoulder of the Ventura Freeway, impatiently scanning the horizon for oncoming traffic. The tops of His flip-flop-clad feet are burning up from near-constant exposure to the sun, the bottoms swollen from walking all day over blacktop and concrete. He considers taking off His flannel shirt and carrying it, but decides being a little warm is better than being sunburnt. "There is no such thing as gridlock," He suddenly says out loud. "There is also no such thing as a lunch rush-hour." He bites his lip and looks nervously up at the sky. "A car will be coming to pick me up shortly," He says. "It will rain soon."

It seems to be getting hotter. Summer insects trill happily in the waist-high yellow grass as the sun climbs higher and higher in the sky, burning away the last traces of early-morning fog. Jesus sits down by the side of the road and wipes the sweat off His forehead with the edge of His shirt. His fingers drag along the sand beside Him, feeling damp gravel beneath the cracked topsoil. He grins at something somewhere in the sky before enlarging the now-damp scratches in the ground. Water seeps into the hole, fills it and runs over the side. It is cool, sweet, and soon Jesus is back on His feet, walking along the road once more. He reaches into His pocket for the empty pack of cigarettes and finds that, amazingly, there is still one left.

He finds he also has exactly one match. "I promise I'll quit tomorrow," He says as He lights the cigarette. Smoke rushes into His lungs, fills them completely from the very first drag.

The hills are high enough for Jesus to see over the smog, to actually see it as a thin yellow strip separating the city from the sky. It's not as bad as it used to be, He reminds himself, but it could still use some work. The ocean glitters white and sapphire in the distance, appearing impossibly close. He cuts diagonally across the road in order to get a better look and is nearly mowed down by a badly dented, white '67 Chevy.

The car screeches to a halt inches away from Him. A scared-looking girl with dirty blond hair and a bad complexion is yelling something at Him, but He can't hear what she's saying through the closed windows. He smiles, waves and walks over to the driver's side of the car. "Hello there," He calls out, tapping lightly on the rolled-up window.

The girl rolls down the window. "What are you, fuckin' nuts? Didn't you see me coming? For chrissakes, what are you doing walking around up here? You're gonna get yourself killed!" She beings to roll her window back up, then stops halfway. "Say," she says. "You're not wandering numbly away from the scene of a terrible accident or anything like that, are you? I mean, should I be concerned?"

"Nothing like that," Jesus says, still smiling pleasantly. "I'm just trying to get a ride back to town. I walked up here, and now I don't feel like walking back down."

The girl snorts and shakes her head. "Crazy! Sounds like something *I'd* do." She reaches over to the passenger's side and flips the door lock. "Get in," she says. "I could use someone to talk to."

Jesus climbs into the vehicle, ducking low to keep from hitting His head. The inside of the car is much cooler than the road outside, the air-conditioner running at a sputtering full-blast. The floor of the car is littered with debris from six or seven different fast-food restaurants. "Excuse the mess," the girl says, shrugging, half-embarrassed, half daring Him to say something about her lifestyle. "I'm on the road a lot, don't get much chance to eat at home."

"Hey, doesn't bother me a bit," says Jesus, struggling with the seatbelt. "I'm just happy to be getting out of here."

"Well, I'm going all the way past Malibu, so I can drop you off just about anywhere. Just tell me when to stop." She reaches across to the seat behind Jesus and produces a black pouch full of cassette tapes. She drops it on His lap. "Here," she says, "pick something."

Jesus stares blankly at the pile of homemade tapes. He tries to read a few of the labels, but can't make out the cramped scribble-handwriting no matter how hard He tries. He gives up, pulls a tape out at random, and hands it to the girl. She squints at the tape, grunts, looking as though He has perhaps failed some sort of test, and pops it into the tape player.

"You can drop me off in Malibu," Jesus says after a bit. "I really don't have a destination. I'm just kind of traveling along the coast, exploring, I guess." He glances sideways at the girl, is relieved to see her grin.

"Crazy!" The car is going very fast now, whipping around the sharp turns going down the hill. "I'm Sheila, by the way. I'll be your captain, pilot, copilot and stewardess for the duration of the flight." She laughs maniacally, both hands wrapped firmly around the rubberized steering wheel. Jesus grips the strap of his shoulder harness, watching the speedometer soar up to fifty, sixty, seventy, eighty.

"I'm Jay," He manages, a little weakly. Yellow hills flash by at a frightening speed, the ground quickly rising and falling beside the car like the lines of an oscilloscope. He can feel the whole car wobble every time the wheels hit a small rock or dip into a pothole.

Jesus is standing in the soft shoulder of the Ventura Freeway, partly shaded by a withered magnolia scrub. Sheila stands next to her car, hands on hips, talking wildly to no one in particular. "If you drive slow, the car overheats, dummy!" she suddenly shouts, kicking the right front tire. "Ouch!" she says, collapsing on the ground, holding her injured foot. "You fucking asshole car! Fuck you, car!"

Jesus walks over to where the girl is sitting and squats down next to her. "Hey," He says. "It's okay. You just got to let the car cool down a bit, and then we can drive some more. It's okay."

"We need water!" Sheila snarls. "We don't have any goddamn water to put in the car. We're not fuckin' goin' anywhere!" She brushes the loose hair back from her face and glares at Jesus angrily. "What're you lookin' at?"

"You're getting a sunburn," says Jesus, softly. "Your face is all pink, and your eyes are a little puffy. You should get out of the road and sit in the shade. I'll push the car to the side of the road and join you in a moment."

Without waiting for her to respond, Jesus gets up and walks around to the driver's side of the car. He opens the door and turns the wheel to the right. In the rearview mirror He sees Sheila get up and obediently walk to the magnolia tree. She sits on the ground beneath the tree and watches Jesus push the car over to the shoulder of the road and up the shallow slope of the hill a little ways. He rolls down all of the car windows and opens the rear hatch.

"Sorry I yelled at you," Sheila says when He comes back to sit beside her. She has begun drawing a series of pictures in the dry earth with the sharp end of a stick, little whirls and stick figures and a three-dimensional box. "I just hate cars, that's all. I like to drive fast because the faster I get to my destination, the less time I have to sit in that damned car."

"I prefer walking, myself," Jesus says. He picks up a stick Himself and pokes it in the dirt. The stick stands upright by itself for a few seconds, then slumps back to the ground. He tries again in another spot with the same results.

"What are you doing?" Sheila asks. She leans closer to Jesus for a better look.

"Making a better tree for us to sit under," Jesus says, trying yet another spot. This time the stick stays upright for nearly a full minute before imperceptible shifts in the sand cause it to fall over again.

"You're a nut!" she says, clapping her hands and laughing. The color on her face has faded from pink to a light tan. "Oh, that's wonderful." She leans back a bit and pulls her knees up to her chest. She reaches into her shirt pocket and takes out a pack of cigarettes. She lights two cigarettes and passes one to Jesus.

Jesus takes the cigarette gratefully. It seems to have grown a little cooler, but that could have something to do with His present state of inactivity. He wipes clean the pictures of stick men and flowers and begins a new sketch, wavy lines and perfect circles. He takes a deep drag on His cigarette and closes His eyes for a moment.

"There was this guy I knew, a long time ago. Pete. Pete Myers. Went to school with him until his parents moved to another city. We kept in touch for a little while, then I got lazy and stopped writing." Jesus takes another long drag from His cigarette

"Pete and I used to ditch school together. We'd get stoned first thing in the morning and go hang out at this little patch of overgrown farmland at the edge of town. There were almost enough trees there to call it a forest. The whole time we were supposed to be in class we'd be playing War, and Urban Commando, and GI Joe. We had these big sticks that we'd pretend were guns, have little pieces of bark for knives and pistols. Fuckin' fourteen years old and we were still playing War."

"It sounds like fun," says Sheila. She rests her head on the tops of her knees and stares out at the hills in the distance, at the far-away ocean.

"It was. Anyway, one day we were out there, making idiots of ourselves, when we came across this girl lying in the middle of the field. She was about our age, maybe a little older, wearing blue jeans and a ripped-up T-shirt, and she was all curled in a little ball around a real gun. We thought she was dead at first, but she sat up real quick when we poked her and pointed the gun at us and said something like, 'Don't move, I'll shoot.'" Jesus shakes His head and absent-mindedly sketches out a stick figure with a top hat in the dirt.

"Turned out she had gone out there to kill herself. Something about her parents getting divorced and fighting over who would get custody of her, and some guy or another dumping her the day before, and her dog or cat getting run over by a car—a whole bunch of shit. Oh, and she was flunking some class as well. She had come out to the middle of our field to shoot herself, got scared, then decided to just lie there and will herself to die. She'd already been there a full night and part of a day when we showed up."

Jesus pauses and leans back against the stunted tree, watching Sheila out of the corner of His eye. Her eyes are still fixed on the ocean in the distance, the cigarette dangling between her fingers, a good inch-and-a-half of ash clinging to the end. Jesus draws a picture of an A-frame house next to the figure with the top hat, followed by a crude picture of a dog with big teeth. It is getting darker, the air growing even cooler. Crickets chirp in the long yellow grasses behind them. He is beginning to think He should have told the fishing story instead, when Sheila suddenly leaps to her feet.

"And what?" she shouts. "Then what? This isn't a story, dammit! What the hell happened to her? Did she kill herself? Did you all end up having sex together? What's the fucking point?!"

"There's no point, Sheila," Jesus says. "I guess I just felt like talking about someone I used to know, and someone I didn't really know at all. I'm pretty sure the girl didn't kill herself. People don't usually want to kill themselves. I think a lot of people kill themselves because they think they're supposed to. All they need is someone to come along and tell them they don't have to."

Sheila comes back and sits down beside Jesus. After a few minutes she leans her head against His shoulder and whispers, "How did you know?"

Jesus wakes up to early-morning sunlight pouring in through the cracked windshield of the '67 Chevy. The girl in the driver's seat moans, fighting hard against consciousness. Jesus reaches over and brushes the thin blond wisps of hair from her face.

"Jay?" She creaks her eyelids open and stares at Jesus through gummy lashes. "You're still here," she says, smiling. "Wow."

"Of course I'm still here. We got water in the car now. A truck driver pulled over during the night. He offered to give us a tow, but I told him we just needed water."

Sheila nods sleepily and turns the key in the ignition. The engine starts right up, as it always will from this day forward, without sputtering or rattling. "Nice car," she murmurs, patting the dashboard, and pulls out onto the road. The dying tree that provided them with shelter the day before has grown taller overnight, dark green leaves and fleshy white magnolia blossoms unfurling like tiny flags in the muted light.

"Did you sleep all right?" Sheila asks Jesus, passing Him a lit cigarette. Jesus thinks about refusing, remembering His promise to the other He, then decides to be polite and takes the cigarette. She continues without waiting for Him to respond. "I've fallen asleep here more times than I care to count," she says. "There aren't any springs in the seats." She punches the side of Jesus' seat lightly. "It's all foam rubber. My idea," she adds, beaming proudly.

"Very nice." Jesus shifts position, somewhat anxious. He is supposed to be some place else right now, and the car is not going in the right direction. At least it doesn't feel like it is.

Sheila notices His discomfort. "Hey," she says. "I appreciate you listening to me last night. I'm not in the habit of picking up hitchhikers in the first place, and I'm especially not in the habit of telling complete strangers my life story. I think I really needed someone to listen to me last night, and I'm glad I ran into you." They are at the bottom of the hill now, almost to the beach. "Can I buy you breakfast or something? I'm starving, so we've got to stop for food anyway."

"Sure."

Jesus isn't really hungry, but Sheila seems so eager to feed Him. The California coast stretches out before them, the Malibu peninsula far away and barely visible through the thick early-morning fog. A few surfers dot the clear green waves, bobbing like ducks just above the waterline. Jesus rolls down His window and breathes in the cool moist air. He can smell the rotting seaweed on the beach, the sweet sea salt, the faint trace of cities in the distance. He almost asks Sheila to stop the car right there and let Him out so He can walk the rest of the way.

"Look!" Sheila says, pointing to a little wooden shack just around the next corner. She pulls the car over to the side of the road and screeches to a dusty halt. "I wonder if it's even open yet. Have you ever eaten here before?" Jesus shakes His head. The smell of lard and potatoes frying reaches Him through the thick fog, hung there in front of Him as if trapped. He is suddenly very hungry after all. "Come on!" Sheila calls, climbing out of the car, gesturing for Him to follow her. "This place is great!"

The stand is located as close to the edge of a cliff as is safely possible, ruling out possible mud slides and floods. Waves crash loudly against the bottom of the cliff, hollowing the rock face a little each time they attack. There is already a small cave dug into the rock, barely visible from where Jesus is standing. A bleary-eyed fry cook greets the pair from inside the stand. "Man, are you two up early!" the cook says. "I just turned the stove on a couple minutes ago!"

"What do you feel like having?" Sheila asks, pulling her wallet out of her pocket and quickly rifling through the faded bills inside it. "Get anything you want."

Jesus scans the menu. At this point, everything looks good. He settles on a large rare hamburger with onions and green peppers ("At this time in the morning, man? You're crazy!") followed by a strawberry milkshake. To assuage His guilt at spending most of Sheila's money, He quickly heals a cluster of deep acne scars on the right side of her face. The miracles are coming easier, He notes. Sheila orders some sort of standard breakfast sandwich and an orange juice.

They sit at a wooden picnic table overlooking the ocean. Directly below them the waves strike the cliff face with such force that jets of sea spray splatter them lightly. Off in the distance the last dolphins of the morning go through their acrobatic routines one more time before heading off to deeper waters.

Jesus is halfway through His burger before He hears the child crying. Sheila notices it first.

She puts her drink down and walks over to the edge of the cliff. "Did you hear that?"

Jesus gets up and stands beside Her, peering down into the ocean. The sound is louder now, impossibly rising above the racket of water smashing into rock. No words, just one nearly continuous wail of terror, the voice warbling now and then as though the screamer were swallowing massive amounts of water.

An arm, a small black head, a bright blue windbreaker. Jesus sees the boy, stares uncomprehendingly for several seconds before realizing He's looking at a child. "Oh my God," moans Sheila, clutching at Jesus' arm. "We've got to do something!"

"Get the guy at the stand. Tell him to call the police. Hurry!" Jesus shakes her a little too roughly. She pulls away and stumbles toward the little shack. Jesus watches her retreat for a moment before turning back to the struggling child.

You can save him, says a little voice in Jesus' head. You could just climb down there and pull the kid out and carry him back up the cliff with you. Hey, You're the Messiah, right? Jesus shakes His head until His ears buzz. "There's got to be a better way," He says out loud. "There has to be." He lies down flat on the rock and inches as far as He can over the edge of the cliff, face down, trying to get a better look at the situation.

The child has both arms wrapped around a rock, clinging desperately. Jesus tries to get a look at the boy's face, tries to catch the child's attention, but there is too much confusion below. You can save him, the voice says again. He looks around, sees Sheila waving her arms excitedly at the bleary fry cook, looks back at the churning waves just beneath Him, at the small white hands fighting to keep a hold on the smooth wet rock. The morning rush hour has just begun, the winding road behind Him gradually filling with compact cars speeding to their destinations. No. He has been here before.

"I'm sorry," he says, then repeats himself, shouting this time, "I'm sorry! Please..." His voice trails off. The child seems to hear Him, turns to face Jesus full-on, and it's not the face of a child down there, not even the face of a human being, it's something so bright and powerful and beautiful that Jesus is momentarily blinded.... A test. Another fucking test.

When His eyesight returns the child is gone. Sheila is staring down at Him uncomprehendingly. "Hey, man," she says, finishing off the last of Jesus' strawberry milkshake. "Are you all right? Are you, like, an epileptic or something?"

"I'm fine." Jesus climbs slowly to His feet and brushes the sand off His clothes. "I'm just fine."

# Another Day

*By* S. Anand


It must be the birds that woke me. The sunlight makes filigreed patterns on the bed and wall. I turn over and see that Latha has already left for work. She always leaves before I wake.

Outside it is drizzling. On the street below, brightly colored umbrellas bob up and down as fresh-faced children head for school. Grumpy middle-aged men jostle with well-groomed college students at the bus stand. The sombre notes of All India Radio's morning news mingle with sinuous ragas announcing the beginning of another day. I stare up at the ceiling fan, its blades creaking with age, sending swirls of dust around the room. I find the dust immensely fascinating. On other quiet mornings like this I watch the particles moving slowly in the sunlight, heading in no particular direction, going round and round in irregular circles. Sometimes I try to follow an individual speck in its peregrinations, to observe it settle on a table, bed or windowsill. But its life seems circumscribed by the shaft of sunlight, its journey always ending at the boundary of light and darkness.

I drag myself out of bed and into the bathroom. I look at myself in the cracked mirror, a wedding present. I see a brown face mottled with the traces of childhood smallpox, a stubble of graying hair on each cheek, a wrinkled forehead, small dull eyes, a nose with no particular shape, thick lips. I open my mouth and look at my yellowing teeth and tongue. I suddenly feel sick. I probably have an ulcer, to have a tongue this color. Or cancer. I try to remember how I looked five years ago when I married Latha. I cannot recall looking any better than this. I wonder why she agreed to marry me. To be sure, it was an arranged marriage and I had a good job at that time. But she could have said no. She was well educated and beautiful. She could have found a thousand men more handsome. True, I'm more broad-minded than most husbands. I have let her pursue her own career and interests. I don't mind her mingling with male colleagues. And even since I lost my job I have been very gentle with her, not allowing my own inner turmoil to burden her.

I finish brushing my teeth and go to the kitchen to fix a cup of coffee. Then I step outside to pick up the newspaper the delivery boy has left. I pull my easy chair over to the window and start to sip my coffee. Outside, the rush-hour hubbub has subsided. The only footfalls are from the odd office worker hurrying late to work. I scan the classified section, looking for any suitable job. For the past two months I have not found a single listing I could apply for, and today is no exception. Hydraulics engineers are not a hot commodity in today's market. I move on to other sections of the newspaper and take in my fill of yesterday's killings, riots, accidents and bombings.

A loud car horn jolts me awake. For a few minutes I am not sure where I am. Outside, the sun is blazing furiously. I can hear children returning home from school for lunch. I walk over to the bedroom window and look out at the neighbor's house. I can see directly into their bedroom. Around this time of day the wife has her bath and dries herself near the window. But today I am not lucky. The shutters are tightly shut.

I think about Latha. When was the last time I saw her naked? It is more than two years since we made love. Even before that our sex life was sporadic. I had come to feel that she was no longer interested. We talked about it a couple of times, but our talks didn't seem to help. And then I must have begun to lose interest as well. I am not the type to force myself on a woman. When Latha comes home from work she's very tired. Then she has dinner to cook. By nine o'clock she is fast asleep.

The cold shower clears my head. I stand under it for a long time, until I start to feel dizzy. I carefully step out and towel myself dry. I feel fresh now and ready for the day. I go to the bedroom and put on clean clothes. Then I go to the kitchen and eat the rice and vegetables Latha has left for me. After lunch I go out for my customary walk. As I lock the door I start to think about my previous job and my prospects for finding another. I wonder what has happened to all the résumés I sent out. Of course, I could take a government job, but I don't want to vegetate for the rest of my life doing nothing of any consequence. There must be plenty of multinational companies in need of someone with my skills.

I feel better now that I am out of the house. This time of day there is hardly anyone on the street and a pleasant breeze is blowing. A few steps down the street I hear some yelps from behind a big garbage bin. I walk around it to see what's happening. I find two dogs there in the midst of a frenzied copulation. I have seen the bitch before, a flea-bitten mongrel, foraging for food near this same bin. The dog is a new-comer. Then I notice something strange. The dog has mounted the fe-male and is trying hard to consummate the act, but he is not able to do so. I move around to get a better view of the situation and then, like a hard slap in my face, I see his limp organ hanging useless as he tries in vain to quench his desire. I see the misery in his eyes, and I am filled with disgust. I rush back to the house and vomit.

Something wakes me from a deep sleep. Latha is standing over me, looking worried. She must have smelled the vomit in the bath-room. I tell her I must be sick. I do have a splitting headache. She brings me a tablet and makes me swallow it. Then she covers me with a blanket, turns off the light and leaves. I hear noises from the kitchen as she prepares the evening meal. Soon I hear the television. I lie in bed staring into the darkness. I drift off to sleep again and see the bitch cowering behind the garbage bin, her eyes glinting in my flashlight. I move closer to her, but she makes no effort to get away. I run my flash beam over her ugly brown coat, torn by numerous encounters with other dogs. She wags her short stump of a tail feebly. On her leg there is an open wound with flies all around it. She looks up at me meekly. I grip the long knife that Latha and I received as a wedding gift. In one movement I grasp the bitch's head with my left hand and with the other slice open her neck. Beside the flashlight lying on the ground I see dark blood flowing into the dust.

The birds wake me yet again. This time it is crows making a racket just outside the window. Beside me Latha is still asleep. It must be Saturday. I get out of bed and go to the window. There is a light mist, but no rain. By the garbage bin I see dozens of crows feasting on some-thing. Others are squatting on electric cables overhead. I turn back to-wards the bed. Latha is still sleeping. I go into the bathroom and look at myself in the cracked mirror. Today, I think, I will shave.

# London Through the Magic Eye

*By* Ramond Ramcharitar

What is unnerving about London are the security cameras everywhere. Around Downing St, around Buckingham Palace, on the buses, in the seediest train stations. More unnerving is the apathy to them. The litigious British psyche, it seems, has negotiated a way around, or through, the cameras and their implications of interrupted privacy, sensory invasion, undefined uneasiness. (Though the very unease is foreign, traceable to American-inspired notions of inalienable rights attached to personal privacy, and recurrences of this differentiation in British-outsider relations appear to be infinite.)

To the outsider—and for once, all outsiders: the American, the Third Worlder, the Easterner, the European—the casual surveillance is a truly alien object, initially invisible to the visitor, eliciting a kind of self-consciousness at first realisation, only later, and then only for some, clarified into a vague discomfort.

In all likelihood, the others' responses divide at the Atlantic: American outrage at unauthorised surveillance; European resignation; Asian stoicism to statist intrusiveness. But for the Third Worlder, once detached from the phantasmagoria of American television, what remains at the prospect of being watched is a mildly pleasant relief.

Since the end of colonialism, what has defined the countries of the South (in Africa, the Caribbean), you must realise, is the absence of watchers. There remains no sense of ubiquitous authority or order. And of late, there's been an overwhelming sensation of the consequences—fantastic political corruption and thievery; the evil of ordinary men living in a society dissolving the notions that hold it together: whispers of devolution to a primal past. No cameras: nobody watches, nobody cares.

Such uncertainty is virtually unknown in England. There is the institutional continuity of the thousand-year history, of course, but something else: a centuries-old sureness, which has osmosed into the collective life. England, to an outsider, is a place so sure of its existence that even the threat of invasion, psychic or otherwise—such fear as led America to enshrine the rights of the individual—is unimportant.

Even the clannish instinct of the British to rebel against threats to their existence has begun to atrophy, leaving an indifference to the smaller, more insidious moments of history. So what if someone looks? Life continues—and hardly in the wretched state Orwell foretold. Life, in its way, even inverts the intimidation of being watched by unknown eyes. American counter-culture has long ridiculed the ethos of the inalienability, or even the desirability, of the wholly private life.

Surveillance has become, rather than an instrument of invasion, an instrument of perversion. Rupert Murdoch's US-based Fox Network and others have, in the past few years, made surveillance the absinthe of the jaded masses—with shows like *Cops*, *Trauma*, *America's Most Wanted*, *Jerry Springer*—where the viewer accompanies the law, or the host (the surrogate superego of the underclass), on sundry invasions of homes, privacy, lives and often the liberty of the invaded.

We can only speculate on the morbid curiosity and stultified existences that fuelled the industry, of course, but worse was to come. A few years ago, out of anonymity and without preamble or theoretical precedent, economics student Jennifer Ringely trained a "homecam" on herself and, transmitting through the Internet, let virtually anyone interested into the minutiae of her life: her menstruation, her sex life, her sleep. The "Jennicam" phenomenon has now become a thousands-strong Internet industry, including sexual liaisons, childbirth, death. From my life into your home: Welcome.

(Paradoxically, it's unlikely that the average British student would entertain such a thing. Even more curious, though, is the schism between what the British see of the real world and what of the world is transmitted to them: no inhibitions at being examined at length, but a certain coolness at examining others' lives in such detail.)

The most effective conveyance of Western civilisation anywhere is American television. Cultural generalisations, ideas, even self-images are formed in relation or opposition to the unreal (and even covert counter-cultural) insinuations planted in phatic situation comedies. An entire generation forms self-images from *Beverly Hills 90210* and *Baywatch*. And every so often, whatever is left of the feminist movement rails against the impossible and frustrating standards engendered there: everybody wanting to fuck Pamela Anderson or Brad Pitt creates a culture of detachment from the real.

Perhaps Britons' ideas of their lives are not so easily defined, but their indifference to the way they are seen begs the question: how do they see themselves? British television is a marvel of opposites—of sophistication/unsophistication, the sublime lying alongside the bathetic. It will nonchalantly show male frontal nudity (always riskier than female nudity), while maintaining enough reserve to essay a "serious" examination of the pornography industry (*Sex and Shopping*). Then, in the same breath, show *God's Gift* (on BBC 1), a dating game for seniors: old geezers croaking out "Unforgettable" to a group of giggling grannies. And as the irony never comes, it strikes you: they're having fun.

*The Game Show* hosts, far from the slick, scripted badinage cued at their American counterparts, banter with each other like the office wiseass having a go at the company awards function. "And now here is the chairman to present the awards for...what was it again, Delilah? Sleeping in the store room...no need, mate, let's just 'and it hover to Edgar...." Then *Comedy Nation* (BBC 2) features surreally funny segments like "Ducks of Doom," "League Against Tedium," and "Buller," a 400 lb yobbo who knocked out a bull once using his gangsta-midget friend, Mikki, in a matador get-up as a decoy.

Clearly, the dialectics of public communication (which invoke such principles as freedom of expression) elsewhere do not figure in England or figure with a radical difference. Freedom here is an operational concept, not a principle that generates ineluctable moral problematics—as does the mythic overarching idea of American "freedom," the viability of which they neurotically and futilely attempt to prove. (Thus the existence of the Ku Klux Klan and the Nation of Islam; but the struggle for the ideal is to no avail: the insistence on principle is constantly disproved by national humiliations, succumbing to such emotional immaturity as the Clinton impeachment scandal.)

If television transmissions can be used as an indicator, Brits are a stoic bunch, satisfied for the most part with their lot. What dissatisfactions they do have they see to be part of their process, viewing them with resignation, if without bland Northern European élan, then with an interesting Anglo-Saxon roughness.

The argument, that the stoic acceptance of surveillance in his life defines the Briton's rough national character, though, will hold only so much weight. Sometimes roughness is just brutality: In America, the governance of the principle of equality, rather than the dynamic of traditionalist hermeneutics, would have exacted a far more just price for the death of Stephen Lawrence, the black teenager killed by British police in 1997. The killing uncovered what British blacks had known all their lives: the traditions of empire tend, like every other human impulse, to randomness and cruelty when order is threatened.

# The Shadow

*By* Abbas Zaidi

The first of every month was a time of great tension and excitement on Blessed Companions of the Prophet Street. Those who had the money for their rents gloated over Khurram Pig's (everybody called him "Pig") abusive treatment of the more impecunious tenants. Some smart alecks, despite not being able to pay on time, got round Pig by relating to him some neighborhood sex story in which he could be a potential participant.

But this time it was to be altogether different. It was the first of October, and every tenant was anticipating some fun. At the end of Blessed Companions of the Prophet Street—the entire street was owned by our landlord—a big stage had been carefully prepared and about a hundred seats neatly arranged. Khurram Pig had let it be known that there would be a lavish dinner preceded by devotional songs followed by a *mujra* of Multan's best dancing girls. He had also announced that the tenants could pay their rents on the seventh, a one-week reprieve. "It is a great day in our lives," he said, but he did not say why.

When I came out onto the street that day expecting some free food and fun, I found instead a commotion in which Baqir's voice was raised above all the others. "I will burn the whole Multan University! I will burn the whole country if I have to! All these mother-fucking pseudo-intellectuals are just jealous of our beloved doctor! Bring me a man in the entire universe who is worth the dust off our doctor's feet!" he was yelling in his high-pitched grating voice.

I pushed a few spectators aside for a better view. All the tenants were there, along with a number of other people from the neighborhood. Khurram Pig was present as well, looking nervous, his Turkish fez tending toward the right side of his head. In the center of the crowd Shamsuddin, our landlord, sat in a high-back upholstered chair. Baqir was standing nearby as if guarding him. Shamsuddin had a serene look on his face and kept telling Baqir in a quiet voice to calm down. "You can't change the world, my dear! Truth-seekers are always undermined. The Shias curse three out of the four pious Caliphs of Islam. The Jews disobeyed Allah again and again and pestered every single one of His apostles. Look what happened to the Prophet Himself. People called him a false prophet! Allah's blessing be on him! Amen!"

"Amen!" Baqir shouted, along with the rest, while Shamsuddin's face oozed stoicism. "You are a saint, but I myself cannot take it anymore! I have requested you many times to migrate to America where they will properly honor you. This unfortunate country does not deserve a genius like you!"

"If every competent person leaves Pakistan, the place will collapse and the Shias will take over," Shamsuddin replied patiently, his head bowed, his reading glasses resting in his cupped hands.

"Then you should lead a *jihad* against the Shias. I tell you..."

While Baqir continued his invectives I pulled Tahir, one of my roommates, away from the crowd to ask what was up. What he told me was this: Shamsuddin had obtained a Ph.D., in the philosophy of science, by correspondence from a university based on some Pacific island. It was in celebration of that Ph.D. that this grand function was being staged. Shamsuddin had invited the Multan University professors and important city dignities to the function, but none had shown up. Some professors had even called Shamsuddin's Ph.D. a fake.

While Tahir was still telling me this, Baqir shouted, "Down with the conspirators! Let us celebrate Doctor Shamsuddin's great academic victory!"

Khurram Pig told us tenants to hurry up, and we quickly sat down in the seats in front of the stage. Everyone else there was a local: laborers, sweepers, stray-dog killers, grass-cutters and drug addicts. They could not read a word, but the prospect of free food and fun had excited them beyond their limits, making the event very lively.

The promised musical shows never took place. Baqir made a lofty speech about Shamsuddin's genius and greatness for Pakistan. He would have gone on forever, but after a bit Shamsuddin raised his hand and Baqir abruptly fell silent. Then an old man, a janitor in a nearby factory, stood up and began praising Shamsuddin. "Now we have our own doctor. We will not have to go to the city for treatment. I request our respected doctor not to charge us like other doctors, as we are poor. I wish he had become doctor before now and saved some of us who died before their time," at which all the other locals applauded enthusiastically. Khurram Pig gave us tenants a threatening look, and we also applauded.

Shamsuddin said that he was too busy with his scholarly research to start a clinic for them ("Maybe some other time.") Then he talked at length about Pakistan's need for scholars, his fascination with the philosophy of science, his four-year stay in England, the ignorance of the Multan University professors, the Jewish-Shia conspiracy against Pakistan and Islam and, finally, his travels abroad where he had got opportunities to learn and teach. Whenever Shamsuddin paused, Baqir raised his hand and the local people clapped. Then Khurram Pig raised his own hand and we tenants did the same.

The food was modest, but we fell on it like hungry animals. Then Baqir left the stage and slipped the linen cloth off a tiny brand-new car parked nearby, an 800 cc Suzuki. Everone oohed and aahed. Then a tractor appeared to which was attached a long, battered trolley. Baqir placed a flower wreath and a five-rupee-bill wreath over Shamsuddin's head and held open the back door of the car. Shamsuddin squeezed in, and Baqir assumed the driver's seat. Khurram Pig ordered the locals and the tenants onto the trolley, and our procession started towards the city center, Shamsuddin's car in the lead. Throughout the journey Khurram Pig called out prompts to which we replied in unison:

"Who will outlive all?"

"Doctor Shamsuddin!"

"Doctor Shamsuddin is the Lion, the rest are...?"

"Sheep! Sheep!"

"Time and tide wait only for...?"

"Doctor Shamsuddin!"

Throughout the ride Baqir's hand remained stuck out of the car window, making a "V" sign. The procession paused near the Multan University Staff Colony so that we could shout, "Down with the pseudo-intellectuals! Down with the conspirators! Down with the Jewish agents!" A number of professors appeared along with their families and some curious passers-by. I slumped down in a rear seat of the trolley in order not to be seen.

Suddenly Baqir sprang out of the Suzuki and flung open its back door. With considerable grace Raiz climbed out as well, raised his hand in appreciation towards us, made a "V" sign with the other hand towards the University people, took off his wreath and threw it in their direction. Then he got back into the car, and the procession started back to Blessed Companions of the Prophet Street.

The next day was Friday. In the late morning Khurram Pig herded all the tenants over to the mosque where a number of locals were already sitting on the carpeted floor. As was his custom every Friday, Shamsuddin was seated on a chair up on the podium. But even though the mosque's prayer room was full after our arrival, he did not start his sermon. Soon a few men arrived in the company of Baqir. Khurram Pig stood up and greeted them. They were strangers to me, but most of the congregation seemed to know who they were. Shamsuddin introduced them as local public school teachers. One of them, Haji Pervaiz, had worked with Shamsuddin in Borneo, and they had come to congratulate Shamsuddin on his Ph.D.

Shamsuddin then gave a long sermon which was actually a synopsis of what he said was his Ph.D. dissertation. He spoke both in Urdu and English. All the locals and most of the tenants were unable to understand a word. To me it sounded like a terrible muddle. But whenever he paused the entire congregation applauded, prompted by the raised hands of Baqir and Khurram Pig respectively. Shamsuddin announced that in a month's time he would be going to the UK to discuss with the relevant authorities the possibility of setting up a Multan campus of Cambridge University under his own rectorship. Finally, after the Friday prayer, Shamsuddin climbed down from his throne and retired to the Sufi Restaurant at the end of the Blessed Companions of the Prophet Street to discuss some academic matters with the public school people.

Blessed Companions of the Prophet Street was situated in the outer suburbs of Multan, an extremely backward village with very few civic amenities. There was no drainage system, and the Blessed Street was soft with filth. But it was entirely owned by Shamsuddin. He made good money in Borneo and with it had bought a piece of the Multan suburbs where he had constructed this little real estate empire. Baqir, his childhood friend, was from the same village as himself, a hamlet about four hundred miles from Multan.

There were fourteen double-storey houses on both sides of the Street. At one end was a small Aurengzeb mosque and at the other the small Sufi Restaurant, both owned by Shamsuddin. The general state of the dwellings was very bad: dilapidated rooms, ineffably dirty communal toilets, moss-ridden bathrooms. No one was allowed to use electricity after seven in the evening. Even so, it was convenient for some us to live there, as it took only a few minutes to get to the city center or the university by bus or van. And the rents were very cheap.

Shamsuddin lived on the ground floor of one of the houses. Baqir lived on the floor above with his wife. Baqir's wife observed complete traditional purdah. No one saw her face or even her hands, because she always wore black gloves. She led such a cloistered life that no one, not even a woman friend, was ever seen visiting her. Khurram Pig lived somewhere outside the immediate neighborhood, but he was present on the Street from morning till night. He was responsible for collecting rents and kicking out undesirable and deadbeat tenants, and he did so in the most disgraceful manner. He also kept all the rooms overcrowded by adding new tenants at will and by requiring existing tenants to move into other rooms, seemingly at a whim. The tenants were struggling students, underpaid clerks, unemployed youth from villages looking for jobs in Multan, and scores of indigent nonentities. No unmarried woman or Shia was allowed even to be seen on the Street, and every new tenant was required to swear that he was not a Shia. But soon I discovered that most of the students there were in fact Shias, like myself.

Every tenant, especially those who were being kicked out of their dwellings, added to the stock of stories about Shamsuddin and Baqir. Those two, along with Khurram Pig, were always the hot topics of conversation. Like every other prospective tenant, I had been interviewed by Shamsuddin in his library in the back of the Aurengzeb Mosque (named after the eighteenth century Mogul King who persecuted Shias). There were two glass cabinets filled with "O" level books, dictionaries and texts on topics ranging from chemistry to literature. During the interview Shamsuddin freely dropped literary terms, watching me expectantly each time he did so. I told him that, despite being an English literature student at Multan University, my grasp of the subject was not half as good as his own. He accepted me immediately as a tenant.

Every evening Shamsuddin's tenants and the locals gathered in the Sufi Restaurant because the electricity restriction did not apply there. That was also where Shamsuddin held court. He always had a book or magazine in his hand and talked incessantly about every topic under the sun. Baqir either arrived with him or showed up shortly thereafter.

He never sat on the same level as Shamsuddin and usually preferred to stand behind him. But at the slightest indication from Shamsuddin he pulled up a small chair and sat down, his hands locked together in his lap and his head cast down. Occasionally he looked up into Shamsuddin's face but only to support a point that his mentor was making, nodding in approval or shaking it to deplore what Shamsuddin was criticising.

"I see innumerable vices about," Shamsuddin would say, and Baqir would look around suspiciously. "That makes me angry." Baqir's face flushed and his lips began to tremble in anger. "But when I ponder on some finer aspects of life, like newborn babies or my own intellectual pursuits, I experience a great sense of happiness," and Baqir's face glowed with happiness, his eyes shining ecstatically. "But the point is that the Shias, being in the minority, cannot take over the government. That's why they are conspiring with the Jews to capture Islamabad," at which Baqir's hands looked like someone restraining himself from doing some terrible violence.

"Can you not form an army of Islam and destroy them?" Baqir asked. And Shamsuddin said, "We must wait for the right time. Let their friends, the Jews, destroy the West and weaken themselves beyond repair. Then we shall deal with them all....

"In London I was solicited by many women. At times they entered my bathroom naked." At which Baqir blushed crimson and could not even bear to raise his eyes. "But I preserved my virginity. My personal philosophy of life is very rigorous," and a proud, victorious Baqir shot us a victorious look and then stared adoringly at his master.

But Baqir was not merely a passive supporter. Sometimes Shamsuddin broke off in the middle of his homily, gave Baqir a meaningful look and his assistant would take over for him.

"What," Shamsuddin said one day after the Ph.D. procession "can I say about the Multan University?" and glanced at Baqir.

"That third-rate university? Where the only thing the professors do is collect their salaries and have a nice time with the female students? And look at the Shias! They are taking over. This will become a Shia University."

"But less than one percent of the teachers are Shia," I said. "I know because I study there."

Baqir stared at me furiously, but before he could say or do anything Shamsuddin added quietly, "No, they are actually in majority. They pretend not to be Shias, but actually they are working against

Pakistan."

"Yes, they are hiding their identity!" Baqir shouted. "Doctor Shamsuddin is right. How dare you challenge him!"

"Calm down," Shamsuddin told him. "He is new and does not know that the Shias are imitating the Jews' tactics." Shamsuddin gave me a kindly look, and then Baqir smiled at me as well.

"There might be some Shias amongst our tenants!" Baqir said.

Shamsuddin darted a suspicious look at Khurram Pig.

"I shall kick them back into their mothers' wombs," Khurram Pig shouted.

Shamsuddin laughed. "Yes! The bastards!"

As the tenants before us did, we gave various names to the relationship between Shamsuddin and Baqir. At first Baqir was called "Shamsuddin's dog" for his faithfulness. "My friendship with Shamsuddin is the most beautiful thing that has ever happened in my life! I shall continue to serve him as long as I have the last drop of blood in my muscles!"

For his womanish expressions of love for Shamsuddin, we called Baqir "Shamsuddin's wife." Whenever we saw them together we whispered about "the odd couple." If one of them was absent we whispered that the wife/husband was missing. But that did not last long because Baqir was married, while Shamsuddin was not. Besides, Shamsuddin was thin, bald and clean-shaven; Baqir was well built, hairy and had a beard. Shamsuddin was over fifty and Baqir was in his mid-forties. Although Baqir's wife observed purdah and no one had ever seen her, some of us seriously and half-seriously speculated that, given Baqir's obsequiousness, Shamsuddin must be sleeping with Baqir's wife. For a while that idea became very popular with the tenants. But Baqir's demeanor in the presence of his wife was quite macho. Whenever he went out with her, he walked a few steps in front, the mark of male dominance, his head held high and his chest expanded, making him look like a very different Baqir from the dog-like sycophant we knew. We all respected Baqir's wife for being a purdah-observing woman, a mark of honor and pride for a woman in an Islamic society.

After the Ph.D. celebration we finally settled on a permanent name for Baqir: "Shadow."

"Why hadn't Shamsuddin married, and why was he so much against the Shias and the Jews?" were the two questions that we Shias used to ask each other in private.

Twice a year Shamsuddin went abroad for "research." At that time Baqir would also leave town and go to his village with his wife. Shortly after the Ph.D. affair, Shamsuddin went to the UK and Baqir to his village, and so we had Khurram Pig all to ourselves. To our amazement we discovered that he had a bachelor's degree in physics and liked to drink alcohol. Almost all of us tenants drank, so he became our comrade. Then, one evening while some other tenants and myself were drinking cheap whiskey with him, we made another shocking discovery: He was an Ahmedi! The Ahmedis were even more persecuted and more despised than Shias. Under some circumstances Shamsuddin might have tolerated a Shia; but having an Ahmedi on his Street was out of the question. And yet, there was Khurram Pig, working for him!

For as long as Shamsuddin and Baqir were away—about a month—Khurram Pig joined us every evening, drinking alcohol and revealing secret after secret. He said that he had to pretend to be anti-Shia and anti-Jewish because he did not want to lose his job, even though Shamsuddin had not paid him a penny for years. But he was clever enough to get even by putting up tenants without keeping any records. He told us that Shamsuddin was once given a government-sponsored "backward area uplift scholarship" to study in London for a B.Sc. Some of his teachers and classmates there had been Jews and Shias. He spent four years trying unsuccessfully to get a degree while everyone else passed their own. He was sure he had failed only because the Jewish teachers were anti-Islamic and anti-Pakistani. When he returned he did a master in science by correspondence from some foreign university and applied for a teaching position in Multan University. The validity of his degree was challenged by a competing candidate who happened to be a Shia. Shamsuddin's application was rejected, and the other man got the job.

Khurram Pig also told us that Shamsuddin was married a long time ago, but soon after the marriage his wife eloped with a Shia. "And now he says he goes abroad for research. Bullshit! He visits foreign brothels for sex, which he cannot do in this country," Pig said. We all laughed, and so did Khurram Pig.

It was a month since Shamsuddin and Baqir had gone away. As the winter was approaching its coldest part and examination time was drawing near, we the student tenants decided to go see a movie before buckling down to our studies. Khurram Pig decided to accompany us to a late show. It was about one in the morning when we returned from the cinema. As our auto-rickshaw pulled into the Street, a taxi entered from the opposite direction. Shamsuddin and Baqir got out and, while the taxi driver was offloading their luggage, the two of them approached us. Shamsuddin demanded an explanation for our presence on the street at such a late hour. We explained to him the circumstances for our unusual behavior.

"If I ever see you out again at this time of night you are out of here," he said.

All of a sudden a very nervous Khurram Pig asked, "Where is your wife, Mr Baqir?"

"You worry about your own!" Baqir shouted back at him.

Next day the entire Street returned to its ugly self. Khurram Pig became again the same malicious law-enforcer. On the third day after his return from Cambridge, Shamsuddin called all the tenants together in the mosque and announced that his visit was a "total success," as the university had agreed to set up a campus in Multan. We students congratulated him and requested that he allow us to use electricity after seven because of our examinations, and he graciously consented. Meanwhile it started to rain. It rained for the whole week—such an unusual event in Multan! The cold became unbearable. Even in late afternoon we all remained tucked away in our rooms.

One of those evenings Khurram Pig came to visit me. Besides my friend Tahir, two other students were also present.

"Do you know Shamsuddin and Baqir have quarreled!"

We were shocked. "You are lying," Tahir said.

"I swear upon Allah they have! I overheard them exchanging hot and indecent words. I bet it is due to Baqir's wife. You know, this time Baqir has not brought her back with him from the village. Shamsuddin must have tried to molest her! Didn't I tell you Baqir is a wife beater? Many times in the evening I hear her moan. I am sure that Baqir got suspicious of her and Shamsuddin having an affair," Tahir said.

We did not believe him. But for days we did not see Shamsuddin and Baqir together. Despite the cold I went to the Sufi Restaurant to spy on them, but neither turned up. By now all the tenants knew what was going on, and the two men's failure to appear in their usual haunt confirmed our suspicions. One day one of the tenants did spot Shamsuddin and rushed to tell us. We saw a very depressed-looking man sitting in an armchair in front of the mosque. Next afternoon we saw Baqir sitting alone on the pavement outside the Sufi Restaurant.

That same evening Khurram Pig told us he had overheard Baqir soliloquizing, "All the great books Shamsuddin reads, nothing is left for us! What kind of justice is it?" which puzzled us greatly.

A bit later we heard someone screaming in the street. As we rushed out we saw Baqir running about in the fog, beating his chest and head.

"Doctor Shamsuddin is dead!"

It was an unusually cold morning, but I felt my entire body begin to sweat. It was the first time a resident of the Street had died.

Soon everyone was out on the street, even the locals. We tried to console Baqir. "It is Allah's will! Who can defy Him?"

"But why our Doctor? He was the gentlest man alive? Why him?"

It was quite some time before Baqir calmed down. Two of the locals went into Shamsuddin's house and brought his body to the prayer hall of the mosque where we all saw his calm face for the last time. Later we offered the prayer for the dead. Then a tenant who worked in the transport office arranged for an ambulance to take Shamsuddin's body back to his village.

By now Khurram Pig had arrived. He offered to accompany Baqir to Shamsuddin's village, but Baqir refused, saying there were hundreds of people in the village who would look after the remains.

Two months later when Shamsuddin's brother came to dispose of his brother's property he told us that Baqir had joined some religious group and gone to Kashmir to participate in a *jihad* against the Indian army. We never heard from him again.

After Baqir left, a kind of depression settled over the Street. For hours on end we talked about the futility of life and the certainty of death. We praised Shamsuddin for his generosity, and Baqir as well, especially for his loyalty. But life goes on, and eventually things returned to normal.

Late in the evening about a week after Baqir had gone, Khurram Pig barged into our room looking very distressed. He said that he had smelt something burning in Shamsuddin's house. "Maybe Baqir did not switch off all the lights, or a heater even!"

We decided to check the house. We took as many tenants as possible in order to save us from a possible problem for breaking the lock without Baqir's permission. When we reached Shamsuddin's house we did not smell anything, but we were so worried that we broke the lock anyway and went in.

It was dark inside, and for some reason we were all very frightened. We switched on all the lights and began searching for smoke from one room to another. We found nothing amiss downstairs, so we went up into what we believed to be Baqir's apartment. The doors were all unlocked except for one, which we had to break open. We were immediately struck by some alien fragrance. "A woman's room!" Khurram Pig shouted. We switched on the lights and saw that the walls were covered with maps and souvenirs from London, Amsterdam, Bangkok, Manila, Kuala Lumpur. There was a large poster over the double bed which seemed to be an advertisement for condoms available in many different colors. To one side of the bed, on the floor, were scattered female wigs in different colors and styles. In a corner there were several pairs of pantyhose. There was neither smoke nor any burning smell.

We were about to leave when Khurram Pig suddenly jerked open a cupboard, and panties, bras and mini-skirts came flying down onto the floor. He pulled open another cupboard, and this time a bundle of some kind fell out. He ripped it open, and a cascade of photographs fell out: naked Chinese, African, Indian and Caucasian women. The last cupboard was stuffed with women's clothes. He rummaged through it and came up with a big album full of snapshots. He sat down on the bed with it, opened it and declared, "Baqir's wife was more beautiful than a fairy!"

We all flocked around to see the pictures. They seemed to have been taken in front of famous tourist attractions all around the world. In each of them Baqir's wife was wearing a provocative dress: leaning against the railing of London Bridge; posing in front of Singapore's Changi Airport, a Manila casino, a Bangkok nightclub, an Amsterdam bistro. In many of them she was sitting on Baqir's lap, and she seemed to wear almost as many different wigs as there were photographs, her face heavily made up with rouge and lipstick.

Then, as if he knew exaclty where to find it, Khurram Pig suddenly pulled a picture out from a hidden pocket in the back of the album. It had been taken in Trafalgar Square. In it Shamsuddin was sitting in Baqir's lap. Baqir's hand was on Shamsuddin's head, holding a red wig in place. The smile on Shamsuddin's face was the same as the one in all the other pictures we had seen.

# The Waters of April

*By* Jojo Malig

A stick, a stone...you know the rest of the song. The cold season has come and gone, and my sweater remains unused in my closet. Before the cold season that never was, was the typhoon season that never had a single typhoon. What happened was the summer of '97 connected with the summer of '98 to form one long continuous summer, drying up dams all over the country and wreaking havoc on crops. Meanwhile, on the other side of the planet, tornadoes turned more murderous than normal and California barely survived its wettest month on record. What's going on here? I can't recall a warmer February—or a warmer January, for that matter. The patch of bermuda grass in our back yard has prematurely browned, and the potted poinsettia has expired, perhaps wondering during its last dying moments why the air was so hot when it was supposed to be winter.

All the Valentine's Days of years past were chilly enough for romance, but this one was all dust and sweat. The temperature kept climbing, and it was only February. I dreaded to think how hot March and April might be. And then...rain. It was a Sunday, I think. Here in Angeles City, the cold wind carried the scent of it at twilight time, and I knew instantly it was pouring somewhere. As it turned out, Clark Field was the lucky beneficiary of the unseasonable downpour. Like a sponge, the parched land quickly absorbed the water, and people rushed indoors, then went to their windows to watch the water with disbelief. They had forgotten how rain looked, how it smelled, how it sounded and felt. The clouds continued to empty, dumping more water than the earth needed to satisfy its thirst. It felt like a benediction. The next day, the brown grass miraculously turned green, and the air smelled of moist soil.

There would be no dust all that day, because the sun hardly shone

198

as the rain clouds stayed overhead. It would rain again, in Angeles and in Manila and who knew where else.

But today, the heat is back, reminding me that summer is just beginning—the long hot Philippine summer, a summer like no other. But I was not afraid anymore. The deadly grip of El Nino was slackened by that week's triumphant rain, and now I have faith that there's still water, if not on earth, at least in heaven.

## Wet Sprockets

Every August in Pampanga province the frogs come out. This means nothing to anyone who hasn't heard their deafening chorus in moonlit eastern swamps. In the spring, they all gather around bodies of water, thousands of them in thousands of swamps, calling out for mates. The sound is not unlike the daytime chorus of cicadas in other parts of the country.

It's a feverish high-pitched throbbing mass of sound that gets so loud and intense that on certain roads in Ithaca it pierces through closed windows and engine noise and Nine Inch Nails on the tape player. If you listen closely you can make out individual chirps as well, but the overall effect is that of a constant, vibrating chorus. It's impossible to get away from the din, but to get the full effect you have to pick your spot carefully. My favorite place is a small pond near the research park. You drive out on Warren Road on a moonlit night, take a right onto the dirt road right after the golf course, and drive slowly uphill for a quarter mile. There the road drops off into a little hollow and a low-lying fog. And the sound is suddenly on top of you, rattling the car windows.

You drive past the hollow to the lot by the stables, and park. Walk past the snorting horses along the split-rail fence, then head back down into the cool dark hollow. To the left of the road is the pond. In wintertime I used to skate over it while doing my periphery-of-the-golf-course run. But in spring the water is high, and in leaky old wellies you can only walk up to the water's edge where murky water meets spongy soil.

Nature worship has never been my thing. I'm a lousy camper, I can't name any of the plants or birds or rocks in the woods where I grew up. I hate being bitten by bugs. Nor do I collect stuff. The only reason I ever venture into the great outdoors is to get away or to metaphorically roll around in the long grass nature provides, not to cut it up into its constituent parts or embalm, analyze and name it. I want to breathe and feel it without thinking, because thinking ruins it.

I once made the mistake of going to the frog pond with some other scientists. They showed up in hip boots and armed with specimen jars and maglites, jabbering about species and populations and sexual selection. They talked and laughed their way through the muck, not hearing a thing. Shut up, I kept thinking, for God's sake, shut up and listen.

At the edge of the pond the sound is overwhelming. It's a swelling wall coming at you from all sides. It's only gradually you notice there are three or four different voices of frogs singing: the low rolling croaks coming off the surface of the water; the warbling mid-tone melodies that seem to fly across the pond diagonally, sometimes hovering over the middle of the water; and then up in the trees the real source of the racket—tree frogs. Little, unassuming brown things that cling to the branches over your head. Their calls seem to fall like a rain of ripe fruit on your head, then roll and bounce over the pond and the surrounding countryside like a million marbles dropped from the sky.

Sometimes you can make out individual chirps, but the noise itself is unceasing and unstoppable. It throbs and vibrates and pulsates with varying rhythms. It gets under your skin and vibrates up and down your limbs and bones till you're physically connected to it. It yanks on your nerves the same way drums can take your heartbeat out of your body. The trees, the heavy air, the swamp, the spongy muck and the thousands of frogs all together—a giant metafrog—it all combines into one, and you are all humming hysterically together in a throbbing, thrumming, unflagging sonic spiral.

This is when I realize: I need silence, but I also need noise, sometimes very loud noise. Just as I need both dark and light. I need to be in control of what goes into my head, the sensory stimulation I can stand to let in. But I also need to be overwhelmed, bowled over, rattled to the soul, have experience wash over me orgasmically and put me temporarily but completely out of control.

# Blood and Champagne

*By* Anjana Basu

Two o'clock in the morning. Dawn is somewhere on the other side of tomorrow. The miniskirts are swinging, the sequins catching the light, and Malini Ramani has got the tallest pair of block heels this side of Suez. For a Thursday—no, early Friday—morning, this is a happening party. All the beautiful people of Delhi have already been here and gone, but there are still Mercedes parked outside. Yes this is "the scene."

What a good idea to have a party where anyone can just walk in. Someone did just that right after the clock struck two. He walked in from the dark, demanded a drink and when the pretty girl behind the bar refused, he shot her in the head and then walked out again. Leaving the music to wind down, the bearers to stare and Malini herself to go teetering over to cover the poor thing's face. Poor Jessica, she died young but quick, let's hide the booze before the police get here. And then it really was Friday morning, with nowhere to run to and Jessica Lall, thirty-four, former model, had been shot in the head over a drink by Manu Sharma, the politician's son.

The last time high society recorded a shooting like this was when Captain Nanavati shot his wife's lover in cold blood. That was in Bombay in the fifties, and it caused such a scandal that it made it into the pages of Salman Rushdie's *Midnight's Children*. Of course, high society has had its corpses since then—a prominent badminton player found mysteriously dead while his wife dallied with a friend of the Gandhis; a politician's wife thrown to the crocodiles by the man's mistress—but nothing so visible, and certainly nothing with blood-in-the-champagne about it.

"Our children don't do this kind of thing in public," was what the mothers sniffed. How could they? The children were brought up by relays of *ayahs* and sent to the right schools. No one who went to the right school could possibly be a murderer!

Even now, no one can quite figure out what combination of ingredients led to the disaster at the Tamarind Court, though ever since it was built the place has been bad news. A bar-cum-restaurant on Heritage property? Unheard of! cried the social activists. The place was built on land reclaimed for a song near the fabled Qutb Minar historical monument. Malini Ramani and her mother Bina were the prime movers of the project. News followed wherever the Ramani women went. Bina Ramani had rehabilitated another piece of Heritage property, the crumbling pleasure houses of the Mughul Emperors, turning the ruins into a "village" where destitute women could stitch pieces of needlepoint embroidery and run up expensive outfits for the jet set.

Hauz Khas Village, part Mughul ruin and part modern-Gothic, became a complex of restaurants and boutiques that made Bina Ramani an entrepreneurial byword throughout the nation. She planned to do the same for the Tamarind Court property and too bad if it was Heritage land—no one wanted it for all these years anyway.

Qutb Colony, as it was called, danced briefly through lines of newsprint, but no one could find a legal reason convincing enough to keep the Ramanis from continuing their plans. And so it was built—charming, chic and very expensive—and then run by Bina's daughter, Malini. The restaurant soon made food-column news and so did the cluster of shops round about that were fabled to be the most expensive of their kind in the capital. It was the latest phenomenon—Hauz Khas Village and its Indo-Saracenic chic were suddenly passé. The beautiful people were now all to be found at Qutb Colony. They were there every night, including Thursdays (the day is significant because on Thursdays liquor cannot be sold in public bars and restaurants) when the Tamarind Court held an open party. Anyone could walk in, buy coupons for food and drink and be part of the moveable feast. "What a good idea!" chorused the butterflies, "It takes a Ramani to think of something like this. You don't have to go to all the trouble of throwing a party. You just hook on to Malini's." There was, of course, a cut-off time—the bar was supposed to shut down at one a.m.—and what most people didn't know was that the Tamarind Court didn't have a liquor licence. But why should they care?

Jessica was behind the bar—most of Malini's friends served behind the bar at some time or other during the evening. It was the impromptu bartending that gave the place its party feel. Sort of like a forfeit in a game: you played and then did time out for playing. Whoever was tending looked after the guests while every one else got down on the floor and shimmied. Jessica just happened to be the one behind the bar at two in the morning on the sixth of May. "The girl must have said something to him," Manu's friends insisted weeks after the event. There was some banter about his having wanted "a sip of" Jessica herself, perhaps he misunderstood. "He wasn't the sort to just kill someone." Of course, they added, when he was drunk he was a lout.

And he was very drunk indeed when he staggered into the Tamarind Court with his two friends. People remember him reeling in; perhaps they heard the altercation over the loud music. But they only really paid attention when he whipped out a revolver and fired the first shot at the ceiling. The second went through Jessica's head.

No one moved a muscle to stop him, they were too busy disbelieving what was happening—though Bina Ramani later claimed that she had confronted him. The people outside were less drunk and more observant. They heard the shots. The licence plate and the make of the car were recorded. Soon the cops were all over the Tamarind Court, looking for someone to blame. It had to be someone else's fault. The politician's son had fallen into bad company. Look at all those shameless girls in miniskirts! The place had no licence, evidence had been tampered with. The list went on and on.

Jessica Lall's sister was interviewed the following night on Star TV News. So was the Delhi chief of police, who announced grimly that his men were on the job. Bina Ramani was arrested even before they arrested Manu Sharma who, in officialese, was "absconding." The police had many reasons for arresting her: the heritage property scam, unlicensed sale of alcohol, the fact that she had a British passport. More noise was made in the press about the party than was made about the fact that a politician's son had committed murder and fled the state. Of course, Bina was out on bail five minutes later and began issuing statements through her friends about her grief at Jessica's death.

Rumors about Bina Ramani began circulating all over again through the upper echelons of Delhi society: She had arranged a marriage for the Hindi film star Rekha that ended with the husband hanging himself after barely a year. She had been friends with a Mafia don. She was divorced and was flaunting her current marriage to a Canadian citizen, Georges Mailhot. She had given up her Indian nationality but insisted that she had not. Basically, she was *besharam*, shameless.

The police shut the Tamarind Court and took away Bina's marriage licence. They said this was so that she could not use the licence anywhere outside the country. Manu Sharma gave himself up a week later, having realised that there was nowhere to run, though he insisted confidently that he had done nothing wrong. He and his friends are currently in custody. In the meantime, the Delhi party scene has been slightly dampened. No one knows if some drunk will walk in and pop open a skull instead of a bottle of champagne.

Someone in Lucknow did in fact shoot a shop attendant just a month later, but that was in a Baskin Robbins ice cream parlour. The killer was drunk, and the attendant didn't have cassatta, the gunman's favourite flavour. So, possibly under the influence of those Delhi headlines, the killer whipped out his gun and shot the ice cream attendant through the head. Like the killer in the Tamarind Court, he was recognised by other people present at the scene and, like the first killer, he had the right connections—the son of a police chief who had committed suicide as a result, people said, of his son's vagaries. The national press tossed it around in two columns but, possibly because there were no sequins or other traces of glamour, quickly lost interest.

Jessica's murder still creeps back into print here and there. The gunman's friend, Vikas Yadav, who accompanied him to the Tamarind Court is complaining about having been tortured while in police custody. Meanwhile, no one has quite decided what to do about the murderer himself. He did, after all, give himself up and he is still the son of a Member of Parliament. And anyway, those Ramanis are a shameless lot. But, given the brevity of people's memories, it won't be long before the Armani suits are out again at midnight and the corks popping once more in Qutb Colony.

# The DMZ:
# Notes from a Journal

*By* Thomas G. Fairbairn

My trip to the northern limits of the demilitarized zone would, I had hoped, overpower the egotistical urge to impose myself on these notes. And it did have some effect, for the charged environment at Imjinkak, where the two titans—Western capitalism and Eastern, albeit Stalinist, communism—stand *mano a mano* and hurl insults back and forth from opposing loudspeakers on either side of the Imjing River, electrifies the atmosphere. Merely the endless, serpentine coils of fifteen-foot barbed wire stretching hundreds of miles along the Freedom Highway should have quenched my curiosity. I have never been able to abide the sight of barbed wire. But even as I stood between those two irreconcilable worlds and felt my eyes brim with sadness, there crept into my mind the memory of Changbalsan Mountain.

Changbalsan is right in the heart of this planned community, Ilsan, and is easily accessible by subway. It is, truthfully, not much of a mountain but would, I knew when I first sighted it, serve my desperate need for sanctuary, a place where I could escape from the tedious horror of mad bus drivers, screaming cars and the ant-like scurrying of 700,000 inhabitants. At the top of the mountain is a pagoda-like building, much like the one at Imjinkak, meant for meditation, prayer, paying respect to ancestral memories.

It was very early in the morning, and there was no one in the temple. Having gazelled my way up the mountain, I was happily exhausted. I slipped off my backpack and, using it for a pillow, was soon fast asleep. A few days before this, in my "Pooh" kindergarten class, one of the children, Sang, had slipped away from me and taken a header off the stairs leading up to the play loft. He broke his arm in two places. My stomach heaved when I saw the bone in his tiny arm (he's the youngest of the class, only four) stretching the paper-thin skin just below his elbow. The night previous to my climb up Changbalsam, I had visited him in the hospital to meet his parents and apologize for having let the accident happen in the first place.

I never got the chance. The father, who could speak a little English, motioned me to follow him out into the hallway where he proceeded to ask my forgiveness for his son's behavior and for having caused me so much worry and pain. "He runees like lizardee!" he said, smiling and bowing.

In my dream in the temple on top of Changbalsan, I stand in an unfamiliar kitchen. Sang's parents are with me. In my hands I hold a large platter with a raised edge like those used for panning gold. In the pan, dashing from side to side, is a russet-coloured chameleon. I am explaining how the lizard has to be cared for, fed, kept cool, cleaned. I pick the creature up, using my fingers like a pair of pliers, and it shoots forth a stream of milky waste. As I bend down to wipe up the mess I glance along the linoleum floor, and there behind the refrigerator is stretched out full length a brilliantly coloured orange snake.

Then all three of us are standing outside in the yard. I am again holding the pan with the lizard in it. In front of us is a house under construction. I can see the foundation beams and the black shadow of the hole under the house which will become the basement. The lizard flops wildly and is suddenly scurrying along the ground, heading fast for the dark shadow. Before anyone can react, the foundation beams of the house shake violently and the ground beneath our feet trembles. From out of the darkness there bursts a monstrous, Galapagos-size lizard that lunges and crashes like thunder into one of the support posts holding up the half-constructed building.

"There's no use!" I cry as I awake, my heart pounding, my breathing coming in desperate gulps. I do not recognize where I am and remain disorientated while that scene of the monster crashing into the support post plays over and over in my head.

At the northern limit of the DMZ where the Han River, flowing north through South Korea, intersects with the Imjin River flowing south out of North Korea, where both converge and ebb tiredly out into the West Sea, in my mind's eye the beast again rocks the foundations of the house. I stare through the coils of barbed wire toward the fake and empty apartment buildings which North Korea has constructed to convince the South Koreans how grand life is over there (the S. Koreans call it Propaganda Village). A light rain begins to fall. The water gathers and hangs on the fishhook prongs of the barbed wire and drop slowly like tears. I think, those are God's tears as He attempts to decide if this, like the dinosaurs, is just another failed experiment.

Sang, by the way, is fine. He's back home and, his mother tells me, darting through the house just like always. The veil has trembled but, for now, the foundation holds.

# Linguistic Cleansing:
# The Sad Fate of Punjabi in Pakistan

*By* Abbas Zaidi

Punjabi is the mother tongue of well over 120 million people. It is the language of two groups: the Sikhs of East Punjab in India (who use Sanskritised script), and the Punjabis of West Punjab in Pakistan (who use Persianised script). The two groups cannot read or write each other's writing, but their oral communicability is one hundred percent.

Before the partition of India in 1947 these two peoples used to live side by side. Some of the richest poetical traditions—the Sufi and romantic—of the Indian-Pakistani subcontinent are to be found in Punjabi. The immortal Punjabi love epic *Hir-Ranjha* is the acme of what Matthew Arnold called "high seriousness." And yet, Punjabi is also the most jokes-inclusive language of the Subcontinent. Even the non-native speakers of Punjabi accept that it is an exceptionally rich language: just one expression couched in the right tonal emphasis or written from the right perspective is worth scores of locutions, and the same expression can convey a variety of meaning in the same and different contexts if given the right twist. It is a language of nuance and double entendre. Sometimes the two meanings are contradictory (e.g., "X is a healthy man" or "X's figure is athletic" can mean just the opposite.). Sometimes one meaning is wit-packed and the second is serious (e.g., "The mullahs efficiently carry out their sacred duties in the mosque" can also mean they do wicked sexual things there). Most of the time one meaning is an ordinary, intended statement, while the other is playfully sexual (e.g., "Shall I pour [milk/water]?" secondarily refers to penetration, and more). If someone wants to experience synaesthesia, let him learn Punjabi.

Recently I met a Sikh in Brunei. He was in his mid-twenties, born in Malaysia and had never been to the place of his origin, i.e., the Indian Punjab. But he could speak perfect Punjabi. He said to me, "If a Sikh cannot speak Punjabi, he is a fake Sikh."

And yet, Pakistani Punjabis must be the only linguistic group in the world that has a dismissive—even derogatory—attitude towards its own language. I have lived in or visited a number of countries. I have talked to countless Punjabis both in Pakistan and outside. Most of them, Pakistani Punjabis wherever they may actually reside, are willingly, even proudly, dumping their own language in favor of Urdu.

The most aggressive anti-Punjabi-ists come from the educated and semi-educated classes. As soon as they acquire the most minimal academic advancement, the first thing they do is jettison their natural language. I have never seen or heard of an educated, or even semi-educated, Punjabi parent who is willing to communicate with his or her own child in their native tongue. Rather, they strongly discourage and often rebuke their children if they even suspect they might be talking to other children in Punjabi, because speaking Punjabi is considered a mark of crudeness and bad manners. A young child speaking Punjabi is at best an amusing curiosity for adult Punjabis. In a posh social or academic gathering anyone speaking that language is either trying to be funny or himself soon becomes the butt of jokes. A poet who writes in Punjabi finds an audience predisposed only to ribald entertainment.

Pakistani Punjabis' negative attitude towards their language can be demonstrated by the fact that there is not a single newspaper or magazine published in Punjabi for the 60 million-plus Punjabi speakers. Historically, every Punjabi journalistic venture has died soon after its launching. The latest venture was a daily newspaper, *Sajjan* ("Friend"), edited and published by Hussain Naqi, an Urdu-speaking Indian emigrant. It only lasted a few months. Yet, all the regional and provincial languages like Sindhi and Pushto have a proud history of publication. Sindhi, a minor language compared with Punjabi, can boast scores of daily newspapers and periodicals. Yet, while Pakistani Punjabis can certainly speak their language, they can neither read nor write it. I estimate not more than two percent of Punjabis can read or write Punjabi. Add to this the fact that, after Urdu speakers, Punjabis on average are the most literate group in Pakistan and you see what irony there is.

Consider the following breakdown of the speakers of the various Pakistani languages:

| | |
|---|---|
| Punjabi | 48.2 % |
| Pushto | 13.1 % |
| Sindhi | 11.8 % |
| Seraiki | 9.8 % |
| Urdu | 7.6 % |
| Other | 9.5 % |

What can one make of this situation? Is it not a linguistic schizophrenia on the part of Punjabis? Urdu is regarded as the "correct language," the language of taste and class, by the Punjabis themselves. Quite apart from what others think, it is they, the Punjabis, who think that Punjabi is an "indecent" or "vulgar" language. Some of them say this is because of the Punjabi accent, the rude way individual words and expressions are uttered, or because Punjabi is the language of the illiterate and the uncouth; or because there are countless swear words and double entendres in Punjabi; or because Punjabi is just plain déclassé. Hence, Punjabi has multiple semiotic indictments against it even before it is expressed.

And yet, a language's capacity for double entendre is actually at the heart of its expressiveness and power, making these objections to Punjabi as ridiculous as General Franco's charge that Basque was a "language of dogs."

The only places in Pakistan where Punjabi is uninhibitedly spoken are the so-called backward rural areas or city slums. These misfortunate people look up to prosperous educated Punjabis—the landed aristocrats, industrialists, the yuppies and the bourgeoisie—as role models. As they become educated they discard their mother tongue along with their uncouth dress and manners. Hence the formula seems simple enough: the more educated a Punjabi is, the more anti-Punjabi and Punjabi-less he or she becomes. Ironically, the illiterate Punjabis are the most genuine Punjabis.

The responsibility for such a state of affairs lies with the Punjabis themselves, especially the "Wake Up Punjabi!" slogan-mongers. Is it not significant that in Pakistan's history no Punjabi leader of stature has addressed a mass rally in Punjabi? Nawaz Sharif, Pakistan's current and twice-elected prime minister is a Punjabi. It was he who some time back raised the "Wake Up Punjabi!" slogan while challenging then Prime Minister Benazir Bhutto's supremacy. Yet his track record on Punjabi is as bad as any other Punjabi leader's. Bhutto, who was also twice elected prime minister, is a Sindhi. She always talks to the Sindhis in Sindhi. Similarly, Urdu-, Pushto-, Seraiki- and Baluchi-speaking leaders and intellectuals always use their own languages when talking to their people either in private or in public.

Sindhi, Pushto and Urdu are compulsory languages for Sindhi, Pathan and Mohajir students, and the Baluchis are working hard to evolve a script for their own language. A number of official activities are transacted in these languages. The Punjabis are the largest linguistic group in Pakistan. They are also the most powerful political and economic group. Pakistan is an agrarian society, and the Punjab feeds the whole of Pakistan ("Punjab" means "the land of five rivers"). But there is not a single school where Punjabi is taught. Nor has Punjabi ever been part of the school syllabi. Pre-university as well as college courses in the Punjab are taught in Urdu. In a majority of cases, the characters, their names and the situations projected in narratives, poems and social descriptions are based on the culture of Urdu speakers and have nothing to do with the Punjab. There are a number of universities in the Punjab, but it is only in the University of Lahore that a small MA Punjabi department exists, and even then the students admitted are more interested in finding a cheap residence in Lahore than in studying Punjabi.

The books published in Punjabi in any given year can be counted on one hand. Compared with scores of Urdu, Sindhi, Pushto, and other minority languages (e.g., Seraiki and Kashmiri), there is not a single full-fledged Punjabi research institution in Pakistan except for a misshapen Punjabi Adabi Board notable principally for its inactivity. The few research works in Punjabi owe their existence to individual efforts. One may argue that this state of affairs can be explained by economics, but why does economics affect only Punjabi in this way?

The average Pakistani Punjabi would answer such questions thusly:

> (i) The reason the Sikhs have never discarded their language is that their holy book, the *Garanth*, is in Punjabi;
>
> (ii) We must use Urdu because it is our national language.

To which I reply:

> (i) The Koran is in Arabic, but its readers have not dumped their own native languages simply because of that fact. Moreover, the Punjabis, along with other Pakistanis, never

learn Arabic; they read the Koran without understanding a word of Arabic;

(ii) All the different ethnic groups in Pakistan know Urdu, but they have not jettisoned their own languages for the sake of a national language whose native speakers make up less than eight percent of the general population.

Language has played a very significant role in Pakistan's history, a fact that makes the Punjabi question all the more ironic and tragic. When Pakistan was created in 1947 as East and West Pakistan, it was claimed by its then rulers—who were Urdu-speaking emigrants from India—that Pakistan would last till the Day of Judgment with Allah's blessing: two (East and West) wings, one religion, one nation, one country and one national language—Urdu.

But the blessing was not realized, and before it could celebrate its first anniversary the whole of East Pakistan was rocked to its foundations with bloody "language riots." The Bengalis refused to accept Urdu because it was an imposed, not their own, language. They said they would lose their identity without their mother tongue. In turn, they were dubbed "anti-Pakistan" for their opposition to Urdu.

The pro-Urdu lobby in West Pakistan then played the Islamic card: Urdu amounted to Islamic identity. Anti-Urdu was anti-Islamic. Calling the Bengalis anti-Islam, the religious scholars of West Pakistan argued that Islamic identity should transcend Bengali identity if the Bengalis were to consider themselves true Muslims.

But the language of theology could not overcome the theology of language, and in 1971, before Pakistan could celebrate its silver jubilee, East Pakistan had become Bangladesh, "Land of the Bengali-speaking People." And as the Bengalis were about to start preparations to celebrate their first independence anniversary, the province of Sindh became a scene of language riots between the speakers of Sindhi and Urdu, shaking the very foundations of the newly-elected government of Zulfiqar Ali Bhutto, the most popular and powerful leader in Pakistan's history (he was both the country's president and chief martial-law administrator). Bhutto appeared on TV and spoke in English, Sindhi and Urdu. He joined his hands together and, pointing them towards the people said, "For God's sake, let it (i.e., language rioting) go!"

Again the religious scholars played the Islamic card. One of them said, "The end of Urdu will mean the end of Pakistan and Islam."

The province of Sindh has continued to be a hotbed of ethnic violence between Sindhi and Urdu speakers. Sindhi nationalists want a separate homeland, Sindhudesh, exclusively for speakers of Sindhi, while Urdu speakers threaten that any "conspiracy" against "Pakistan and Urdu" would meet with an "iron fist." They themselves had planned to establish "Jinnahpur," an Urdu-speaking province within Sindh itself. Their scheme was thwarted by an army action against the Mohajirs in 1992.

Since Pakistan's creation, the Pathans have been lobbying for Pakhtoonistan, the "Land of the Pushto speakers." Nowadays they talk about separating from Pakistan itself and forming a greater Pakhtoonistan with Afghanistan, a majority Pathan country, even though severe differences exist between medieval religious obscurantist Talibaans and so-called liberals. The nationalist movement in the South of the Punjab is based upon the Seraiki language. Other examples can be multiplied. Yet, no similar debate exists amongst the Punjabis about Punjabi. They are secure in the belief that their language is merely a source of embarrassment rather than of a proud common identity.

Amrita Pretam, a Punjabi poet and fiction writer, once invoked the soul of Waris Shah (the Hir-Ranjha poet) when hundreds of thousands of Punjabi women had been raped by their own countrymen during India's partition. One is tempted to again invoke the name of this great Punjabi bard whose language is being consigned to an historical black hole by the Pakistani Punjabis themselves. What are the inheritors of the language of Waris Shah and numerous other Punjabi literary titans, both inside and outside Pakistan, doing about this shameful neglect of the Punjabi language? Will Punjabi ultimately become like Latin, a dead language with no one left who can actually speak it?

We find throughout history that dictators who want to terminate a target group are assiduous in their attempt to first efface the language of that group. Pakistani Punjabis are their own dictators. If they continue to treat their language the way they are doing at present, in future there will be a strange, baffling mass of "ethnic" Punjabis who will not know their own language. Or, if somehow miraculously Punjabi isn't lost in Pakistan, it will become at best a pidgin.

Love for one's native tongue is a universal phenomenon. At minimum, a language is a mark of personal as well as national identity. It's a glue that holds its speakers together as a people. This is why language has been so pivotal in the history of nations, a stronger bond than religion, land and even race. At present, written and spoken Punjabi is heavily punctuated with Urdu words and phrases that are foreign both semantically and phonetically. Mohajir (i.e., the Urdu-speaking people) and Punjabi temperaments are poles apart in terms of cultural values and attitudes. Many would argue that Islam is the common bond among all Pakistani people, which in the course of time will transcend all the differences. I am not sure this is true, but what, however sadly, I am sure of is that at the rate things are going, Punjabi will have disappeared before the end of the next century.

# A Death in the Family

*By* Arlene Ang

When I think about it now, everything started when Eldest Brother died. He was thirty-four years old and drunk that night he smashed his car into a wall. Dead drunk, as they would say. During the funeral we threw roses onto his coffin before they sealed him away forever behind a slab of marble. I had picked the lot because it faced the east. Mother had coached me endlessly about how important it is that the morning sun shines on his grave and that I must specify that we wanted a Chinese burial—that Eldest Brother must not be buried beneath ground.

It was raining that day. Looking up from my muddy shoes, I glanced at the family and friends who had gathered in sympathy. At least my parents had not had to hire professional mourners.

But my parents themselves were noticeably absent. Father had locked himself in his room in silent outrage. Mother reluctantly decided to stay with him—for propriety's sake. It was considered a slapping insult if a child should die before his parents. And so they could not attend the funeral. I never questioned these customs. I had heard my parents claim that our traditions made us the most cultured race in the world. Though I secretly believed that most of these traditions were mere superstitions and old wives' tales, I didn't dare challenge my parents' beliefs. I endured them without question.

Such as the pains they took to follow every geomancer's whim in the construction of our house—which eventually meant reconstructing everything from scratch because one of the geomancers decided that every overhanging beam would bring about a death in the family, and there were forty beams in all. I didn't dare to mention the fact that there were only ten of us, including my sister, her husband and their children.

I didn't even mind celebrating Chinese New Year, the ban on

wearing black shirts, working eight hours a day seven days a week, and only going out with Chinese girls (as far as my parents knew).

But their not attending Eldest Brother's funeral grated. He may have had his weaknesses, but he was still their son. And I knew he loved them and did his duty as Eldest Son more than I myself can ever imagine doing. The old excuse of saving face angered me tremendously. The day of the funeral, looking at the guests tiptoeing through the mud, I wondered: Can this be all there is to life? Going through the motions because custom demands it of us? Wouldn't it be better to live life in a box?

I've watched friends and relatives, always Chinese, even though we are by now the second generation born in the Philippines, stick strictly to the dictates of a Sino-centric life: attending Chinese schools, speaking Chinese, eating Chinese food, working for the family business or for Chinese corporations, marrying fellow Chinese and in the end even being buried in the Chinese way.

In my anger, born partly out of panic and partly despair, I thought about going back to my old job as a journalist. It seemed a waste to throw away my degree. I had a good position at one of the national newspapers. But the family business needed me now and, young and dutiful as I was, I thought I had all the time in the world to go back to my career. I thought bitterly, Eldest Brother finished a degree in archaeology at the university, but being the eldest son the responsibility for the family business was turned over to him and he never got to pursue the real passion of his life.

I phoned my old editor who luckily still remembered me. I asked if he had any vacancies. He immediately offered me my old job back, and I gratefully took it. That night I told my parents I was going back to work as a journalist. Father exploded. "You are not thinking of your family! With your worthless brother dead, you must now take care of the business."

I tried to explain about wanting to do something on my own, that I never liked running the family business, and that taking care of his broken-down supermarket depressed me.

"It's not about liking it. This is business—you're not supposed to enjoy yourself! And what kind of job is it being a journalist? You won't earn your bread that way. You have no future there. How can you get married with a job like that? No woman would accept you! Think how I sweated to keep that supermarket alive, you ingrate! You can't throw away everything I've worked so hard for. "

As a last note, he threatened darkly, "If you go back to your job, I'll disown you. You won't get a cent out of me. You will be nothing."

"So be it," I replied.

I went to my room and started packing. Mother stood by the door watching me. "You're so young, Youngest Son," she whispered, tears in her eyes. "You don't know yet what you want. Apologise to Father, he will forget and take you back."

"No, Mother," I said, "I don't want to do Eldest Brother's work and end up dissatisfied like him. I'll be all right." I kissed her awkwardly on the cheek, "Go to bed. It is late. I'll be fine."

Early the next morning I left the house before anyone else was awake.

# Life and Death on Shiva's Beach

*By* Paul Spencer Sochaczewski

*Pulau Enu, Aru Islands, Indonesia*

A newly hatched green turtle wanders into my tent this evening, attracted perhaps by a lantern that he thought was the reflection of the moon on the sea.

A few hours later I wander the beach on the windward side of this small island, blown sand gritting my contact lenses, looking for the tractor-like tracks that indicate an adult meter-long turtle has visited the low dunes to lay her eggs.

It is a night with stars like I've rarely seen, and I half expect Alfred Russel Wallace, the Victorian naturalist-explorer-philosopher to appear out of the shadows, gaunt and curious and quietly eager to join me. I've been on his 150-year-old trail for some time now, and I feel his presence as I examine small piles of sand that mark where one of these green turtles has laid her eggs. But, perhaps in too much of a hurry, she has deposited the eggs below the high-water line, where they are certain to become waterlogged and spoiled. I finally unearth her sixty fresh eggs, still slimy with turtle juices, and transplant them into another hole I dig a few meters beyond the reach of the high tide.

Yet, amidst this exuberance of life I smell death. I wander the beach and, like a dung beetle, am drawn to the rotting carcasses and bleached skulls of turtles which have been slit open by fishermen after the two hundred or so eggs in the reptile's egg cavity, fishermen either too impatient or too greedy to be satisfied with catching the fifty-odd eggs as they plop out during the normal cycle. The tasty turtle flesh has been left uneaten to rot; the only part taken is the stomach, which makes a fine bait.

Earlier today the research group I am with chased reputedly vicious Indonesian fishermen away from Sulawesi, men who lay nets to capture green turtles in the waters of this unguarded nature reserve. From a distance of a hundred meters we saw that their boat was full of live turtles, perhaps a hundred of the animals, all destined for Bali. Another Western conservationist and I urged the Indonesian captain to give chase. We made an attempt, but the captain's heart wasn't in it.

"Those men are armed and dangerous," said a frustrated Ating Sumantri, the person in charge of the Indonesian government's efforts to conserve sea turtles. "We don't have any soldiers, no weapons."

Just then, Fata, an Indonesian game warden, jumped overboard and swam ashore to rescue the turtles which had been abandoned on the island when the poachers first spotted our boat. He flipped over eight of the 100-kilogram animals and watched them escape into the sea before the three grounded poachers caught up with him. Fata himself had to hide in the woods until we could rescue him. What is a turtle worth? Worth getting stabbed for? Worth shooting someone for?

I've been thinking about many things on this trip. How is it, I asked the memory of Alfred Russel Wallace, that we humans will travel halfway around the world and suffer physical discomforts in order to study a beach where green turtles come ashore to lay their eggs? Why do we watch another creature's life cycle—laying and hatching—with such emotional intensity and intellectual curiosity? Why should it disturb us that others of our race—the Balinese in this case—enjoy eating this ancient reptile? Why do we have such protective attitudes toward another species?

Later, in Bali, I wanted to find out just how important turtle meat is to that island's Shivaistic Hindu culture. This was not merely a question of being environmentally and politically correct. It's also good conservation to understand what emotional and spiritual values lie behind what seems to outsiders to be senseless consumption—some 18,000 turtles a year, according to one estimate.

"Turtle meat adds something to our ceremonies," explained I.B. Pangdjaja, head of public relations at the Bali governor's office.

"But it's not essential to the religious ceremony?" I said.

"It's like you eating turkey at Thanksgiving. Except it makes us strong."

Odd, isn't it. Transported to Bali for barbecue, or worse, slit open for their eggs and then left to die on the beach. And then, against all odds, life goes on—more turtles come ashore to lay their eggs. Because we happen to be present on Pulau Enu on this particular night, the bad guys stay away, and just maybe tonight's crop of eggs will hatch. I call this contradictory place Shiva's Beach. A beach of destruction and creation. Shiva dances on a beach of skulls. Ecstatic Life breathes below.

Alfred Russel Wallace travelled some fourteen thousand miles in the Malay Archipelago during the period from 1854 to 1862. Why did he put up with bedbugs and homesickness and upset stomachs and the risk of drowning and malaria? Why travel so far for that? I asked Peter Kedit, director of the Sarawak Museum, which was created by Wallace as a favor for James Brooke, the first White Rajah of Sarawak, whether Alfred's odyssey was comparable to the Iban concept of *berjalai*, the rite of passage for young men that often ended with the taking of a human head. Kedit, an Iban, thought Wallace's ambition was more typically British: the Protestant work ethic, missionary zeal, socialistic tendencies.

I stood on a ridge near the border between Malaysian Sarawak and Indonesian Kalimantan in Borneo. I had been gone half the day and had not brought food; time to return, my inner-mother admonished. "What happens if I go down there instead?" I thought, heading towards a steep, trackless hill that my instincts told me would eventually meet a tributary of my campsite river.

I scampered, skidded and bounced down the side of the mountain, finally reaching a meter-wide stream and a series of small, ridiculously pristine waterfalls, which I slid down with otter-like joy. Chasing waterfalls, I was making no contribution to humanity, but I was fulfilling one of my basic needs—to get away from the crowd and spend time with myself.

Alfred Russel Wallace said that the reason he went to Asia was because of his "vocation" as a collector and naturalist. I suspect he was driven to leave England, first for the Amazon, then to Southeast Asia. He argued that he was in it for the money, but reading between the lines of a letter he wrote while in Indonesia to his friend George Silk back in England, I sense a passion:

"Besides these weighty reasons [for my staying in Southeast Asia] there are others quite as powerful—pecuniary ones. I have not yet made enough to live upon, and I am likely to make it quicker here than I could in England. In England there is only one way in which I could live, by returning to my old profession of land-surveying. Now, though I always liked surveying, I like collecting better, and I could never now give my whole mind to any work apart from the study to which I have devoted my life. So far from being angry at being called an enthusiast (as you seem to suppose), it is my pride and glory to be worthy to be so called. Who ever did anything good or great who was not an enthusiast? The majority of mankind are enthusiasts only in one thing—in money-getting; and these call others enthusiasts as a term of reproach because they think there is something in the world better than money-getting. It strikes me that the power or capability of a man in getting rich is in inverse proportion to his reflective powers and in direct proportion to his impudence. It is perhaps good to be rich, but not to get rich, or to be always trying to get rich, and few men are less fitted to get rich, if they did try, than myself."

Alfred left something unsaid: By leaving home and going off to the distant corners of the world, he put down a marker. He announced to his friends and family that when he returned he would have been changed. It is his expression of a desire to move towards individualization. He left, and did exciting things that his left-behind friends could only dream about; they stayed and worked in the post office. Think of Kipling: "All things considered there are only two kinds of men in the world—those that stay at home and those that do not."

Alfred, you are driven. You are Odysseus and Rama, Don Quixote and Lancelot. You live and breathe adventure but, paradoxically, you equally long for stability and inner peace:

"As to health and life, what are they compared with peace and happiness?" you wrote, adding that happiness is best obtained by "work with a purpose..."

Anthropologist Robert Sapolsky discussed exile in the context of young male primates leaving the nest. "Another key to our success must have something to do with this voluntary transfer process," he wrote, "this primate legacy of getting an itch around adolescence. How did voluntary dispersal evolve? What is going on with that individual's genes, hormones, and neuro-transmitters to make it hit the road? We don't know, but we do know that following this urge is one of the most resonantly primate of acts. A young male baboon stands riveted at the river's edge; an adolescent female chimp cranes to catch a glimpse of the chimps from the next valley. New animals, a whole bunch of 'em! To hell with logic and sensible behavior, to hell with tradition and respecting your elders, to hell with this drab little town, and to hell with that knot of fear in your stomach. Curiosity, excitement, adventure—the hunger for novelty is something fundamentally daft, rash, and enriching that we share with our whole taxonomic order."

Here's a wild theory, based on no evidence whatsoever. Alfred, had you returned from the Amazon with your entire collection and notes intact instead of losing virtually all your new species, all your sketches, drawings, daily journal and three massive notebooks (and almost your life) when the ship burned at sea in 1852, you would never have gone to Southeast Asia. You wouldn't have needed to. By virtue of your Amazon collection you would have earned your stripes as a serious and effective researcher and, like Darwin, could have stayed in England for the rest of your life, writing books. You could have dined out on that single mission just as Darwin dined out on his travels aboard the Beagle. But the fact is you came home from the Amazon empty-handed, except for the few hundred specimens (400 butterflies, 450 beetles, 400 "others") you had previously sent to Samuel Stevens, your agent.

Amazingly, with few notes and with a niggling number of specimens, you still managed to write two books on your travels within ten months of your return. One volume, *A Narrative of Travels on the Amazon and Rio Negro*, gave you a foothold in the literary world, while the other, *Palm Trees of the Amazon*, helped establish you in the scientific community. You could have stopped there. But something inside you forced you to get back on the horse after you had been thrown. Only then could you return a hero. Your Amazon "failure" must have caused you great turmoil. Remember what Nietzsche said: "You must have a chaos inside you to give rise to a dancing star."

While you go out of your way sometimes to appear drearily practical, I know you were a dreamer. Only a dreamer would have written: "Strength grows in one who grasps the skirts of happy chance/And breaks the blows of circumstance/And grapples with his evil star." What is the dream that forces some people to travel hard? Bruce Chatwin found that "'Travel' is the same word as 'travail'—bodily or mental labour, toil, especially of a painful or oppressive nature, exertion, hardship, suffering, a journey."

Let's play with this a bit more. We travel to test ourselves, to cleanse, to rejuvenate. This could be termed *catharsis*, which is Greek for "purging" or "cleansing." According to Chatwin, one controversial etymology of the word derives from the Greek *katheiro*, "to rid the land of monsters." We want to rid the land of monsters? External and internal demons? Sounds to me like we're trying to relive the great epics.

We modern boys and girls lack rites of passage, rituals and ceremonies where we clearly shift from childhood to adulthood. Our life-passages are unclear. Girls in Western societies begin to menstruate many years before they are old enough to bear children in a socially acceptable context. Boys might be old enough to drive but not to drink, old enough to kill and be killed in the army but not to vote, old enough to father children but not old enough to leave school of their own volition. Alfred, maybe your butterfly-chasing and my waterfall-schussing were aspects of our own rites of passage, rituals we created ourselves because our society gave us few hints and forgot to stage a ceremony just for us. We were denied the vigil in the desert, where we were expected to kill a lion, fast for three weeks, have a vision, return to the village to get circumcised, become cleansed in a sweat lodge and be decorated with feathers and body paint and invited, finally, to eat with the grownups. The vision, for me, is the most important part of the rite of passage. The illumination of a higher purpose. The dream. Martin Luther King and all that.

T.E. Lawrence wrote: "All men dream: but not equally. Those who dream by night in the dusty recesses of their minds wake in the day to find that it was vanity: but the dreamers of the day are dangerous men, for they may act their dreams with open eyes, to make it possible."

I awake before dawn the following morning and watch a bunch of just-hatched turtles, shorter than my thumb, scamper like reptilian puppies to the sea. After they all reach the sea safely I strip so I can wash off the sand and bathe in new-turtle water. Back at the nest site a straggler emerges from the quickly heating sand half an hour behind his nest-mates. I follow his clumsy but determined flipper steps into the sea, and swim with him for maybe thirty meters. He paddles aggressively, sticking his little head out of the water every four seconds. The water is clear and warm, free of hungry fish or crabs, the sky blue and free of birds of prey. The little fellow swims towards a group of seven fishing boats. I tell him not to, but he doesn't listen. The sea is big, though, and perhaps he will pass his life free of hassle. Eventually I let him find his own course and he paddles out of sight. Just a boy. He isn't going to listen to me.

He doesn't really know where he is going, but he knows he has a journey to make. I wish him well, as much for my sake as for his own.

# Author Bios

**Razi Abedi** is Pakistan's foremost literary figure. He was chairman of the Punjab University in Lahore and has published extensively on the literatures of both East and West. His particular interest is the study of Urdu literature in the context of third-world literature and the literature now being produced in the West.

**Vasilis Afxentiou** has worked as an engineer, technical specifications writer and, for the past fourteen years, English-as-a-Second-Language teacher. His writing has appeared in *Greek Accent, National Herald (Proini), CrossCurrents, 30-Days, Key Travel News, Greece's Weekly, Athena Magazine*, and online in *The Domain, Ibn Quirtaiba, Cosmic Visions, Aphelion, Dark Planet* and other publications.

**Subra Anand** is a chip designer living in the Bay area of California. He grew up in India and came to the US for graduate studies in engineering. This is his first published story.

**Arlene Ang** was born in Manila of Chinese parents. She writes poetry, short stories, articles and translations. Her work has been published in *LiNQ (AUS), RE:AL, Black Bear Review, Oyster Boy Review, American Tanka* and *Dandelion*.

**Anjana Basu** does advertising work in Calcutta. Formerly, she taught English Literature at Calcutta University. A volume of her short stories, *The Agency Raga*, was published by Orient Longman, India. Her poems have been featured in an anthology brought out by Penguin India. Her work has also been published in *The Wolfhead Quarterly, The Amethyst Review, The Blue Moon Review, Kimera* and *Recursive Angel*.

**Viktor Car** is a native Croatian, naturalized Canadian. He studied civil engineering at the University of Zagreb and also edited a university magazine. His short stories have been published in *Blood & Aphorisms* and on the Web.

Made in Japan and born in California, **KC Chase** spent several years in the military before finally coming to the realization that it's difficult to write in a foxhole. Between writing and assorted eclectic pursuits, KC rarely finds time to eat or sleep but spares enough energy to shout at traffic lights and chase cars.

**Richard Cumyn** is the author of three collections of short fiction: *Viking Brides* (Oberon Press, 2001), *I Am Not Most Places* (Beach Holme, 1996), and *The Limit of Delta Y Over Delta X*, (Goose Lane, 1994). He lives in Halifax, Nova Scotia.

**Richard Czujko** has lived with his family in Pietermaritzburg for almost twenty years. He is employed as a senior administrative executive at the Pietermaritzburg city library, from which he observes firsthand the social and cultural changes taking place.

**Holly Day** lives in Minneapolis, Minnesota, with her son, Wolfegang, and her cat, Calypso. She works as a music journalist for *Guitar One* and *XLR8R* magazines and was invited to pen the intro for the new guidebook, *Jimi Hendrix: Bluesman.*

**Thomas G. Fairbairn** left home in Canada when he was fifteen to hitchhike to Mexico. Later he emigrated to the US. He has worked as a journalist in Toronto, Los Angeles and Winchendon, Massachusetts. He currently lives in Seoul, Korea, observing and recording the phenomenon of globalization, watching East meet West.

**David Herman** was born in South Africa in 1950. He left in 1965 and has spent the past thirty-four years on the road. Along the way he won an EMMY for an independently produced documentary in the USA and farmed a 100-acre mixed dairy farm in Ireland. He is currently living in Holland with his wife and two children and is writing a novel about the struggle for truth during the dying days of apartheid.

**Thomas J. Hubschman** is the publisher of Gowanus (www.gowanusbooks.com), from which the essays and stories in this collection are drawn. He has also published four novels and numerous short stories, most recently *Billy Boy* (Savvy Press).

**Fanuel Jongwe** is a journalist whose work appears in the *Harare Daily News*.

**Miroslav Kirin** was born in Sisak, Croatia, and lives in Zagreb. He is the author of two volumes of poetry and a collection of short fiction. He has also translated into Croatian the works of the American writers Paul Auster, Paul Bowles, Sam Shepard, David Mamet, Siri Hustvedt, Bret Easton Ellis, et al. "Snapshot" is part of a new collection of short fiction about post-war Croatia.

**Norma Kitson** is the author of the acclaimed autobiography *Where Sixpence Lives*, Chatto & Windus, 1987; *Zimbabwe Women Writers Anthology No. 1 - English,* 1994, Southern African Research and Documentation Centre (SARDC); and *Creative Writing—A Handbook,* Academic Books, 1997; and numerous articles, reviews and short stories.

**Ellen Larson** is a freelance writer and editor living and working in Cairo, Egypt. She has published short fiction, essays and reviews in the USA, Egypt and on the Net. Her first short story appeared in *Yankee Magazine* in 1971. She has two mystery novels in print, *The Hatch and Brood of Time* and *Unfold the Evil,* published by Savvy Press.

**Le Van Thao** is a writer and editor of *Arts and Letters Weekly Magazine* in Ho Chi Minh City. He was born in 1939 in Long An, South Vietnam, and served as a guerilla in the War.

**Ly Lan** was born in Binh Duong, grew up in Sai Gon, graduated from the University of Hochiminh City and now does writing and translating. Among her published works is a short story collection, *Di Mong.*

**Joselito "Jojo" Pasion Malig** is a twenty-five-year-old journalist, essayist, poet and freelance writer based in Pampanga, some fifty kilometers north of Manila. He is editor-in-chief of *Philippine Web Ex-*

*change*, a technology and e-commerce newsletter. He is into Zen Buddhism, existentialism, Moslem literature, literary journalism, technology, philosophy and metaphysics—not necessarily in that order.

**Anthony Milne** was born in Trinidad and Tobago in 1951, educated there at St Mary's College, and subsequently in Canada and at the University of the West Indies, St Augustine, Trinidad and Tobago. He has worked as a journalist with *Trinidad Express* newspapers since July 1981, covering politics, parliament and just about everything else under the sun.

**Vallath Nandakumar** was born and grew up in India. At the age of twenty-one, he came to the United States for graduate studies. He now works as an electrical engineer in Silicon Valley, where he writes short stories in his spare time. Inspiration for many of his stories is drawn from his experiences in the state of Kerala, South India.

**Raymond Ramcharitar** earns his living as a journalist in Trinidad and Tobago, West Indies. He has been published throughout the Caribbean and the United States.

**Rasik Shah** was born in Nairobi, of migrant parents from India. He grew up in a large family in a Kenya not very different from apartheid South Africa, speaking Gujarati, Hindi, Urdu and Swahili. He studied law at the Inns of Courts in London and practiced in independent Kenya for about ten years, and then in Canada where he now lives and writes.

**Keith Smith** was born and grew up in Laventille, East Port of Spain, and still lives there. He was educated at Fatima College and at the University of the West Indies, St Augustine, and has now been engaged almost as long as anyone else in Trinidad and Tobago in the pursuit of journalism. He is Editor-at-Large at *Trinidad Express* newspapers.

**Paul Spencer Sochaczewski** lived in Indonesia for twelve years and writes regularly on nature conservation. His co-authored book, *Soul of the Tiger: Searching for Nature's Answers in Southeast Asia*, is published by the University of Hawai'i Press. His novel *Redheads*, about orangutans, is published by Sid Harta. This essay is taken from a forthcoming book that traces the travels of Alfred Russel Wallace, the Victorian explorer, naturalist and philosopher.

**Paul A. Toth** lives in Michigan and has been published in *Blue Moon Review, Pif, Satire, WebDelSol/InPosse* and elsewhere. His short story "Fizz" is available from Powell's Books as a Pick Pocket chapbook (Phony Lid Publications).

Born and raised in Bombay, India, **Vasanthi Victor** now lives in the California Bay Area with her husband and children. Her fiction has been published in anthologies and online in *IndiaWorld* and *Monsoon* and the Canadian anthology *Bolo! Bolo!*.

**Abbas Zaidi** was editor of *The Ravi,* Pakistan's premier and oldest academic magazine, published by Government College, Lahore. He also edited *Interface* for the Program in Literary Linguistics, University of Strathclyde, Glasgow. Zaidi has taught English Literature in Multan University and worked as assistant editor for *The Nation*, Lahore.

Printed in the United States
2778